D1221530

Time Machines

Time Machines

The World of Living History

Jay Anderson

The American Association for State and Local History
Nashville, Tennessee

Library of Congress Cataloguing-in-Publication Data

Anderson, Jay.
  Time machines.

  Bibliography: p.   *1075 1948*
  Includes index.
  1. Historical models. 2. Historical museums.
3. History—Research. I. American Association for
State and Local History. II. Title.
D16.A556 1984   907'.2   84-9332
ISBN 0-910050-71-6

Designed by Gary Gore

Publication of this book was made possible in part by
funds from the sale of the Bicentennial State Histories,
which were supported by the National Endowment for
the Humanities.

To my mom,
who stitched up my first "Confederate uniform,"
way back in 1950;
and my dad,
who patiently hiked with me
around historic sites
as various as Culloden Moor and Gettysburg.
They incubated my lifelong interest
in living history.

Contents

Preface:
Tripping through Time

MY great-grandfather, Joseph Maier, was a child of the Great Revolution. He grew up in Belfort, Alsace Lorraine, in the tumultuous world of 1870s France. Every aspect of the life he knew—economic, political, social, cultural—was changing. We look back and describe that epoch as an industrial revolution. For Maier, a man given to poetry, Europe was Matthew Arnold's "darkling plain/Swept with confused alarms of struggle and flight,/Where ignorant armies clash by night." When he was impressed into the French navy after the Franco-Prussian War of 1870–71, Maier decided he had to escape. A few years later, his crew made a courtesy call at New York, and he jumped ship. He spent the rest of his life in Brooklyn, working as a chef and tending his garden. I can still see him leaning on his hoe, puffing a huge Meerschaum pipe, and bitterly recalling the "barbaric" German soldiers who had invaded his parents' home in France and slept in their beds with muddy boots on. Maier used these memories as a reminder of the revolutionary world he had left behind. That world had turned him into a liberal progressive. He welcomed the future and spent his later years reading Jules Verne.[1]

Tante Valie, my mother's Swiss aunt, reacted to this same changing world in exactly the opposite way. She came from La Chaux-de-Fonds, the watch-manufacturing center in Neuchâtel Canton, near the border of France. She also had emigrated in the 1870s and had worked for years as a governess in New York City. Tante Valie never felt at home in America and preferred the close company of her Swiss friends at the French Protestant Church. There, they could sip chocolate, compare needlework, and quietly chat in French. I visited Tante Valie's apartment on the Upper East Side in the late 1940s, and except for the view of 72nd Street, out the window, it might have been Switzerland. Everything in that room seemed foreign, especially the towering wardrobes and the walls seemingly papered with old faded photographs of the Jura Mountains, Swiss peasants, and street scenes of her beloved Chaux-Fonds. For me, it was a fascinating visit. Tante Valie chatted away in French with my grandmother, while plying me with chocolate and wedges of Swiss Knight cheese. The more the world changed, the more conservative she became. Valie spent her final years returning, in memory, to the days when her father would take her as a child to pick wild flowers on the high alpine meadows.[2]

Thinking back, I believe that my great-grandfather and my aunt were culture-

9

shocked by the revolutionary changes they saw occurring around them in Europe and America. At times, they each needed to escape. Joseph Maier chose the future, while Valie Burger selected the past. Both retreats served their purpose. Getting away by means of a Jules Verne fantasy or an old photograph helped them survive.

*   *   *

This book is about a particular way in which people have chosen to slip away from the modern world. I call it *time traveling*. Some people travel by means of a "head trip," assisted by a photograph album, a historical novel, or a science fiction film. Others attempt a more physical experience, by simulating life in another time at a living-history museum, aboard a re-created Viking ship, or in the din of a re-enacted battle. Although it's usually a great adventure for the participants, time traveling can also be a significant historical exercise, and much can be learned from talking to time travelers and studying their trips.[3]

In this book, I'll deal chiefly with the latter, the complex simulated trip. But first, some background.

The idea of deliberate time travel originated with the English author (H. G.) Wells. Between the years 1888 and 1894, in a series of short magazine articles, Wells worked on the idea of a time machine that could take a person to a particular point of time, past or future. Other contemporary authors had played with the notion of time travel, but they resorted to accidents or nonscientific means of transportation. Edward Bellamy hypnotized his hero Julian West, in *Looking Backward* (1888). West woke up in a utopian Boston, on September 10, 2000, and liked what he saw. A year after Bellamy's book appeared, Mark Twain whacked his hero's head with a crowbar, and Hank Morgan awoke in Camelot, 1351 years earlier than the time frame he was born in, and became *Connecticut Yankee in King Arthur's Court* (1889). Morgan disliked

the Dark Ages and longed to return to his munitions factory in Hartford, Connecticut. Wells was also interested in comparing historical periods, but in *The Time Machine* (1895), the real hero is the device itself. In fact, we never learn the name of the "Time Traveler." He is simply an English scientist fascinated with the possibility of building a machine that will take him through time, the fourth dimension. He eventually travels 800,000 years into the future, where he encounters a strange world peopled by conflicting Eloi and Warlocks. The latter creatures steal his machine, and he barely escapes to tell the tale. On his return, the time traveler's friends don't believe him, and at the end of the book, he disappears again into time, never to return.[4]

Despite Wells's skill as a storyteller, the book's real interest comes, not from the plot, but from the idea of plausible time travel and the creative possibilities such travel opens up. Wells's time machine gave writers and readers a mechanism for breaking out of the present and living vicariously in other times, other places. And by including the scientific theories underlying the concept, Wells made time travel more believable.

The Time Machine was a tremendously popular and influential book.[5] People readily understood its attractive idea of man's mastery of time, even if they couldn't quite grasp the scientific explanation of the reason that this might be possible. They correctly realized that time traveling would allow them a new perspective from which to view historical events. Suddenly, the context of history was much greater; man had the freedom to move about in it and to look at specific periods of history from varying points of view. Wells used the device to move far into the future, answering perhaps an anxiety about the nature of life to come. (In chapter 8, he even describes a museum of dated artifacts from the Industrial Revolution.) However, time travel could also be used to go *back* and clarify our picture of life in the past, allowing us to reassure ourselves that civilization *is* improving; or, if we take the opposite view, giving us the opportunity to escape from the present and visit a lost Golden Age.

Still, there was the problem of credibility, especially in an increasingly skeptical age. Time travel defies our common sense, which cautions us that time is real and well-grounded in the individual's own experience of the natural cycles of day and night, moons, and seasons, and the irreversible stages of life. There is also the matter of evolution!

I doubt whether the concept of time travel would have retained its vitality, had it not been for Albert Einstein. In the same year that Wells published his book, Einstein was asking such questions as "What would the world look like if I rode a beam of light?" Ten years later, in his Special Theory of Relativity, Einstein theorized that, if a traveler could actually enter the domain of light, time for him would stop—since light is timeless and lives in the eternal present. From this eternal perspective, he wrote, "For us believing physicists, the distinction between past, present, and future is only an illusion, however persistent."

I'm not a physicist, so I won't attempt to explain Einstein's theory. I can try to illustrate it in humanistic terms, however: imagine all the events of history—not in a linear time line, but rather on a large painting by an artist like Peter Bruegel. (Bruegel's *Children's Games* or the *Netherlands Proverbs* are apt examples.) Every creature, person, and historical event has a place on history's teeming, colorful canvas. Time travel now becomes a simple trip from one part of the picture to another. Relationships are no longer linear, but relative to you, the traveler. The new historical adventure comes from looking for hitherto hidden patterns, examining neglected background details more carefully, and comparing in new ways, people and events among whom there was previously considered little relationship.

Some examples: Did Irish monks sail across the Atlantic in leather boats? What was Stone Age life in Holland like? How have soldiers throughout history relaxed after battle? *The answers are all in the painting.*

Armed with Einstein's theory, or with humanistic interpretations of it, four generations of twentieth-century writers and film makers have experimented with the possibilities of time travel in the realistic tradition of H. G. Wells.

Many writers have used the concept of the time machine. Among the better known are Jack Finney, Ray Bradbury, and Robert Silverberg. Of the many recent books on the subject of time, the most useful, as an introduction for the layman, is Michael Shallis's *On Time: An Investigation into Scientific Knowledge and Human Experience.* The classic is Jack Finney's *Time and Again,* which appeared in 1970. Ray Bradbury's *Dandelion Wine* contains a poignant section on a "happiness machine," describing the author's ironic comments on the negative aspects of the attempt to escape from the present. Time travel itself is exuberantly dealt with in Robert Silverberg's *Up the Line.*[6]

In 1981, Robert Forward explained, in laymen's terms just how a time machine could actually be built, and Gregory Benford—in his novel *Timescape* (1980)—demonstrated how English scientists in 1998 could send messages to their California colleagues in 1962, thereby saving the world from a catastrophic ecological crisis that had already occurred, but could still be averted! Although this sounds extremely paradoxical, Benford makes such communication sound reasonable. The same can be said of the work of the other masters of the time-machine motif.[7]

The desire to slip out of our own time is often strong. We willingly suspend disbelief. Perhaps that is why even fantasy is so appealing. Films such as Terry Gilliam's *Time Bandits* (1980) or the novels of Clifford Simak reassure us.[8] In Simak's *The Goblin Reservation*

(1968), time travel has been mastered, and all his creatures—legendary and real, from miniature Neanderthals to trolls—freely roam the Cosmos. The tone is comic, but the message is serious: modern man should try to transcend his own times, even though his dated philosophy and common sense resist that notion. Simak gently prods us toward relaxing our rigorous fixation with abstract digital time, stretching our creative minds, and using the tools that Wells, Einstein, and a school of speculative fiction writers have given us.

Paralleling this literary tradition is another far more loosely organized group of time trippers who have been interested in studying, interpreting, and experiencing different periods of history through simulation. They seldom use the terms *time travel* or *time machine,* and they vary so greatly in their reasons for wanting to simulate the past (or future) that they have communicated with one another only infrequently.

This mixed company of scholars and laymen, practising "experimental archaeology," "living history," and re-enacting, is the subject of this book.

Most of these time travelers would accept the premise that time travel is a useful intellectual tool, and that their museum, re-created raft, or encampment could be interpreted as a "time machine," a vehicle that enables people to re-enter another period of time, vicariously, and to simulate life there, if only for a short period.

Beyond that, superficially, they have little in common. They come from a variety of backgrounds. Some are trained archaeologists, others weekend warriors. Some use simulation as a serious research method or mode of interpretation, others trip for fun and the joy of just getting away from modern life. There are those who yearn to know more about pre-history and build Neolithic villages to find some of the answers; others don medieval armor and test their martial and courtly arts. Some are futurists; others grow nostalgic about nineteenth-century family farms. Most are fascinated with folklife and social history—the everyday lives of ordinary people—but at least one group prides itself on re-creating the Middle Ages the way it ought to have been; that is, without peasants. The world of these time travelers, or practitioners of simulation, if portrayed on a Bruegelesque canvas, would vibrate with activity.

*   *   *

Three major groups do emerge, differing from one another on the basis of their purpose for simulating life in other times. One group is primarily interested in using simulation as a mode of interpreting the realities of life in the past more effectively, generally at living museums and historic sites. These interpreters "animate" a restored fort, farm, or village, and invite visitors to involve themselves in the daily activities of the time it represents. *The site becomes, then, both the time machine and the destination of the time travel.* The goal of this group is essentially educational, and these interpreters often consider themselves master teachers.

A second group uses simulation as a research tool. Many of these are scholars, come from archaeology and the social sciences, and they have tried to develop archaeological and historic sites as outdoor laboratories—settings for testing ethnological theories or generating new data about material culture. Many of these scientists and their projects are well publicized—Thor Heyerdahl and his voyages on *Kon Tiki* or *Ra I* and *Ra II*—but there are scores of other, lesser-known but comparable projects.

The third and most colorful group is made up of "history buffs"—people who time-travel for personal reasons, often for play and the joy of getting away. Many of these enthusiasts identify with particular, real, or composite individuals of the past or future and fabricate "impressions" of them. Buffs are sticklers for "authenticity," especially with regard to clothing, grooming styles, and idiosyncracies of speech. Buffs often liken themselves to method actors, steeped in a role, and therefore able to improvise, comfortably and accurately, the behavior of a medieval squire, a Confederate sniper, a French *voyageur*.

I have devoted a section of this book to each group. The sections are roughly chronological and consists of case studies of museums, projects, and organizations. The point of view I use is often that of a participant-observer, for I believe it's important to evaluate these time machines from both the insider's and the outsider's perspective. Therefore, I've used, whenever possible, oral history and field notes as sources. At the end of the book is an appendix—an annotated list of sources and resources—books, sites, people, organizations, and so on, a "baker's dozen" of each.

In the final chapter, I ask myself the tough questions: What's the historical significance of these modern time machines? What is their function in our world? Do they have a future? In this final chapter, I introduce a thesis, relating the concept of time travel to the "Third Wave" that Alvin Toffler argues is engulfing us, and the recent thoughts of social historians on nostalgia.

One last note. Because I have been actively involved in all three aspects of simulation as a museum interpreter, an experimental researcher, and a buff, I often draw on my own experience and that of my family, colleagues, and friends. Many thanks to all of them. Special appreciation to Dale Jones and Luanne Gaykowski Kozma, my graduate assistants at Western Kentucky University, and Jan Anderson, whose husband I'm fortunate to be. All three patiently worked with me on Time Machines *and provided enthusiastic assistance. The memory of many happy days spent with my children Iain, Anna, and Coll at living museums was a continuing comfort.*

NOTES

1. Allan Anderson, telephone interview with author, August 1, 1983. This conversation helped me verify my childhood memory of Maier.
2. Joyce Anderson, interview with author, June 24, 1983.
3. This inclusive approach to living history was first put forward in my article "Living History: Simulating Everyday Life in Living Museums," *American Quarterly* 34:3 (1982), the annual bibliography issue.
4. H. G. Wells, *The Time Machine: The War of the Worlds* (1895; reprint, New York: Oxford University Press, 1977); Edward, Bellamy, *Looking Backward, 2000–1887* (1888; reprint, Cambridge: Harvard University Press, 1967); Mark Twain (Samuel Langhorne Clemens), *A Connecticut Yankee in King Arthur's Court* (1889; reprint, New York: W. W. Norton & Company, Inc., 1982).
5. See Isaac Asimov's introduction to *The Time Machine* (New York: Fawcett Premier, 1968), pp. 9–22.
6. Michael Shallis, *On Time: An Investigation into Scientific Knowledge and Human Experience* (New York: Schocken Books, 1983; Jack Finney, *Time and Again* (New York: Simon and Schuster, 1970); Ray Bradbury, *Dandelion Wine* (New York: Doubleday & Company, 1957); Robert Silverberg, *Up the Line* (New York: Ballantine Books, 1969).
7. Robert Forward, "How to Build a Time Machine," *Omni*, May 1980; Gregory Benford, *Time-Scape* (New York: Pocket Books, 1981).
8. Clifford D. Simak, *The Goblin Reservation* (1968; reprint, New York: Daw Books, Inc., 1982).

Part 1
Memory Machines:
Living History Museums

1

Over There

TEN YEARS ago, on a warm August evening, I visited a Finnish open-air museum on the island of Seurasaari, just outside of Helsinki. Although it was still midsummer bright, the tall pines that had been planted to screen the old buildings from one another darkened the scene, reminding me of Longfellow's "forest primeval," with its "murmuring pine and the hemlock." Walking up a lane, I heard a fiddler tuning up. Following the music, I entered a rectangular cluster of log farm buildings and saw him, sitting there, surrounded by other musicians and dancers, all dressed in traditional folk costumes. They nodded hello, and I sat down to watch and listen. Informally, they began to play—at times, solo, but mostly together. Occasionally, a dancer would initiate a set, and they would reel a while in a very relaxed way. One older man also sang a few very slow, sad-sounding songs.

A Finnish colleague, a folklorist, joined me. I asked him about the music, especially the songs. No, he said, they weren't particularly sad. Rather, they were slow, determined, *protest* songs. Against whom, I asked. He gestured toward Russia and indicated that the music, the dance, in fact all the folklore here—costumes, buildings, artifacts, even the re-enacted customs and festivals— helped Finns to remember who they were

and to keep in mind the eastern power that perennially threatens them. Looking back on that moment, I think that the museum's originator, the ethnographer Axel Heikel, might well have called his creation a national "memory machine."[1]

Open-air museums can function as powerful time machines, with the potential to transport visitors mentally and emotionally into the past, where important lessons can be learned. That achievement certainly was the intention of Artur Hazelius (1833–1901), founder of Skansen, the prototype of all open-air museums. The motto Hazelius chose for Skansen was "Know yourself by knowing the past."[2]

Hazelius was the son of a Swedish general who had strong ideas about education. The elder Hazelius wanted his boy to be educated in the country, away from the negative urban influences of Stockholm, close to nature and hard-working farming folk. The education took: Artur Hazelius became a linguist, interested in Swedish vernacular speech. He traveled throughout the country collecting regional dialects and narrative folklore. In 1872, he returned to Dalecarlia, on the Norwegian border, a particularly isolated region that he had known as a schoolboy. He was shocked at the changes that had taken place in the folk culture there since he had last

Fig. 1.1. Drawing on the example of local color painters, Artur Hazelius, in the late nineteenth century, created tableaux of regional Swedish folklife, complete with authentically costumed figures and appropriate artifacts. Often unabashedly sentimental, these tableaux established Hazelius's Nordiska Museet (Nordic Museum) as an enormously popular Swedish institution.—*Nordiska Museet, Stockholm, Sweden*

visited the area. Under the twin assaults of Victorianism and fundamentalist religion, the old regional traditions of dress, song, art, and custom were either being turned into affectations, for the sake of tourists; or—worse—tabooed, in the cause of puritanism. Hazelius's reaction was immediate: he applied for a grant from the Swedish Antiquarian Association and returned to Dalecarlia that autumn, to begin documenting the endangered Dalecarlian folklore. Hazelius enlisted a network of "informants" and started recording and collecting oral traditions and folk art. His young wife joined him, and their diaries reflect a joy at record-

ing material they believed was both beautiful and of national significance. In 1873, they opened a museum of Scandinavian folklore in Stockholm, and Hazelius was full of enthusiasm and hope for his Nordiska Museet, or Northern Museum.

The following spring, his wife died in childbirth. This loss had a profound effect on him, and at the age of forty-one, Hazelius dedicated the remainder of his life to one mission: establishing the Northern Museum as a major state institution that could create a national consciousness in the Swedish people and foster a sense of identity rooted in the country's traditional folklore. Hazelius quickly gained the support of Parliament, wealthy patrons, and—most important—the Swedish people. A major indoor museum was built, and by 1880, its exhibits were immensely popular.

Hazelius believed that artifacts of the kind that he and his wife had collected in Dalecarlia should be exhibited in their cultural contexts. Drawing on the example of regional local-color painters and documentary photographers, he moved entire rooms from the provinces into the museum and turned them into tableaux, complete with authentically costumed wax figures and appropriate furnishings and smaller artifacts. Some of these "folklife pictures" were unabashedly sentimental; one called *"Lillans sista bädd"* (The Little Girl's Deathbed) recreated a domestic funeral of a child and contained accurately costumed figures of a minister, mother and father, two sisters, and the dead infant in the crib—all in a restored Dalecarlian peasants' sitting room.

Hazelius, like Dickens, knew what the public liked. A friend wrote that "Hazelius felt and worked with the public like a theater director or department store manager would have done. He identified himself with its tastes and wishes in the area in which he worked."[3] Hazelius himself wrote that he hoped, through these provincial folklife pictures, to give Swedes a "live impression of people's moods and customs" and thereby foster better understanding between the country's different regions. Even today, historic photographs of these life-sized dioramas communicate their stories to the viewer. One can't help being drawn into their intimate tragedies or domestic celebrations.

An indoor museum, Hazelius concluded, could never be a national center where "Swedes could see their great lovely country in summary."[4] He therefore—literally—invented Skansen, the first *freilichtmuseen*, or open-air museum.[5]

During the 1880s, Hazelius began to collect, from throughout Sweden, entire farms, churches, manor houses, cottages, an assortment of workshops and stores, windmills, and wooden bell towers. He also sought out native plants and animals from each region, for he was determined to set each structure in its natural as well as its historical and cultural context.

As a functionalist, Hazelius believed that material culture could be understood only in terms of its cultural environment. A charcoal-burner's hut should be exhibited in its own peculiar landscape, just as open-fire cooking utensils needed the context of a peasant kitchen. His policy was to acquire structures and artifacts representative of each of Sweden's regions, classes, and major historical periods, from the 1600s to the present. There were half-timbered farm houses from Skåne in the South, Lapp huts from the far north, and appropriate animals—red deer and reindeer—for each.

Skansen became, in the public's eye, part natural history park, part historical museum, and part zoo. From its inception, Skansen's success was assured. It was a "pocket edition" of Sweden and a natural attraction. It opened Octboer 11, 1981, to enthusiastic crowds.[6]

Hazelius went one step further. Without activity, he felt, Skansen would be nothing but a dead museum, a dry shell of the past. In 1898, he wrote "We want to exhibit folklife in living style."[7] Hazelius brought in musicians to play their fiddles, Lapps to herd reindeer, Dalecarlian peasants to live in their mountain chalets. Old popular customs were revived: girls with candles in their hair sang on St. Lucia's Day, and museum staff and visitors alike danced around the Mora farm Maypole on Midsummer's Eve. There was folk music and dancing on warm evenings, and handicraft markets and fairs in the winter. Skansen became the first "living museum."

Almost immediately, the museum achieved Hazelius's goal of being the cultural center of

Fig. 1.2. Without activity, argued nineteenth-century museum master Artur Hazelius, open-air museums would be dry shells of the past. At his Skansen, prototype of all open-air museums, Hazelius introduced the *living* exhibit. Traditional rural customs and music attracted the attention of an increasingly urban public, searching for its cultural roots.—*Nordiska Museet, Stockholm, Sweden*

Fig. 1.3. Artur Hazelius's Skansen became Sweden in summary, a unique collection of native buildings, plants, animals, and people. Especially popular were folk singers and dancers who performed on long summer evenings.—*Nordiska Museet, Stockholm, Sweden*

Fig. 1.4. Old calendar customs such as Saint Lucia Day and Midsummer's Eve were revived at Skansen during the 1890s. For Swedes, this open-air museum was a folk park, an ideal setting for a family outing or a patriotic celebration. —*Foto Expressen*

Sweden. With its 150 buildings on seventy-five acres in the heart of Stockholm, Skansen is a veritable kaleidoscope of time machines, capable of transporting visitors over space and through time into the traditional farms and shops and churches of old Sweden.

Within twenty-one years of Skansen's opening, major national open-air museums were established in Norway (Norsk Folkemuseum, Oslo, 1894), Denmark (Frilandsmuseet, Copenhagen, 1987), and the Netherlands (Nederlands Openluchtmuseum, Arnhem, 1912).

Despite two devastating world wars, the number of museums grew, and in 1974, the Association of European Open Air Museums commissioned Adelhart Zippelius to compile a comprehensive guide.[8] Zippelius described 314 significant open-air museums in twenty-one European countries, covering the continent from Iceland to Hungary, Ireland to Bulgaria.

Ironically, while these open-air museums are all "children of Skansen," few attempted even modestly to simulate life in the past, and so cannot therefore be called "living museums." They are like superb historical stage sets, without the actors. Visiting most European open-air museums is akin to time-traveling through the past, only to find vacant and silent homes and shops. Seldom do you encounter an old man singing protest songs, as I did in Finland, or a miner's wife heating up water for her husband's bath—a scene that sometimes takes place in the North of England Open Air Museum in Beamish. This is not to say that these museums aren't popular and don't function as major preservation projects and research institutions; most are considered by visitors to be "folk parks," comfortable places you can take the family to for a picnic and a stroll. Throughout Europe, open-air museums are crowded with visitors enjoying the fresh air and sun in a pleasant, old-timey context. And most of these institutions undertake significant fieldwork and research. However, it is in the area of interpretation—or "didactic simulation," as the Nebraska folklorist Roger Welsch calls it—that they hold back from Hazelius's daring experiments with live interpreters.

I discussed this situation with Konrad Köstlin, a German folklorist and colleague, as we walked around the open-air museum of Schleswig-Holstein, near Kiel, in northern Germany.[9] Köstlin ascribed this lack of live interpretation to a fear of *folklorismos,* a German term for what Americans call "fakelore"—pseudo traditions being passed off as the real thing. *Folklorismos* is a dreaded word. Hazelius himself was bitterly criticized for hoking up the past at Skansen, but he was able to defend his programs. Other museum directors, however, feared the charge that they were cheapening their nation's or region's cultural heritage. The understandable result was several generations of conservative administrators, often architectural historians with a fine arts backgound.

Twice, when I was in Europe, I experienced this antipathy toward *folklorismos.* Once, after showing slides of Plimoth Plantation, an unabashed living museum, to an international conference of regional ethnologists, a curator came up to me and said that he had enjoyed the photos, but weren't they really examples of *folklorismos,* and therefore unsuitable models for European museums? A second time, I was watching a performance of singing and harp-playing in a restored historic inn in Wales. The audience included several dozen social historians from Wales, Ireland, Europe, and America. It was a magical moment; I really felt transported back in time to medieval Wales. Most of the other guests shared the same enthusiasm for the interpretation—or the entertainment, if you like. But a Scottish colleague of mine caught my eye—and pinched his nose. "It stinks of *folklorismos,*" his gesture said, unmistakably.[10]

Other, less emotional reasons are given for this reluctance to simulate life in the past at open-air museums. One is the curator's understandable concern for his collection. Might not activities, however educationally valid and traditional, endanger his artifacts? The answer, of course, is yes, and so the decision is often made to forgo live interpretation in favor of guidebooks. A second objection was raised by Iowerth Peate, Curator of the Welsh Folk Museum near Cardiff, one of the finest open-air museums in Europe. Reviewing a proposal to establish a series of living historical farms in the United States, he asked, "How far can a folk museum go in reconstructing the past?" He answer was: not very far. The scope of most European museums is too broad. Peate's museum, for example, covers the whole of Wales and its evolution from prehistoric times to the present. Peate's comment:

If in a folk museum we re-created the full working of, let us say, a seventeenth-century farm, we should also have to re-create life of an eighteeth-century Nonconformist chapel, with presumably a congregation in suitable costume, etc., etc. We revert again to the question of how far can a folk museum go?[11]

Peate went on to say that such ideas were unacceptable to most European museums on practical and financial grounds.

There was a compromise position, one that Artur Hazelius had taken in the 1890s: *Selectively use living activities at particularly suitable sites and times.* Folk music and dancing in the farmyard won't endanger your buildings, break your budget, nor—if it is done authentically—will it elicit charges of *folklorismos.* Still, few have followed Hazelius's example. In 1980, G. Ellis Burcaw reported on a long tour of European open-air museums. His conclusions:

I recalled that the great majority of open-air museums on the Continent do not regularly employ even the demonstration of equipment or the normal work practices of a farm or village. (Skansen is a notable exception.) On the living history continuum, history on the Continent is dead; beautifully embalmed, but dead. The farmsteads are empty husks of peasant culture, collected as curiosities, not as settings for the explication of social history.[12]

The same situation is definitely not the case in North America, where Hazelius's influence is still felt and the example of Skansen emulated.

NOTES

1. Interview with a colleague who prefers anonymity, on August 15, 1973, in Helsinki, Finland.

2. Nils-Arvid Bringeus, "Artur Hazelius and the Nordic Museum," *Ethnologia Scandinavia* 3 (1974): 5–16.

3. Bringeus, *Hazelius,* p. 10.

4. Nils Erik Baehrendtz, "Skansen—A Stock-Taking at Ninety," *Museum* 36:3 (1982): 173–178.

5. Bo Lagercrantz, "A Great Museum Pioneer of the Nineteenth Century," *Curator* 7:3 (1964): 179–184.

6. Mats Rehnberg, *The Nordiska Museet and Skansen* (Stockholm: The Nordiska Museet, 1957).

7. Bringeus, *Hazelius,* p. 10.

8. Adelhart Zippelius, *Hanbuch der Europäischen Freilichtmuseen* (Koln: Rheinland-Verlag Gmb H, 1974).

9. Konrad Köstlin, interview with author, August 25, 1973, in Kiel, West Germany.

10. The first of these interesting experiences took place in Helsinki, on Tuesday, August 14, 1973; the second, near Cardiff, South Wales, on Friday, August 26, 1977.

11. Ioworth C. Peate, "Reconstructing the Past," *Folk Life* 6 (1968): 113–114.

12. G. Ellis Burcaw, "Can History Be Too Lively?", *Museum Journal* 80 (June 1980): 5–7. See also Ormond Loomis, *Sources on Folk Museums and Living History Farms* (Bloomington, Indiana: Folklore Forum Bibliographic and Special Series, 1977).

2

An "American Way of History"

DURING the summer of 1876, Artur Hazelius sent to the United States a set of six folklife tableaux, "illustrating the habits and the dress of the peasantry," for the Swedish exhibit at the Centennial Exhibition in Philadelphia. Included were scenes of elk-hunting, courtship, christening, life among the Laplanders, Bible reading, and the death of a little girl. The *Illustrated History of the Centennial Exhibition* noted that the "Swedish exhibit was one of the most complete and tastefully arranged in the Exhibition. The show-cases were handsomer than was the rule with the European nations."[1] For an American public familiar with John Rogers's statuary groups, the Swedish tableaux generated warm recognition and friendly cross-cultural comparison.

One American exhibit also focused on traditional folklife: the New England states built a "New England Farmer's Home" and a "Modern Kitchen." The structures were considered "one of the most interesting features of the Exhibition." The editors of the centennial's *Illustrated History* wrote, of them:

The New England Farmer's Home was a plain one-story log house, and was built and arranged in the style of the New England farmhouses of a century ago. It contained a parlor, or "settin-room," a kitchen, and bed-rooms, all of which were furnished with veritable heirlooms contributed by the people of New England . . . . Everything in the house had the ripe flavor of antiquity, and the visitor might see in the place an exact reproduction of the homes that his ancestors, the Minute Men of the Revolution, left so promptly and bravely when the news of the battle of Lexington called them to arms. The farm-house was occupied only by ladies, who were dressed in the quaint costumes of their great-grandmothers and who conducted visitors through the house, and explained to them the story and uses of its contents.[2]

Visitors to the Log House could compare it with the modern kitchen, which "contained all the improvements of the present age, and showed the progress of the century in the department of domestic economy."[3] Here, then, were the twin American themes, both positive: *the good old days were indeed good, but we have progressed since then. These are the good old days, too!*

This pioneer experiment with living interpretation, which actually predated Skansen by fifteen years, was followed up by other innovative projects, also carried out by New Englanders.

One of the first innovators was George Francis Dow (1868–1936).[4] Dow was an antiquarian particularly interested in the folklife of New England. Born in New Hampshire and educated at Wakefield Academy, he was

25

Fig. 2.1. Featured at the 1876 U.S. Centennial Exposition at Philadelphia were six of Artur Hazelius's Swedish folklife tableaux. For an American public familiar with John Rogers's statuary groups, the Swedish exhibition generated friendly cross-cultural comparison. — *Nordiska Museet, Stockholm, Sweden*

Fig. 2.2. A popular American exhibit at the U.S. Centennial Exposition in 1876 was "Ye Olden Times," a one-story colonial log house that projected the "ripe flavor of antiquity." Costumed guides from New England conducted visitors through the house, commenting on its heirlooms. — *The Smithsonian Institution, Washington, D.C.*

a businessman before deciding to devote his energies to the study, preservation, and interpretation of New England material culture. Dow was essentially a public historian. He became secretary of the Essex Institute in Salem, Massachusetts, in 1898 and was enthusiastic about applying there the interpretive techniques pioneered by Hazelius at Skansen. In 1907, Dow installed, in the Essex Institute's main hall, three period rooms: a 1750 kitchen and an 1800 bedroom and parlor. He attempted to create the illusion of reality by "casually placing on the table before the fireplace in the parlor a Salem newspaper printed in the year 1800 and on it a pair of silver-horned spectacles, as though just removed by the reader."[5]

Two years later, Dow acquired for the institute one of Salem's oldest structures, the 1685 John Ward house. It was moved to a lot adjoining the museum. In his reports to the board, from 1909 to 1913, Dow told of his progress in restoring and interpreting the Ward house. His goal was to furnish the house in a realistic way, so as to present "a truthful picture of 17th century household life in Salem."[6] In 1912, with restoration well under way, Dow noted that:

Where original furniture or utensils of the period have not been available, reproductions have been made, the finished result is believed to be highly successful, giving much of the atmosphere of liveableness. Miss Sarah W. Symonds and her assistants occupy the second floor and act as custodians, showing the house to visitors when the cow bell signals its call from the front entry. They will be dressed in homespun costumes of the time when the house was built.[7]

And in 1913, Dow was able to report on his attempt to re-create the lived-in atmosphere of the home:

The experiment of showing visitors about "the old house" by Miss Symonds and her two assistants dressed in Homespun costumes of the time when the house was built, has proved to be a great success, as the appropriately costumed figures

Fig. 2.3. In 1912, the New England antiquarian George Francis Dow restored the 1685 John Ward house for the Essex Institute in Salem, Massachusetts. Dow attempted to re-create a historically realistic atmosphere through the use of "custodians dressed in homespun costumes of the time when the house was built." This early experiment in living history proved a great success.—*The Essex Institute, Salem, Massachusetts*

add much to the effectiveness of the restored interior. A gentleman from New York City, who has a country estate in Virginia, has recently dressed his house servants in careful reproductions of these 17th century costumes worn by our assistants during their summer season. The old house with costumed attendants has also been photographed for moving pictures, and thus will be seen by many thousands in distant cities.[8]

Dow also moved to the Essex Institute's "lot" an apothecary shop, a spinning-and-weaving room, a shoemaker's, a cent-shop or general store, and a lean-to shed for housing agricultural implements, a chaise, and a sleigh. He then planted an "old-fashioned" flower garden and two pear trees, upon which were grafted "scions from the Endecott (1630) and Winthrop (1640) pear trees."[9] In four years, he had established America's first open-air museum.

In 1919, Dow joined the staff of the Society for the Preservation of New England Antiquities (SPNEA) and began editing its journal, *Old-Time New England*. With the support of William Sumner Appleton, its secretary and a strong advocate of the Skansen type of open-air museum, the SPNEA opened up communication with the Northern Museum in Stockholm. In a 1919 article in *Art and Archaeology,* Appleton discussed the Swedish open-air museum and its use of realistic recreation of the past. It was, he suggested, a potentially useful model for American museums.[10]

Henry Ford took the suggestion. He visited the Society for the Preservation of New England Antiquities in 1923, to look over the association's collections and to talk with Dow and Appleton about old buildings and museums. Ford was in the midst of restoring his boyhood home to its 1876 condition. He was also thinking of building an open-air museum in nearby South Sudbury, Massachusetts, around the Wayside Inn made memorable by the poems of Henry Wadsworth Longfellow. Ford's motives were both patriotic and personal. A Ford company carpenter, Ron Schumann, who helped restore Ford's boyhood house noted that Ford enjoyed "working" in the past.

He'd take the old equipment out and thresh. He often used to do that down at the homestead. He would invite some of the old-timers who were still around the neighborhood, and they'd watch him thresh. Mr. Ford would go over and meet them, talk with them, and different things like that.[11]

Another employee, Edward Cutler, said about Ford's restored house:

They'd have parties over there, and they'd get all dressed up. The men and women were in the old costumes, and they'd dance, and they'd have an orchestra over there.[12]

When Ford eventually restored the Wayside Inn, in 1926, at the cost of millions, he immediately held a country dance with everyone in colonial costumes. He invited Alice Longfellow, the poet's daughter, and they literally danced the night away. When it became obvious to him that South Sudbury was too far away from his home and business in Dearborn, Michigan, Ford restored, at the cost of a half million dollars, the Botsford Inn, a few miles outside Detroit. Here, he had danced as a youth, and when the inn was completed, it too became the setting for evenings of old-time music and dancing. For Ford, old buildings—whether famous or humble—were potential time machines, in which the life of the past could be simulated and celebrated. He clearly understood the educational potential of a "living museum," but he also appreciated the sheer joy of reviving old-time customs and intensifying them by the use of an authentic setting, costumes, music, and so on.

Two years after the completion of the Botsford Inn, Ford began work on Greenfield Village, in Dearborn, Michigan. Opened in 1929, Greenfield Village was the first really large American open-air museum based on the Skansen model. Ford wanted the village to be a truly living museum. His goal, he wrote, was to reproduce

American life as lived; and that I think, is the best way to preserve at least a part of our history and tradition. For by looking at things people used and that show the way they lived, a better and truer impression can be gained than could be had in a month of reading.[13]

Ford hoped that the museum would "demonstrate, for educational purposes, the development of American arts, sciences, customs, and institutions by reproducing or re-enacting the conditions and circumstances of such development in a manner calculated to convey a realistic picture."[14]

Despite the Great Depression that began on October 29, 1929—the day Greenfield Village was dedicated—Ford was able to relocate and restore more than fifty historic buildings by 1935. They included a church; town hall; school; courthouse; post office;

Fig. 2.4. Made famous by Henry Wadsworth Longfellow's *Tales of a Wayside Inn,* the Wayside Inn of South Sudbury, Massachusetts, was restored by Henry Ford in 1926. Ford invited the poet's daughter Alice to the inn's grand opening, which included a country dance. Guests all wore colonial clothing and frolicked the night away.—*Henry Ford Museum, the Edison Institute, Dearborn, Michigan*

general store; carding mill; and the homes, shops, and factories of many of his personal heroes: Noah Webster, William McGuffey, the Wright Brothers, and—of course, most important—Thomas Edison. Ford personally continued to direct the village's development until his death in the spring of 1947. Edward Cutler, who supervised much of the museum's day-to-day development, remembered Ford's response to his American Skansen:

It was a relief for him to get down there. For years he wouldn't let me have a telephone. When I would ask him about it, and I had a lot of running around to do, he would stay, "Oh, forget that stuff. I came down here to get away."[15]

While Henry Ford was assembling his "pocket edition" of America, complete with a facsimile of Independence Hall, John D. Rockefeller, Jr., was similarly engaged on *his* monumental project in Williamsburg, Virginia. In 1926, Rockefeller agreed to provide funds for the restoration, reconstruction, and refurnishing of the colonial capital of Virginia. Eventually, five hundred structures were rebuilt in an accurately re-created historic landscape.

The idea of re-creating an entire historic city had come from William Goodwin, rector of the 1715 Bruton Parish Church. Goodwin had come to Williamsburg just after the turn of the century and supervised the restoration of his church. In 1907, he documented the project in his *Bruton Parish Church Restored and Its Historic Environment* and set out his goal of restoring the complete capital. Williamsburg, he believed, was "the Cradle of the Republic" and "the birthplace of her liberty." He wrote:

If you have ever walked around Williamsburg lake on a moonlight night, when most of the people . . . are fast asleep, and felt the presence and companionship of the people who used to live here in the long gone years, and remembered the things that they did and the things they stood for, and pictured them going into or coming out of the old houses . . . you would then know what an interesting place Williamsburg is. You would realize that it is about the most interesting place in America.[16]

In 1924, Goodwin suggested to the Fords that the historic area of Williamsburg could be purchased for a "mere four or five million." Ford turned the idea down, for a number of reasons, chief among them being his involvement in his own open-air museum at Dearborn. Goodwin then turned to Rockefeller, who visited the city on November 26, 1926. Rockefeller found the opportunity to re-create the entire capital "irresistible." Although he had decided to acquire and restore the community building by building, what fascinated him was the dream of restoring the "whole area." Rockefeller asked Goodwin to prepare a master plan, and on November 21, 1927, in a meeting in New York, Rockefeller studied it.[17] Goodwin remembers that Rockefeller

. . . went through the whole town, following the map, explaining the location of every prominent building, giving its history, and significance to the plan, and the reasons why the Restoration appealed to his imagination and interest. I felt, as I listened to him, that if he were presenting the plan to me and I had the means, I would be glad to give any amount to see it through.[18]

In 1937, in an article in *National Geographic*, Rockefeller reiterated his reason for financing the project.

The restoration of Colonial Williamsburg enlisted my interest and support because to see beautiful and historic places and buildings disintegrating has long caused me real distress. It was this feeling that moved me to aid in Versailles, Fontainebleau, and Reims. To undertake to preserve a single building while its environment has changed and is no longer in keeping has always seemed to me unsatisfactory—and much less worthwhile.

The restoration of Williamsburg, however, offered an opportunity to restore the complete area and free it entirely from alien or inharmonius surroundings as well as to preserve the beauty and charm of the old buildings and gardens of the city and its historic significance. Thus it made a unique and irresistable appeal.[19]

Rockefeller also had definite ideas on the educational purpose of the project. Cary Carson, present director of research at the Colonial Williamsburg Foundation, notes that the restoration's first official statement of purpose, written in consultation with Rockefeller, asserted that "an authentic, three-dimensional environment was essential to understanding the 'lives and times' of early Americans and appreciating their contribution 'to the ideals and culture of our country.'"[20]

But it was Goodwin who advocated greater planning in the area of "interpretation." In a 1930 letter, he even used this word when he argued for a staff position for "someone who would be put in charge of meeting the public, gearing his approach to the different age groups that would be represented." He warned that "future visitors would want to

Fig. 2.5. Predicting that "future vistors would want to know about the *people* who lived in Williamsburg just as much as they would want to know about the architecture," Kenneth Chorley, Colonial Williamsburg's director of restoration, established a corps of interpreters in 1932. Live interpretation was immediately popular among visitors to Williamsburg.—*Colonial Williamsburg, Williamsburg, Virginia*

know about the *people* who lived in Williamsburg just as much as they would want to know about the architecture. . . . "[21] In 1932, Kenneth Chorley, who had been hired to direct the project, suggested that local people be employed as hostesses on a part-time basis. On a warm Friday evening, September 16, 1932, Martha Dovell and Doris Macomber, dressed in colonial costumes, welcomed visitors to the Old Raleigh Tavern, the first of Williamsburg's exhibitions to open. Live interpretation was immediately popular among visitors. Governor Pollard of Virginia said, of his first visit in 1932, that "as you enter the tavern and walk through the parlor and the ladies' withdrawing room, you feel the presence of those 'fair and accomplished ladies of Williamsburg.'"[22] The guides helped him visualize the historical figures who had once frequented the tavern.

This feeling of being in a time machine carried over to the hostesses, as well. Mildred

Fig. 2.6. Colonial Williamsburg's use of live interpreters to simulate life and work in the colonial Virginia capital inspired a similar approach at numerous other American restorations and outdoor museums in the 1940s and 1950s. Williamsburg's living-history program pioneered an "American way of history."— *Colonial Williamsburg, Williamsburg, Virginia*

Arthur, one of the early interpreters, described this experience.

Sometimes I feel that I am actually walking among those staunch individualists of that exciting era . . . I pass the Peyton Randolph House and envision Mr. Randolph and his wife, Betty, entertaining the newly arrived governor, Robert Dinwiddie. At the Geddy House, I can see the silversmith, his wife, and five children crowded into those few small rooms, the youngest child asleep on the trundle pulled out from beneath the main bed. All the exhibition buildings—all my houses, as I call them—are as familiar to me as the one to which I retreat at night, when my costume comes off and I have to renew my acquaintance with the present.[23]

By the 1940s, Williamsburg was employing an entire "corps" of interpreters to simulate life and work in the city's many homes and shops. The impact of Williamsburg's experiment with live interpretation on other American open-air museums, taking shape during that period, cannot be under-estimated. Plimoth Plantation and Old Sturbridge Village in Massachusetts, the Farmer's Museum at Cooperstown, New York, and Mystic Seaport in Connecticut were all inspired by Williamsburg's use of costumed interpreters and historically accurate craft demonstrations. Each of these regional institutions sought to become a "living museum," built on the premise that the folklife of a region is historically significant, and its material culture should be collected, preserved, studied, and especially interpreted. At each of these open-air museums, selected buildings were relocated or re-created in a village landscape, and the lives and activities of ordinary townsfolk were simulated. Some museums went further than others, but a definite "American way of history," based on the example set by Skansen, the Essex Institute, Greenfield Village, and Colonial Williamsburg, was clearly emerging.

NOTES

1. James McCabe, *The Illustrated History of the Centennial Exhibition Held in Commemoration of the One-Hundredth Anniversary of American Independence* . . . (Philadelphia, 1876; reprint, Philadelphia: The National Publishing Company, 1975). Hazilius's tableaux are reviewed on pp. 144–146.

2. McCabe, *Centennial History*, pp. 239–240.

3. McCabe, *Centennial History*, p. 240.

4. The definitive history of the historic preservation movement in the United States is found in Charles B. Hosmer, Jr.,'s *Presence of the Past* (New York: G. P. Putman's Sons, 1965) and *Preservation Comes of Age* (Charlottesville: University Press of Virginia, 1981).

5. Hosmer, *Presence*, p. 214.

6. Hosmer, *Presence*, pp. 215–216.

7. George F. Dow, "Report of the Secretary," *Annual Report of the Essex Institute* (May 6, 1912), p. 16.

8. Dow, *Report* (May 5, 1913), pp. 17–18.

9. Hosmer, *Presence*, p. 216.

10. William Sumner Appleton, "Destruction and Preservation," *Art and Archaeology* VIII (May 1919).

11. Cited in Upward, Geoffrey C. *A Home for Our Heritage* (Dearborn, Michigan: The Henry Ford Museum Press, 1979), p. 11.

12. Upward, *Home*, p. 12.

13. Cited in Edward P. Alexander, *Museums in Motion* (Nashville: American Association for State and Local History, 1979), p. 92.

14. Upward, *Home*, p. 75.

15. Upward, *Home*, p. 22.

16. Cited in Edward Alexander's *The Interpretation Program of Colonial Williamsburg* (Williamsburg: The Colonial Williamsburg Foundation, 1971), p. 7.

17. Hosmer, *Preservation*, p. 18.

18. Hosmer, *Preservation*, p. 27.

19. John D. Rockefeller, Jr., "The Genesis of the Williamsburg Restoration," *National Geographic* 71:4 (April 1937): 401.

20. Cited in Cary Carson's "Living Museums of Everyman's History," *Harvard Magazine* 83 (July-August 1981): 25–26.

21. Hosmer, *Preservation*, p. 43.

22. J. Douglas Smith, "A Solemn Obligation," *Colonial Williamsburg Today* 5:1 (Autumn 1982): 15; and correspondence with Bland Blackford, Director, Department of Archives and Records, June 20, 1983.

23. Mildred Arthur, "The Joy of Hostessing," *Colonial Williamsburg Today* 5:1 (Autumn 1982): 8.

3
Living History

WILLIAMSBURG may have been winning kudos among museum professionals for its life interpretation, but it scared the devil out of me, on my first visit. It was just after the Second World War. My dad had been discharged from the Marine Corps, and we headed north from Parris Island, South Carolina, to Buffalo, New York. Williamsburg was on the way, and we stopped. The restoration had achieved the status of a secular shrine by then, and many servicemen had made the pilgrimage. In 1942, a young army private wrote: "Of all the sights I have seen, and all the books I have read, and the speeches I have heard, none ever made me see the greatness of this country with more force and clearness than when I saw Williamsburg slumbering peacefully on its own foundation."[1] My dad had heard similar endorsements from his buddies and wanted to see the colonial capital for himself. I was five years old, and the place terrified me. Quite literally, I thought we had entered another world, and its strangeness was threatening, especially the gaol. Suppose someone closed that heavy door and I was trapped in this dark, damp room the rest of my life? I worried about the possibility of getting lost and having to talk to these strange people in their incredible clothes. Even the red-coated soldier in the guard-house was fearsome. I was used to soldiers in uniform, but he was something else. For me, the past, as re-created by Williamsburg, was all too real.

Adults were not so apprehensive as that about the realism re-created at Williamsburg and the other new open-air museums. In the late 1940s and the 1950s, these sites became popular tourist attractions. These years were great for traveling; family cars were big, and gas was cheap. Like hundreds of thousands of other families, we stopped by at Greenfield Village, Cooperstown, Old Sturbridge Village, and other sites, on the way to the seaside or a north woods vacation. A generation of families throughout those two decades realized that an enjoyable encounter with history was indeed possible.

A few academic historians sensed the potential of the new "living museums." In 1944, Herbert Kellar of the McCormick Historical Association in Chicago proposed that Americans establish a series of living museums, "to portray vividly and realistically not only the past but, in many instances, the present."[2] Kellar was particularly interested in the possibility of regional agricultural and economic museums. He noted that, although 1880s Dakota wheat farms and Wisconsin lumber camps no longer existed, "it would still be possible to acquire wheat land and timber and to re-establish and operate a bonanza wheat farm or an old-time lumber camp."[3] His inspiration was Lincoln's New Salem, near Springfield, Illinois. Kellar remembered the effect the re-creation had had on him as he stood in the middle of its main street.

You are suddenly in another world. The feeling grows as you explore in succession dwelling houses, a cooper's shop, a hattery, a country store, a doctor's office, an inn, a grog shop and other edifices, and see each one fully equipped and—if peopled—ready to take on accustomed activity at a moment's notice. The illusion is complete, and you realize you have been transported back a hundred years.[4]

A decade later, the National Park Service began seriously to consider using live interpretation. In 1957, its leading spokesman for interpretation, Freeman Tilden, wrote his classic guide to the field, *Interpreting Our Heritage.* Tilden challenged rangers and interpreters to "people" their sites: "Architecture and furnishings are much; we admire and draw conclusions from them, but we must find the art to keep them from seeming to have been frozen at the moment of time when nobody was home." He advocated demonstrations, participation, and animation. Tilden was impressed by the sight of visitors to the Farmers' Museum at Cooperstown watching the old-time process of breaking flax, of weaving, and of candlemaking. He liked it even more when visitors could participate physically in a historic activity, even if it was just a leisurely carriage ride at Williamsburg. And he particularly was moved by animation, or the realistic simulation of life in the past.[5]

Tilden illustrated the effective animation of history in his chapter "Past into Present":

On a Sunday afternoon I went to the Custis-Lee Mansion, "Arlington House," just across the Potomac from Washington. As I entered, someone was playing the piano. It seemed so perfectly natural that somebody would be playing a piano in a house that had sheltered the Custises and the Lees, or indeed in any historic house where people had lived! I had been many times in this famous home and had delighted in its beautiful maintenance. I had, in truth, never actually felt it to be cold; but like so many other precious relics of the past, its treasures have to be safeguarded, and most of the rooms can be seen only from the doorways. That is the penalty we must pay for preservation.

But now, I felt that this house was peopled. Not by visitors like myself, but by those who had been right there—the men and women who loved the place because it was home. In the drawing room an attractive girl, costumed in the period of 1860, was playing the very tunes that were current at that time. It could have been a neighbor lass or Miss Mary Custis at the instrument, which itself was the very period. There was nothing obtrusive about the music, and I noted with pleasure that most of the visitors were not curious about it, a sure sign that it was in perfect harmony and accepted as part of the re-creation.[6]

The National Park Service took up Tilden's challenge and animated many of its sites, although it soon replaced that word with the term "living history." (The bilingual Parks Canada, the Canadian counterpart of the U.S. National Park Service, still prefers *animation,* because it conveys the same meaning in French and English.) In 1970, the National Park Service widely distributed a basic guide, *Keep It Alive! Tips on Living History Demonstration,* by William Kay.[7] although only twenty-eight pages long, the guide covered most of the topics of interest to a site manager considering living history as a mode of interpretation. Four years later, in a second guide, *The Audience and You: Practical Dramatics for the Park Interpreter,* Gordon Hilker spelled out in detail the elements that go into the "craft" of demonstration, borrowing heavily from the theatrical arts.[8] Hilker went into scripts, settings, equipment, direction, speech, and presentation. The seriousness of the guide reflected the enthusiasm and concern of the National Park Service for living history. By 1976, the Park Service was able to publish an

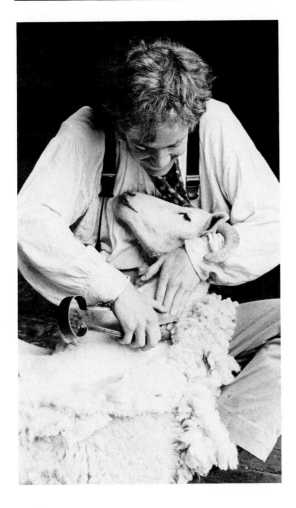

Fig. 3.1. An Association for Living Historical Farms and Agricultural Museums was founded at Old Sturbridge Village, Massachusetts, in 1970. During the following decade, scores of farms sprang up in all parts of North America, providing the continent with a "harvest of history."—*Old Sturbridge Village, Sturbridge, Massachusetts. Photograph by Robert S. Arnold*

Fig. 3.2. Sturbridge housewives prepare deep-dish apple pies for their hungry menfolk, as a dinner of corned beef, potatoes, and onions comes to the boil over an open farmhouse fire.—*Old Sturbridge Village, Sturbridge, Massachusetts. Photograph by Robert S. Arnold*

inventory of the seventy-one farms, prehistoric sites, historical parks, battlefields, and forts where significant living history projects were underway. The inventory, *Living History in the National Park Service*, is surprisingly useful as a guide to visitors a decade later, since most of the sites still continue to use living history as a mode of interpretation, despite budget reductions and the mode's obvious labor-intensive cost.[9]

However, it was outside the National Park Service that the living history museum movement really took hold. Marion Clawson, a foundation director, took up Herbert Kellar's idea again and proposed that twenty-five to fifty actual, operating "living historical" farms representing the nation's major regions, historic periods, and types of agriculture be re-created. In a 1965 article in the journal *Agricultural History*, Clawson outlined his recommendation.

Within the limits necessarily imposed by a sampling of time and geography, the farms should be reasonably typical of the time and place each is chosen to represent. The farm size, its crops, livestock, production methods, the products sold—all

Fig. 3.3. The annual round of seasonal work attracts visitors to the Pliney Freeman Farm at Old Sturbridge Village throughout the year. Spring plowing with oxen amid the splendor of April's New England budding provides a visual delight for contemporary time travelers.—*Old Sturbridge Village, Sturbridge, Massachusetts. Photograph by Robert S. Arnold*

these and other details of the farm should be as accurate as it is possible to make them. The critical aspect of this proposal is that each farm should be operating—a living farm and a living home. A family, or families, would actually live on them, operate them, and live as nearly as possible like the prototype.[10]

Clawson realized that developing these "living historical" farms would not be easy. He foresaw problems with visitors getting in the way of the farm families' routine, difficulties obtaining authentic crops and livestock, and the challenge of interpreting rural life for urban tourists who had never been on a farm

and didn't have a clue as to what they were looking at and why it was important.

Clawson's proposal was strongly supported by John Schlebecker, Curator of Agriculture at the Smithsonian Institution. In the next few years, Schlebecker wrote two reports, *The Past in Action: Living Historical Farms* (1967) and *Living Historical Farms: A Walk Into the Past* (1968), which not only filled out Clawson's proposal, but generated widespread interest in the living-history movement in the academic and museum communities.[11]

In September 1970, a cross section of

Fig. 3.4. Few visitors encounter the chilly tedium of winter logging at Old Sturbridge Village. For this Sturbridge farmer, "getting a sense of the past" is a lonely but ultimately fulfilling task. And his work report may help footnote the farm, filling in blanks in the historical record.—*Old Sturbridge Village, Sturbridge, Massachusetts. Photograph by Robert S. Arnold*

museum specialists, agricultural historians, geographers, folklorists, and farmers met at Old Sturbridge Village and founded an Association for Living Historical Farms and Agricultural Museums (ALHFAM). It soon became the umbrella organization for the living-history movement. Based in the Smithsonian, ALHFAM published a bimonthly *Bulletin;* held annual conferences, generally at living-history museums in the United States and Canada; and encouraged state, provincial, and local organizations interested in living-history interpretation. Most of the theoretical and practical writings on living

history have come from ALHFAM's members. These include John Schlebecker and Gale Peterson's *Living Historical Farms Handbook* (1972) and an inventory of *Selected Living Historical Farms, Villages, and Agricultural Museums in the United States and Canada*, compiled by Darryl Chase (1976).[12]

In 1981, ALHFAM decided to open up the organization to all living history projects, not just farms. The variety of institutional members now includes villages, historic houses, forts, ships, urban neighborhoods, and archaeological sites. Since a complete directory of sites using living history as a primary

Fig. 3.5. Interpretations at living-history farms and villages focuses on the everyday lives of ordinary people. Old Sturbridge Village placed special emphasis on the world of women in early nineteenth-century New England.—*Old Sturbridge Village, Sturbridge, Massachusetts. Photograph by Robert S. Arnold*

Fig. 3.6. All play and no work would not be historically realistic. Some homely routines, such as stuffing a mattress with fresh straw, appear exotic enough to some twentieth-century visitors for them to stop and take pictures of it.—*Old Sturbridge Village, Sturbridge, Massachusetts. Photograph by Robert S. Arnold*

Fig. 3.7. Summer haying at Old Sturbridge Village engages all members of the family. The early nineteenth century in America was a period of rapid progress in agriculture. Producing enough fodder for growing herds of livestock was one measure of a farmer's industry and a farm's success.—*Old Sturbridge Village, Sturbridge, Massachusetts. Photograph by Robert S. Arnold*

Fig. 3.8. Annual meetings, such as that of the Female Charity Society, featured picnics and community-wide recreations. Here, Sturbridge ladies enjoy both camaraderie and regional specialties, as they spend a pleasant afternoon eating on the job.—*Old Sturbridge Village, Sturbridge, Massachusetts. Photograph by Bob Welsh, Jr.*

mode of interpretation has never been compiled, no one knows for certain just how many true living museums there are in North America. In 1978, I estimated there were about eight hundred. Needless to say, the movement is a significant one.

For many members of the Association for Living Historical Farms and Agricultural Museums, the model living historical farm was the Pliney Freeman Farm at Old Sturbridge Village. Although it had been developed in 1952, the farm truly realized its

potential only after Darwin Kelsey began to direct it in 1965. Kelsey was a cultural geographer with strong ideas about the power of living history to teach agricultural history. His theories were presented in a series of thoughtful articles published in the mid-1970's.[13] Kelsey first pointed out the limitations of living historical farms. Such farms, he said, are

historical in the broadest sense of the word, offering a patterned coherent account of the past that is intended to be true. They are thus analogous to

Fig. 3.9. Community life became a significant theme at recreated historical villages. Here, Old Sturbridge Village elders gather to toast the president at a recreated celebration of George Washington's birthday, a patriotic holiday that helped to foster social unity during the early days of the young republic. —*Old Sturbridge Village, Sturbridge, Massachusetts. Photograph by Robert S. Arnold*

written history and exhibits in the traditional history museum. Even though they often appear concrete and complete, that is, real, they are only accounts of the past and not the past itself. . . . Living history farms represent theories—that is, generalizations—about the past. As in any historical account, they are based on incomplete evidence. They are subjective, as any "model" produced in the arts, humanities, or science.[14]

Kelsey made certain that his farm at Sturbridge was based on the most complete body of evidence his architects, curators, horticulturists, and social historians could provide. The final "account," a "well-footnoted" farm, took years for Kelsey to assemble, but the end result was a powerful statement.

In late 1976, Kelsey took stock of the living historical farms movement that he himself had done so much to inspire. In an article in *Historic Preservation,* called "Harvests of History," he identified their primary strength:

Individual living historical farms represent different mutations of the old varieties of historic preservation. Collectively, however, they seem to be developing into a new and vigorous hybrid. As they progress, they may help us make sense of that often used but inadequately explained phrase, "getting a sense of the past." They provide, in addition to strict intellection and cognition, experiential modes of knowing—knowing directly through sight, sound, smell, touch, taste, The "sense" we get is only an account of the past, to be sure. But it is a holistic sense constructed from holistic preservation.[15]

Recently, I took my teen-aged daughter to visit an indoor museum exhibit that interpreted, through the experiences of a young girl, the realities of growing up in the South a century ago. It was a fine account of a Victorian childhood, rich in artifacts and various exhibit techniques. After we had watched the emotionally moving slide show at the end, I asked her how she liked the exhibit. "It was fine," she said diplomatically, "but after you've been to a living-history farm and really *felt* what it was like back then—well, an indoor exhibit doesn't really get to you. I'm glad we came, really, but I'd like to go back to Plimoth or Living History Farms."

NOTES

1. Cited in *The Colonial Williamsburg Interpreter: A Handbook,* prepared by the Department of Interpretive Education and edited by Jeanne Whitney and Jane Strauss. (Williamsburg: Colonial Williamsburg Foundation). The quote is on page 157.

2. Herbert Kellar, "Living Agricultural Museums," *Agricultural History* 19 (1945): 186–190.

3. Kellar, "Living Agricultural Museums," p.189.

4. Kellar, "Living Agricultural Museums," p. 187.

5. Freeman Tilden, *Interpreting Our Heritage* (Chapel Hill: The University of North Carolina Press, 1957; revised edition, 1967), p. 69.

6. Tilden, *Interpreting,* p. 76

7. William Kennon Kay, *Keep It Alive! Tips on Living History Demonstrations* (Washington, D.C.: National Park Service, 1970).

8. Gordon Hilker, *The Audience and You: Practical Dramatics for the Park Interpreter* (Washington, D.C.: National Park Service, 1974).

9. *Living History in the National Park System* (Washington, D.C.: National Park Service, 1976).

10. Marion Clawson, "Living Historical Farms: A Proposal for Action," *Agricultural History* 39:2 (1965): 110–111.

11. John T. Schlebecker, *The Past in Action: Living Historical Farms* (Washington, D.C.: Living Historical Farms Project, Smithsonian Institution, 1967); and *Living History Farms: A Walk Into the Past* (Washington, D.C.: Smithsonian Institution, 1968).

12. John T. Schlebecker and Gale E. Peterson, *Living Historical Farms Handbook* (Washington, D.C.: Smithsonian Institution Press, 1972); Darryl Chase, editor, *Selected Living Historical Farms, Villages, and Agricultural Museums in the United States and Canada* (Washington, D.C.: ALHFAM, Smithsonian Institution, 1976).

13. Darwin Kelsey, "Outdoor Museums and Historical Agriculture," *Agricultural History* 46 (1972): 105–127; "Historic Farms as Models of the Past," *ALHFAM Annual* 1 (1975): 33–39; "Harvests of History," *Historic Preservation* 28:3 (1976): 20–24.

14. Kelsey, "Harvests," p. 22.

15. Kelsey, "Harvests," p. 24.

4

Pilgrim Fathers and Iowa Mothers

PLIMOTH PLANTATION and Iowa's
Living History Farms are two excellent
but very different examples of the
living-history museum in America today.
Plimoth re-creates the daily life of the Pilgrims, medieval farmers roughing it on the
coast of Massachusetts in 1627. Living History
Farms also focus on farmers, the pioneers
who settled Grant Wood's country in the
mid-1800s and transformed the tall-grass
prairie into a breadbasket for the continent.
Both museums are successful in interpreting
a "sense of the past." At Plimoth, the interpreted past is a single year, while at the
Farms, the visitor experiences several hundred years of Midwestern history.[1]

Both museums pioneered new techniques
in living-history interpretation, an accom-
plishment that can best be appreciated if considered in the context of earlier interpretive
techniques. The first museums were "cabi-
nets of curiosities," collections of cases filled
with an odd mixture of history's flotsam and
jetsam, awaiting little more than the visitor's
idle inspection.

These early collections were followed by
the formal exhibit, which grouped objects
in categories—Civil War uniforms here,
arrowheads there, and so on.

Next came the interpretive exhibit, with the
goal of placing artifacts in context, especially
the human, cultural context in which they
originally functioned. The underlying questions raised by interpretive exhibits were—
how did people obtain, make, use, and value
these objects? The basic mode for the interpretive exhibit was a unit of bounded space,
such as a diorama, a period room, or, later,
entire blocks of historic space: a house, farm,
village, or landscape.

Living history moved into the exhibit continuum at this point. Preserve an Idaho ghost
town, and you have *an interpretive exhibit*.
But—set it in motion, with the addition of
well-trained interpreters who do what townsfolk originally did—file claims, shoe pack-
horses, tend bar, serve meals, and so on—
and you have *the living-history museum*, a life-
sized diorama realistically simulating life in
the past.

As a rule, museum visitors have always
liked dioramas; it should be no surprise,
then, that they really enjoyed living-history
museums, life-sized dioramas that they actually could enter, and where—through
demonstration, involvement, and animation—they could experience a sense of the
past.[2]

The sensual dimension was crucial. Once
inside, the visitor could use all his senses:
could look at the horses being shod, smell the
aroma of frying steaks and perking coffee,

Fig. 4.1. The crunch of snow echoes off the palings and palisades of Plimoth Plantation as an interpreter, portraying a Pilgrim housewife, trudges out on a winter morning to slop the hogs.— *Plimoth Plantation, Inc., Plymouth, Massachusetts*

Fig. 4.2. In the chill of a prairie autumn, Iowa Living History Farms interpreters at the 1900 Farm select seed corn to keep for planting the next year's crop.— *Iowa Living History Farms, Des Moines, Iowa. Photograph by Mimi Dunlap*

Fig. 4.3. Iowa Living History Farms interpreters at the 1900 Farm begin the agricultural year by harrowing a field of corn stalks. The tough stalks and their tenacious roots are left in the ground after the fall harvest, to hold and protect the farm's rich topsoil from winter's wind erosion.— *Iowa Living History Farms, Des Moines, Iowa. Photograph by Mimi Dunlap*

Fig. 4.4. The timeless smell of broom-corn permeates the summer air, as this young woman portrays an Iowa pioneer plaiting brooms in the cool of her 1840 dogtrot house.—*Iowa Living History Farms, Des Moines, Iowa. Photograph by Mimi Dunlap*

Fig. 4.5. A skilled Pilgrim thatcher at Plimoth Plantation plies his trade along the comb of a roof made of cattails harvested from the marshes along Cape Cod bay.—*Plimoth Plantation, Inc., Plymouth, Massachusetts*

hear the clinking of spurs, feel the texture of new-planed timber, taste the sourness of flap-jacks, and so on. Many museum educators believed that living history was the antidote to museum fatigue. *Living history was both didactice simulation and stimulation,* a pedogogical tool that could enliven their programs and help visitors vicariously feel the past. Plimoth and Living History Farms were especially enthusiastic about the potential of the new mode of interpretation.

The re-created Pilgrim Village of Plimoth was established in 1947, on fifty acres of land near the town of Plymouth, Massachusetts.[3] the site was ideal, similar in terrain and orientation to the original settlement, which lies underneath the modern town. One by one, the village's structures were re-created; first, the meetinghouse-fort; then the homes and outbuildings of individual families—Brewster, Bradford, Winslow, Standish,

Alden—names that are engraved in American legend. By 1959, Plimoth Plantation was ready for visitors, its buildings peopled by life-sized mannequins and by guides giving short lectures on various aspects of Pilgrim life. The museum was popular with visitors, but it lacked the look and feel of a lived-in village.

In 1967, James Deetz joined the staff as assistant director. Deetz was already a respected archaeologist, well known for his work with historic sites. Working with archaeologists, folklorists, "new" social historians, and interpretive specialists from other open-air museums, Deetz began to "revise" Plimoth's account of the Pilgrims. He was interested in not only advancing living history as an interpretive mode, but also experimenting with its potential to communicate a wide range of humanistic themes. Deetz argued,

Fig. 4.6. The agricultural year climaxes with harvest time in the fall. Racing against a late summer thunderstorm, interpreters portraying an entire family at Iowa Living History Farms' 1900 Farm set to the task of getting the wheat in and under a dry barn roof before it's drenched with rain. —*Iowa Living History Farms, Des Moines, Iowa. Photograph by Mimi Dunlap*

Fig. 4.7. An antidote to museum fatigue: watching farmers with a Daisy reaper at Iowa Living History Farms' 1900 Farm harvest a field of khaki-colored oats. —*Iowa Living History Farms, Des Moines, Iowa. Photograph by Mimi Dunlap*

Fig. 4.8. The aroma of living history: a Pilgrim interpreter at Plimoth Plantation removes crusty loaves of bread from her outdoor bake-oven with a long-handled oven peel. —*Plimoth Plantation, Inc., Plymouth, Massachusetts*

Fig. 4.9. An intimate moment in the 1840 Pioneer Farm at Iowa's Living History Farms. A modern visitor might be dismayed by what may seem, to modern eyes, the clutter and squalor of this pioneer log cabin. For the pioneers, however, the closeness of the cabin was security against the wildness of the prairie.—*Iowa Living History Farms, Des Moines, Iowa. Photograph by Mimi Dunlap*

Fig. 4.10. A Pilgrim housewife begins a joyous ritual: beer-making. For Englishmen, beer was liquid bread, and they drank up to two gallons a day. Brewing was, for the Pilgrims, a respected craft. For visitors to Plimoth Plantation today, the aroma of malt and hops is didactic stimulation.—*Plimoth Plantation, Inc., Plymouth, Massachusetts*

In his book, *the Image*, Daniel Boorstin develops the concept of the "pseudo event," meaning the re-creation of reality to the extent that the image becomes the standard by which reality is judged.

Every functioning historic house museum that addresses a point in time past is, in fact, a pseudo event and should aim at making the experience the best pseudo event possible within the limits that can be commanded.

To be "live," a museum is not simply operating, with someone spinning in the corner or splitting shingles in the yard. To function properly and successfully, a live museum should convey the sense of a different reality—the reality of another time.[4]

Plimoth, Deetz notes, needed to re-create the "reality of the Pilgrim fathers," and he suggested that the Plimoth Plantation's time capsule should evoke a living community of Pilgrims, complete with household clutter, the smell of smoke and sweat, and the buzz of flies. In a staff memo, Deetz outlined his approach:

One can interpret *in* the Village, or one can interpret the *Village*. It is the latter method which we wish to develop. In this context, the Village is viewed as a material assemblage which must be used dynamically, not passively, to convey to the visitor, first, a sense of the physical world of early colonial Plimoth, and then, of the culture which existed in that environment. This method in no way denies nor de-emphasizes such abstract institutions as government, religion, or family life, yet such concepts must be developed interpretively within the context of the physical environment. To do otherwise makes it difficult or impossible to justify the time, effort and expense devoted to the creation of thoroughly researched, documented, and carefully reproduced buildings, artifacts and costumes.[5]

Addressing the question of what themes Plimoth should stress, Deetz suggested that "shrines" like Plimoth couldn't help making political statements, and he hoped that the "story of the Pilgrims and their fellow colonists could be told like it was." In 1969, he mused:

Fig. 4.11. A Pilgrim interpreter harvesting barley with a straight scythe outside the palisade walls of Plimoth Plantation. The end result of this man's work will be a mug of beer brewed by his wife. — *Plimoth Plantation, Inc., Plymouth, Massachusetts*

It is strange, indeed, that many Americans invoke values in the name of the country's founding fathers, including the Pilgrims, that these men of the past would find somewhat peculiar. Some of the dissent that has recently disturbed much of the nation is not essentially dissimilar from that which caused our first settlers to remove themselves from familiar ways and set out into an unknown world.[6]

By the mid-1970s, Plimoth was indeed controversially alive—rough-hewn, fly-ridden, people with long-haired, bare-footed dissenting Pilgrims, and totally open to visitors. You could, if you so desired, crawl into a bed, sit on a sea chest, chase chickens, or help hoe a garden. There were no labels or ropes across doorways. In fact, all the museum's original antiques had been auctioned off and replaced with less valuable but far more usable reproductions. For visitors, Plimoth did indeed convey the "sense of a different reality."

The village also began to work its magic on the staff. Deetz noted that "interpreters, without a word being said, were beginning to shift the whole presentation from third person, past, to first person, present." Guides frequently said, *"We do,"* not *"They did."* In

Fig. 4.12. Small-grain crops such as oats, wheat, and barley demanded a rapid harvest. Entire families turned out to bring in the crop. The celebration that followed, the "Harvest Home," was the parent celebration of our modern Thanksgiving.— *Plimoth Plantation, Inc., Plymouth, Massachusetts*

Fig. 4.13. From the dusty confusion of the harvest field to the cool quiet of the farmhouse, a Pilgrim woman's work was never done. Beside the kitchen table, this Plimoth Plantation interpreter catches up on her mending.— *Plimoth Plantation, Inc., Plymouth, Massachusetts*

1978, the museum officially adopted "first person" interpretation, with individual staff members actually taking on the roles of particular Pilgrims.[7] That step was only logical, Deetz wrote in a 1981 article.

It occurred to us that the live interpreters ought to be re-creations at Plimoth, too. We had them speak in period dialect, which we were able to research, in first person. At that point the visitors became the interpreters, and we started calling the interpreters *informants*. It was as if the visitors coming into the exhibit were anthropology fieldworkers going in to experience a community and elicit from it what they could.[8]

In short, Deetz contended that living-history museums should re-create, within the limits of their boundaries and resources, facsimiles of entire cultures—not just houses, fences, fields, and other appendages of the cultural, man-made landscape, but the social context, as well: people going about their everyday lives, working, playing, praying, bickering, and so on. With museums like this, any of the popular new social history

Fig. 4.14. Catching the last warm rays of the late-afternoon sun, this Pilgrim girl contemplates her Plimoth Plantation kitchen garden, an important source of salad "herbs."— *Plimoth Plantation, Inc., Plymouth, Massachusetts*

themes could be explored: ecology, sex roles, the changing nature of the family, aging—to name a few. The requirements were money, many years spent on research, and a well-trained staff capable of acting the part of "informants" from other, dated cultures.

Does it work? For visitors willing to suspend disbelief, it does. But it takes both physical and imaginative work to re-enter the cramped, crowded, complex medieval world of a colonial village, enclosed by palisades and teeming with pigs, sheep, and people speaking an archaic vernacular English. *Plimoth is not a folk park, a pleasant place to take the family for a picnic and a stroll. Its paths are rocky, its streets splattered with the dung of the resident livestock, and its inhabitants busy. It is filled with culture shocks, and after a day there, it has you yearning for the twentieth century.*

On a hot June afternoon in 1982, I visited the village with my family and watched the village catalyze their curiosity.[9] I could describe a dozen examples of visitors being drawn into cross-cultural comparison, but one incident will illustrate Plimoth's success. After a few hours of playing participant-observer in the village, I ducked into George Soul's house and stretched out on the feather bed. It was heavenly. As I lay there in the dark, a Pilgrim came in and helped himself to a "compound salad" of lettuce, radishes, onions, and cress mixed with "raw" (olive) oil, vinegar, and coarse salt. As he was eating the salad, with his hands, a modern time-traveler came through the door. He was wearing Madras shorts, sneakers with blue wings on the side, and a polo shirt. He asked the Pilgrim, "Why do you enclose your garden beds with wooden boards?" The Pilgrim's jaw dropped. "You mean you don't?," he replied. *Now* it was the visitor's turn to be incredulous. "Of course not," he said. "Well," prompted the Pilgrim, "tell me how you garden." There followed a meeting of the minds and some fundamental questioning of late twentieth-century customs on the part of the visitor.

Plimoth interpreters are skilled at drawing visitors into dialogue. Freeman Tilden wrote, in his *Interpreting Our Heritage,* that, "The chief aim of interpretation is not instruction, but provocation."[10] Plimoth provokes thought, lots and lots of thought.

So, too, does Living History Farms in Des Moines, Iowa, a thousand miles and more than two hundred years away.[11] William Murray, a professor of agricultural economics at Iowa State University, established the Farms in 1969. Murray knew exactly what he wanted: an agricultural museum for Iowa that would tell the story of farmers and farming in the nation's heartland. He had visited open-air museums in Europe and America and liked what he saw. Living museums like Plimoth convinced Murray that living history was the only mode of interpretation that could enliven the story of agriculture. Murray also felt that just one farm couldn't do the job; he would need at least three—an 1840s pioneer log farm, using oxen; a 1900s horse-farm; and a contemporary "farm of the future." Hence, his choice of the name, Living History Farms.

During the 1970s, Murray worked on his "time tunnel with three stops." A determined man, he familiarized himself with the work of his colleagues in the Association for Living Historical Farms and Agricultural Museums and the National Park Service, especially the achievements of Darwin Kelsey at Sturbridge. In 1977, Murray asked me to join the staff as chief of research, interpretation, and collections.

By 1979, Murray, had actually completed *four* time machines at the Farms. The first was a forty-acre Pioneer Area, containing an 1840s stagecoach station, a small trading post, and an adjacent, working, ten-acre farm. The farm consisted of a log cabin, stable/barn, corncrib, smokehouse, poultry hut, garden, three fenced fields, a prairie-grass pasture, and a woodlot.

The second site was a one-hundred-acre

Fig. 4.15. A Pilgrim garden, consisting of a series of raised, curbed beds carefully "husbanded" by the housewife. Such gardens, providing a variety of vegetables and herbs, were women's domain.— *Plimoth Plantation, Inc., Plymouth, Massachusetts*

Fig. 4.16. After a long day in the fields, Plimoth Plantation Pilgrims enjoy each other's companionship and the fruits of their families' labor: beef, bread, and beer. A visitor walking in on this meal would immediately notice that the men eat most of their food with their hands, the tradition at that time. To modern sensibilities, Plimoth Plantation has a decidedly Third-World atmosphere.— *Plimoth Plantation, Inc., Plymouth, Massachusetts*

Fig. 4.17. The first of the Iowa Living History Farms' time machines, the 1840 Pioneer Farm. Here, interpreters prepare for another frustrating day of trying to train steers to think of themselves as oxen.—*Iowa Living History Farms, Des Moines, Iowa. Photograph by Mimi Dunlap*

Fig. 4.18. The wood-fired kiln and pottery at an 1870s railroad town, the second time machine cre-ated by Iowa Living History Farms. Here, the town's potter examines the salt-glazed churns, pots, jars, and milk dishes produced in recent firings. In a few years, the ancient craft practiced by the potter of the 1870s will—we know—be undercut by less expensive, factory-made stone-ware imported from England.—*Iowa Living History Farms, Des Moines, Iowa. Photograph by Mimi Dunlap*

1900 farm containing a frame house, barn, granary, hog pens and poultry houses, sheep shelter, windmill, garden, and fields. The farm operated year round, with horse-power, and was self-sufficient.

A third stop was an 1870s rural marketing town called Walnut Hill. At one end was a late-Victorian farm, containing a two-story brick mansion with a summer kitchen; a three-story, six-bay frame barn; and other outbuildings. At the other end of town, there were a number of typical buildings, including a one-room schoolhouse and shops for the potter, cabinet makers/undertakers, veteri-nary, and blacksmith; a general-merchandise store; and offices for an attorney and a doctor.

Living History Farms' last site was un-doubtedly its most unconventional. Murray constructed a futuristic farm with two mas-sive, earth-covered buildings drawing their energy from a solar pond and wind gener-ator. In addition, he included a two-hundred-acre field, built on the latest principles of soil-and-water conservation. It featured til-ing, terracing, minimum tillage (a method of cultivation that requires little ploughing or harrowing), and the use of experimental "Green Revolution" crops and implements. All four sites were staffed with interpreters simulating life in the past—and in the case of the last farm, the near future.

In short, a visitor to the Farms could move back and forth in time, making comparisons all the while, and coming away with a better understanding of social, cultural, and tech-nological change within one region. Initially, the Farms had stressed the progessive aspect of change in the Midwest; however, the staff gradually adopted a more realistic approach, concluding that visitors should be free to decide for themselves which changes were positive and which negative. In the late

Fig. 4.19. Early morning chores for the husband-and-wife team at the 1900 Farm of Iowa Living History Farms. The 1900 place is the last of the LHF time machines. Older visitors seeing this farm routine seldom fail to mention to the interpreters the old farm adage that "That work will warm you twice." — *Iowa Living History Farms, Des Moines, Iowa. Photograph by Mimi Dunlap*

1970s, staff began to rotate from farm to farm, and period to period, with interesting results. They felt a culture shock when away from their interpretive homes for even a day. I remember 1840s farm wives complaining about the sterile coldness of the Farms' 1900 kitchen, while 1900 farm hands were struggling with a team of oxen at the 1840 site. And all the staff from the historic area found work at the futuristic farm a chore, lacking in human contact and far too technological. The general attitude was, "I didn't come to work

at a living-history museum to be future-shocked. I get enough of *that* in the outside world!"

Visitors, too, were often overpowered by the realism they experienced in the Farms' various historic areas. One summer morning, a member of the Farms' board of directors asked to me to take some VIPs around. The distinquished visitors turned out to be the director of the Vatican Museum and his wife. When we walked down to the 1840 pioneer farm, with its log cabin, hand-split rail fence, and tall-grass meadows, they shouted with delight: "Little House on the Prairie! Little House on the Prairie!" They had, they told me, read Laura Ingalls Wilder's books to their children, as a pleasant means of teaching the youngsters English. Now they had the opportunity to visit a real pioneer farm. It didn't matter that it was a re-created facsimile, they told me: what counted was how real the farm *seemed*. They spent two hours examining every plot and pasture, implement and animal. I don't think they missed a quilt, a Dutch oven, a draw knife, or a flax hackle. We visited the other sites, and they easily made the expected comparisons among them. But their interest was really on the trees, not the forest. The theme of regional change over time didn't interest them as much as the realistic textural nuances of the individual sites.

Frequently, visitors were catalyzed by the Farms' major theme of historical change. Interpreters often came upon visitors arguing about the relative merits of modern agriculture.

Wasn't the mixed farm of 1900 really better, over all, than the agribusiness of today? Farming might be more efficient today, but at what cost? The family farm was becoming an endangered species. What good was increased yield per acre if market prices didn't equal your costs of putting in a crop? Life might have been tough and uncomfortable in 1840 and 1900, but at least Iowa had topsoil. At · *the present rate of erosion, would there be any good, black earth left, in a generation or two?*

Often, Living History Farms functioned as a forum, in the best tradition of the Midwestern folk school.

On October 4, 1979, Pope John Paul II visited the Farms and delivered a homily that touched on a theme common to each of its sites: man's responsible use of the land. He suggested, to almost a half-million other visitors, that America's good earth should be appreciated, conserved, and used to provide food for a hungry world. John Paul's visit was seen by many to be a confirmation of the Farms' mission as an educational institution.[12]

Plimoth Plantation and Living History Farms both experimented in different ways with the time-machine concept. Plimoth took visitors as far into a historic culture as it is possible to go, at a living-history museum, while the Farms moved them rapidly through Iowa's history in a series of stops that recaptured the region's agricultural rites of passage. Both claimed that their use of living history allowed them to provoke thought and stimulate feeling in new and dynamic ways. Although many visitors and museum evaluators would agree, still others would challenge the effectiveness of any living-history museum, including these two pioneers in the field, truly to enliven the past in a truthful manner.

NOTES

1. In the early 1970s, I worked with Jim Deetz at Plimoth Plantation as a consultant in foodways and interpretation. From 1977 to 1980, I was chief of research, interpretation, and collections at Living History Farms. The basis for this chapter is my first-hand experience at both of these living-history museums.

2. The best introduction to museums from an interpretive perspective is Kenneth Hudson's *A Social History of Museums: What the Visitors Thought* (Atlantic Highlands, N.J.: Humanities Press, 1975).

3. Jean Poindexter Colby, *Plimoth Plantation* (New York: Hastings House, 1970).

4. James Deetz, "The Changing Historic House Museum: Can It Live?," *Historic Preservation* 23 (1971):50.

5. James Deetz, "Pilgrim Village Interpretive Program: 1974 Season" (Staff memo, Plimoth Plantation, 1974).

6. James Deetz, "The Reality of the Pilgrim Fathers," *Natural History* 78 (November 1969):44

7. Deetz, "Changing Historic House," p. 54.

8. James Deetz, "The Link from Object to Person to Concept," in Zipporah W. Collins's *Museums, Adults and the Humanities* (Washington, D.C.: American Association of Museums, 1981), p. 32. Also see James Deetz's "A Sense of Another World: History Museums and Cultural Change," *Museum News* 59 (1980):40–45.

9. A similar experience is described in "Beginnings Around Boston," an article on "Living History: Jamestown to Plymouth," by Dudley Clendinen, in the *New York Times* Sunday Travel section, July 4, 1982.

10. Tilden, *Interpreting*, p. 9.

11. William G. Murray's "The Martin Flynn Farm: From Public Land in 1845 to Living History Farms in 1970," *Annals of Iowa* 40:7 (Winter 1971):480–493, is Bill's history of the project's early years. My later history of the Farms is based on my own files.

12. See Betty Doak Elder's award-winning article "Behind the Scenes at Living History Farms," *History News* 34:2 (December 1979):331–349; and *John Paul II Visits Rural America* (Des Moines: Meredith Publishing Services, 1979), edited by Jean Lem Mon.

5

The Medium is the Message

MARSHALL McLuhan's dictum, "The medium is the message," was on the minds of many researchers and interpreters at living-history museums in the late 1960s and the 1970s. [In answer to an editorial comment about the way McLuhan spelled the title of the book that appears here as the title of this chapter, the author would like to say that, in two early additions, I found it spelled both *Message* and *Massage*, so I selected the first and use it, here, as being the more apt for this chapter.—The Author]

It was painfully obvious to critics inside and outside the museum profession during the sixties and seventies that some living-history museums were historically inaccurate distortions, with programs that lacked conviction and effectiveness. Interestingly, few critics questioned the popularity of these museums. Most granted that living history was a potent instrument of popular culture and a force to be reckoned with. They agreed that living-history museums were here to stay and would continue to function in the world of public history. Beyond these general points of agreement, critics differed considerably in what bothered them about living history. Some focused on the medium itself, the re-created sites and their historical activities. Others were concerned with the interpretive themes that the new living museums were attempting to communicate.

Richard Sellers and Dwight Pithcaithley of the National Park Service were bothered by the inaccurate impressions they believed that reconstructions such as Plimoth Plantation were giving the public. "At best," they argued,

reconstructed buildings only illustrate how the past may have looked, not how it did look. Reconstructions are plagued, on the one hand, by insufficient data to allow a truly accurate reproduction and, on the other, by an almost unavoidable desire to beautify what was not always a beautiful past.[1]

Mark Leone, a Maryland anthropologist, echoed that, when he visited Shakertown at Pleasant Hill, Kentucky, and found the restoration "beautiful, even perfect. . . . Nothing needs to be fixed, raked, painted; there is no dung, no puddles, no weeds; it is all on display just for you."[2] And David Lowenthal recorded that Williamsburg had "the flavor of a well-kept contemporary suburb." There is, he said, an "American way of history," and one of its chief characteristics is a penchant for cleanliness.

One historian argues that colonial folk themselves would have liked fresh paint if they could have gotten it—but after all it is the reality and not the dreams of the past that Williamsburg supposedly portrays. In fact, it is the sanitary needs of the

Fig. 5.1. The Fortress of Louisbourg, as it appeared in 1744—now restored by the Canadian government, at a cost of more than twenty million dollars. This project, on Cape Breton Island in Nova Scotia, has been compared to the rebuilding of Warsaw's Old Town, in Poland, after World War II.—*Courtesy Parks Canada, Fortress of Louisbourg National Historic Park, Louisbourg, Nova Scotia, Canada*

present that prevail: eighteenth-century odors would be such a shock to twentieth-century noses that every other impression might be blotted out. And without paved streets, visitors would keep Williamsburg in perpetual dust and soil their clothing in mud. Cleanliness itself is the prime consideration; people feel that just because a thing is old is no reason for it to look dirty.[3]

Whether living museums were inaccurate because of a lack of research or fear of displeasing visitors, the fact remains that in the late 1960s and the 1970s, many museums,

including Williamsburg, decided that their physical sites were indeed bowdlerized and needed a more earthy realism. That was a dangerous course to take, as those familiar with Plimoth's experience knew. When James Deetz revised the village, it was not the "radical" view of the Pilgrims that upset visitors but, rather, the long hair and the dirty feet of the interpreters. Tourists could accept an intellectually feisty Pilgrim more easily than an authentically sweaty one. I vividly remember the words of a well-known pro-

Fig. 5.2. A moment in time: re-enacting a common scene from the history of the Fortress of Louisbourg, an interpreter-sentry halts several fishwives outside the fort's gates.—*Courtesy Parks Canada, Fortress of Louisbourg National Historic Park, Louisbourg, Nova Scotia, Canada*

fessor of American Civilization who visited Plimoth and, when asked what he thought of it, tersely said: "I found it vulgar, tasteless, and dirty. It will give the museum field a bad name if it gets any more popular."[4]

Undeterred by their interpretation being considered a revisionist "nostalgia for the mud," many museums began the long, hard effort to re-create an accurate historical atmosphere evoking a lived-in look that would suggest to visitors that actual people had once really lived and worked there. A partic-

ularly good example is the Fortress of Louisbourg, at the eastern tip of Nova Scotia's Cape Breton Island.

John Fortier, who took over the research program at the fortress in 1968, and seven years later became its superintendent, identified his museum's goal:

Our job at Louisbourg, as with any outdoor museum of this nature, is to re-create a moment in time. This is an elusive goal, if not an impossible one. The most we can hope to achieve is a setting where visitors may sense the immediacy of the past and be moved to think about it . . . . About the best we can manage for them is an evocation of the past, and this is a momentary thing—a whiff of woodsmoke, the slam of a shutter echoing across the King's Bastion, or a glimpse of costumed staff when they happen not to be posing for pictures. It is a peculiar task, calling for a particular skill and feeling for the job.[5]

Fortier and his staff had both the skill and the feeling and, with the help of more than twenty million dollars from the Canadian government, they re-created the heart of the fortress as it had been in 1744, when war was declared between France and England. Their effort has been compared to the rebuilding of Warsaw's Old Town after World War II. The Fortress of Louisbourg had been systematically demolished by the English in 1760, and for the next two centuries, it remained a deserted ruin. In 1961, a Royal Commission decided to reconstruct it, for economic and cultural reasons. Like the reconstruction of Warsaw, it was a monumental job, involving hundreds of historians, architects, craftsmen, and workers. Millions of artifacts were meticulously excavated, and several hundred archaeological and historical research reports prepared. Outside of Colonial Williamsburg, the staff of Louisbourg laid perhaps the most complete research base for any historic site in North America.[6]

One of my advanced graduate students in museum studies, Bill Brooks, visited Louisbourg in 1980. He was awed by the fortress. The research department at the museum reminded him of a "small university." Bill had seldom encountered a project of such breadth and depth. He was taken behind the scenes and shown "acres" of excavated artifacts and some of the nearly one million pages of documentation on microfilm and note cards. He saw many of the five hundred maps, plans, and views of the fortress. The research staff at Louisbourg, Bill felt, were able to document just about every physical change at the fortress during its fifty-year history.[7]

Bill's assessment was correct. John Fortier and his staff had built an extensive library and archive filled with detailed records dealing with building construction; contracts; rental agreements; inventories of households; sales of private estates; lists of storehouses; diaries and journals; census returns; records of births, deaths, marriages, baptisms, and adoptions. There were also legal records of crimes, trials, lawsuits, and inheritances. In short, there was enough data assembled to "allow a truly accurate reproduction" and one that was about as far away from a "well-kept contemporary suburb" as one can imagine. I will resist the temptation to call this the "Canadian way of history," for Fortier, an American from Michigan who studied at William and Mary, was well aware of the recent American attempts to re-create realistic cultural environments at Old Sturbridge Village, Plimoth Plantation, and Colonial Williamsburg, whose Governor's Palace revision stands as a landmark for the outdoor museum field.[8] Still, the efforts at Louisbourg to re-create a huge, complex site accurately has few parallels in North America. For example, the fortress covers seventy-five acres and contains more than sixty-two structures. They include massive gates, bastions, ramparts, batteries, barracks, stables, a bakery, laundry, ice house, forge and kiln, wood lots and gardens, a fish factory, quay and harbor, an inn and cabaret, and more than two dozen

houses of varying size and distinction, ranging from the opulent governor's apartments to the humble soldiers' quarters. Each structure is outfitted with appropriate furnishings. What strikes the visitor to Louisbourg is not just its magnitude, but also its detail. Peter Bruegel would like the fortress; like his paintings, it is broad in concept and scope, but precise in its particulars. The Citadel looms large, but so also do the accurately cast buttons on the red coats of the Swiss mercenaries.

But does the fortress work? Does its material medium communicate a truthful message? John Fortier, who has lived near the fortress in a sixty-year-old restored farmhouse for almost a decade, is the museum's most perceptive critic. He has written eloquently of the project in a variety of books and articles, and he often describes the fortress on days when only a few visitors are to be seen and "Louisbourg, glimpsed through the fog, a chill wind almost always blowing across the site, maintains a feeling of timelessness." Yet, even on those rare days, he writes,

We have no illusions that visitors will really think they have left the twentieth century; in any case, our purpose is to inform people, not to trick them. Beyond that, we hope the physical setting will move visitors to think about the things we have in common with our ancestors, whoever they were, wherever they lived. . . . Perhaps a moment out of time is all anyone wants, for a gulf between past and present remains in spite of all we have done, and few visitors would really wish to cross it. At best, life in the past was full of discomfort and uncertainties. Even now, Louisbourg is an uncomfortable place to visit, yet one that will reward the persistent visitor with a rare feeling that here the past is not only very close but has something important to tell us.[9]

Fortier's modesty is matched only by his achievement. The cold, raw, salty atmosphere of the fortress is just right. It does indeed reward visitors with a moody feeling

Fig. 5.3. Louisbourg was the largest garrison town in eighteenth-century North America. Re-creating the many elements of its social history presented monumental challenges to the restoration's historians. Soldiers and marines here catch a moment of relaxation before yet another drill.—*Courtesy Parks Canada, Fortress of Louisbourg National Historic Park, Louisbourg, Nova Scotia, Canada*

that they have somehow got lost in time and landed on this forsaken, yet fascinating, beachhead of 1744.

About two thousand miles west of Louisbourg lies another major Canadian re-creation, Old Fort William. Located in a 120-acre forest site on the north shore of Lake Superior, Old Fort William simulates life at the inland headquarters of the Scots-run North West Company, which, in the late eighteenth and early nineteenth centuries, developed a complex fur trading empire that

crisscrossed Canada from Montreal to the Arctic and the Pacific. When the Ontario Provincial government decided to re-create the fort in 1971, the legislators realized that the task of reconstructing fifty-four different historic buildings would be difficult. Akin to the challenges of Louisbourg. the Old Fort William re-creation was accomplished with great effort, and an expenditure of nearly fifteen million dollars. Today the completely recreated fort bears comparison with the most historically accurate of North American sites.

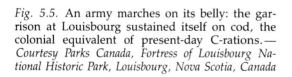

Fig. 5.4. Soldiers and civilians promenade up and down along Louisbourg's stony streets, creating a palpable feeling of timelessness.—*Courtesy Parks Canada, Fortress of Louisbourg National Historic Park, Louisbourg, Nova Scotia, Canada*

Fig. 5.5. An army marches on its belly: the garrison at Louisbourg sustained itself on cod, the colonial equivalent of present-day C-rations.—*Courtesy Parks Canada, Fortress of Louisbourg National Historic Park, Louisbourg, Nova Scotia, Canada*

Fig. 5.6. Two thousand miles west of Louisbourg, another major Canadian fort has been re-created: Old Fort William. This restoration of the North West Company's inland headquarters contains almost sixty buildings on its 120-acre site. — *Old Fort William, Ontario Ministry of Industry and Tourism, Toronto, Ontario, Canada*

However, Old Fort William's director, William Lee, was as concerned with the fort's less tangible medium of communication, its living-history program, as with its physical authenticity. If the "medium is the message," as Toronto professor McLuhan argued, then a living history museum like Old Fort William needed both a realistic site and believable activities for successful simulation of life in the past.

Lee was aware of the critics who scoffed at reconstructions like Old Fort William and Louisbourg, calling them "expensive life-size toys, manufactured for children of all ages who have forgotten how to read," and who derided living-history interpretation as "childish amusement" for a "gullible, history-hungry public." I served with Bill on an evaluation team in 1979, and we discussed the problems many museums were having

Fig. 5.7. The raison d'etre of Old Fort William in the early nineteenth century was the fur trade, especially brisk in beaver fur for European hats. This *voyageur's* load of pelts weighs more than sixty pounds.—*Old Fort William, Ontario Ministry of Industry and Tourism, Toronto, Ontario, Canada*

Fig. 5.8. Relaxing with a twist of tobacco was one of the modest pleasures a *voyageur* could enjoy at Fort William.—*Old Fort William, Ontario Ministry of Industry and Tourism, Toronto, Ontario, Canada*

Fig. 5.9. Most activity at Old Fort William consists of hard work, especially the packaging and transportation of fur.—*Old Fort William, Ontario Ministry of Industry and Tourism, Toronto, Ontario, Canada*

Fig. 5.10. Fort William lay at the center of a vast trading empire stretching across Canada.—*Old Fort William, Ontario Ministry of Industry and Tourism, Toronto, Ontario, Canada*

with their living history programs.[10] We recalled that, whenever directors of living museums got together, there seemed to be bouts of criticism. We both remembered heated discussions on the merits of first- or third-person interpretation; the problems of getting craftsmen, busy with their pewter, pots, and barrels, to talk to visitors; the difficulties of enforcing dress codes that proscribed beards, modern eyeglasses, and makeup; the seemingly impossible job of training seasonal interpreters to come across as believable colonial farmers, Civil War soldiers, or *voyageurs*; strategies for defending expensive, labor-intensive living history in-

Fig. 5.11. A variety of boats and canoes were built in the fort's shipyards and factories.—*Old Fort William, Ontario Ministry of Industry and Tourism, Toronto, Ontario, Canada*

Fig. 5.12. Chippewa Indian women were recruited to build birchbark canoes for the North West Company. Often, these women married *voyageurs* and provided their husbands with food, clothing, and even shelter.—*Old Fort William, Ontario Ministry of Industry and Tourism, Toronto, Ontario, Canada*

terpretation to skeptical bureaucrats always concerned about the bottom line; and— finally—the gnawing question about whether this mode of interpretation was well worth the effort put into it. Bill is a deeply patriotic Canadian who was trained at the Royal Military Academy and believes that the best way to get across the central message of Old Fort William—for Canada to prosper, all its varied peoples, be they French, Anglo-Celtic, or Indian, need to work together—is through the medium of re-created historical activities, involving interpreters of varied eth-

nic and cultural backgrounds: when visitors see a Scottish merchant rubbing shoulders with a French *voyageur* in a thirty-six-foot birchbark canoe built by Indians, they get the message. Bill Lee is confident of this result.[11]

Because Old Fort William was developed only recently, Lee and his staff were able to borrow freely from the collective experiences of other older living history museums. From Colonial Williamsburg and Old Sturbridge Village came ideas on interpreting traditional crafts in context; from Plimoth and Conner Prairie, the use of first-person interpretation; from Fort Mackinac and Fort Snelling, the staging of large and small dramatizations of historical events; and from the National Park Service, employment of uniformed guides (rangers). The Fort William staff mixed these various modes of interpretation, experimented with different audiences, and tried out a variety of themes and clusters of information.[12] With his military background to guide him, Bill deliberately used a mixture of tactics to achieve his objectives. Innovation and flexibility were his bywords. The result is an unusually dynamic living-history program, characterized by a sense of adventure that can be felt by staff and visitors alike.

When I visited Old Fort William on a surprisingly cool day in the summer of 1983, the effort of Bill Lee and his interpretive staff was apparent. Three contrasting interpretive events now stand out in memory. The first took place after we entered the site along a path that curved around groves of white birch, aspen, and pine. Nearby, there was the flowing sound of the Kaministikwa River. We came to a fork in the path and saw, to the left, a small Indian encampment. We saw a circle of lean-to shelters on the river's bank. A cooking fire was smoking, and racks of stretched beaver pelts in the last stages of tanning were hanging nearby. Five Indians were working nearby, four women weaving baskets and a young man carving a spoon. We chatted with the man, Peter Wabose, who spoke English with a strong Chippewa accent. The wooden-ware he was working on also had strong Chippewa overtones. He had learned the tradition from his elders and enjoyed working at the fort because it allowed him to practice his craft and to pass on his knowledge to an apprentice. He showed us the ornamented spoon he was carving. Someday, I mused, he might trade his spoon to a *voyageur* who would end up eating pea soup with it. He smiled politely in response to my thought. But I think he meant to keep it, right there, in its more natural home. Natural, in fact, was the best word to describe their interpretive style. *These Indians didn't have to simulate life in the early 1800s. They were already comfortably living history. As with the Amish, it was the contemporary world of the twentieth century that was the anachronism.*

The second event I remember at Old Fort William was just as relaxed as the first. After entering the main gate of the fort and being literally overwhelmed by the magnitude of the historic complex—eight acres of imposing, very European-looking buildings enclosed by three thousand feet of towering silver palisades—we escaped to the North West House, a summer living quarters for the company's clerks, and a space that was more familiar in scale. Here we met a very lean young man who greeted us formally in a slight Scottish accent. I asked him why his clothes—cut on Beau Brummel lines, to my untrained eyes—were different from those of some of the other European gentlemen we had seen walking around the fort. In a deferential manner he explained that clothing styles were used to indicate rank. "We clerks wear this type of hat, partners that, and the voyageurs . . . " within thirty seconds, we had suspended our disbelief and actually imagined that we were talking to a North West Company clerk and that the year was around 1816. We didn't feel uncomfortable, threatened, out-of-time, or out-of-place. The youth had succeeded in drawing us into his

Fig. 5.13. A Scottish clerk at Old Fort William enjoys a glass of port before a business luncheon. In the original fort, three cultures coexisted comfortably.—*Old Fort William, Ontario Ministry of Industry and Tourism, Toronto, Ontario, Canada*

world, his simulation almost unnoticed. Freeman Tilden would have enjoyed its "perfect harmony." We talked about twenty minutes, in all, and he continued to surprise me with information about the social history of the fur trade, a subject I knew very little about; the conversation made me wish I knew more.

The third event I recall was quite different. We had been told by a uniformed guide, a personable young girl in a crisp white blouse and a kilt of the fort's own tartan, that there would be a "dramatization" in the dry goods store at 3:00 P.M. In the early 1970s, I had experienced what we used to call "street theater" at Plimoth, and I recently had talked at length with Bill Tramposch, Director of Interpretation at Colonial Williamsburg, about Williamsburg's use of professional actors to cover usually neglected aspects of social history, such as the experiences of black slaves, working women, and indentured servants.[13] So I was interested in seeing how Old Fort William would use drama.

There were two characters in the three-o'clock dramatization—"Simon Frazer" and a sales clerk. The plot was almost too simple. Fraser, a partner in the company—and a name familiar to any Canadian schoolchild—entered the store, chatted with the clerk about fashion in Montreal, and bought a new beaver hat. The drama lasted six or seven minutes. Because the store interior was crowded with other tourists, I had trouble suspending disbelief. However, the two actors seemed to have no trouble whatsoever getting into their roles, and their banter about life at the fort, hat sytles in Montreal, and who-is-doing-what-to-whom seemed both historically accurate and realistic. It was also entertaining, and when the play ended, everyone applauded. Again, I was amazed at the amount of information communicated in such a short time and at the skit's success at provoking my curiosity. *It was excellent interpretation.* The same was true of the other less intimate dramatizations we saw at Old Fort William: the arrival of a trade canoe from Montreal, a business meeting of a group of North West Company partners, and the arrest of blacksmith Alexander Frazer for drunkenness—the last rather ribald and a popular favorite. Each dramatization was a serious exercise in helping the visitor understand and appreciate the life and times of the fur trade. Each playlet worked, in its own way, and complimented the entire complex living-history program.

Old Fort William is not, of course, the only open-air museum or historic site experiment-

Fig. 5.14. Fort William's most dramatic event was the arrival of thirty-six-foot trading canoes from Montreal.—*Old Fort William, Ontario Ministry of Industry and Tourism, Toronto, Ontario, Canada*

ing with the medium of living-history interpretation. It is, however, one of the best examples. I left with the thought that a living-history program is a powerful medium for involving people in the day-to-day life of another time. And when it is done professionally, as in the case at Louisbourg and Old Fort William, living history overwhelms criticism.

NOTES

1. Richard Sellers and Dwight Pithcaithley, "Reconstructions—Expensive, Life-Size Toys?," *CRM Bulletin* 2:4 (December 1979):6.

2. Mark P. Leone, "The Relationship between Artifacts and the Public in Outdoor History Museums," *Annals New York Academy of Science (1981)*, p. 301.

3. David Lowenthal, "The American Way of History," *Columbia University Forum* 9 (1966): 31.

4. Interview in Philadelphia, October 15, 1976, with a colleague who, I believe, should remain anonymous.

5. John Fortier, "Patterns of Research at Louisbourg: The Reconstruction Enters Its Second Decade," *Canada* 1:4 (June 1974):13.

6. John Fortier is one of the most prolific writers in the living-history museum field. Three excellent examples of his thoughts on Louisbourg are: "What To Do after the Architect Leaves," *Gazette: Quarterly of the Canadian Museums Association* 9:2 (Spring 1976):6–14; "Thoughts on the Re-creation and Interpretation of Historical Environments," *Papers: The Third International Congress of Maritime Museums* (September 1978), published by Mystic Seaport; and "Louisbourg: Managing a Moment of Time," *National Museum of Man: History Division*, Paper No. 32 (Ottawa: National Museums of Canada, 1981), pp. 91–124.

7. Bill Brooks, interview with author, June 16, 1980, at Living History Farms, Des Moines, Iowa.

8. The revision of the Royal Governor's Palace was reviewed in a special edition of *Colonial Williamsburg Today* 3:3 (Spring 1981).

9. John Fortier and Owen Fitzgerald, *Fortress of Louisbourg* (Toronto: Oxford University Press, 1979), p. 21.

10. Bill Lee and I served on a self-study team for the Minnesota Historical Society, August 19–24, 1979. We talked every evening for a week about our common interest, living-history museums.

11. Bill Lee, interview with author, July 26, 1983, at Old Fort William, Thunder Bay, Ontario.

12. Armin Weber, Old Fort William Manager of Programs and Plan, interview with author, July 26, 1983, also at Old Fort William.

13. Bill Tramposch shared with me several dozen recent publications and staff training papers dealing with Williamsburg's interpretation of the "new" social history. Especially useful were issues of *The Colonial Williamsburg Interpreter*, a bimonthly publication first published in July 1980 by the Department of Interpretive Education.

6
History Lives

AFTER a visit to Williamsburg in 1955, James Agee observed to a friend that, although the historians there were "good scholars," he sensed "a little of the sadness of faculty people [my age and younger] without a great enough subject to involve their best energies."[1] Other friends of living-history museums have been similarly disappointed by the themes they saw being interpreted. Many liked the medium of living history, with its earthy realism and enlivening activity, but they felt that the history being artfully simulated was often oversimplified, shallow, or wrong.

Robert Ronsheim, who worked with Jim Deetz at Plimoth in the 1970s, questioned the basic claim that many living-history museums were making: that somehow they were bringing the past alive. He argued, in 1974, that

The past is dead, and cannot be brought back to life. Those beliefs and attitudes, conscious and unconscious, rational and irrational, that provided a foundation for institutions, governed conduct and controlled behavior cannot mean to us what they meant to those who lived then. Some of the elements are missing; others have a different color and shape when viewed from our pattern of beliefs. So, too, with the affective life of individuals and families. Nor can any material re-creation ever be complete or authentic.

Any historian, social scientist, or curator dealing with the past must tell his student, the museum visitor, that the past cannot be recovered.[2]

Thomas Schlereth, head of the American Studies program at Notre Dame, was more concerned with living museums' "wrongheaded accounts of the past" that were often elitist, chauvinistic, rigidly periodized, sexist, and naive. In a 1978 article, "It Wasn't That Simple," Schlereth wrote:

Historical museum villages are still, with a few exceptions, remarkably peaceable kingdoms, planned communities with over-manicured landscapes or idyllic small towns where the entire populace lives in harmony. The visitor to such sites, who usually does not see the artifacts of convict laborers, domestic servants, hired hands or slaves in the statistical proportion in which such material culture would have cluttered most communities, comes away from the museum village with a romanticized, even utopian perspective of the popularly acclaimed "good old days."[3]

Schlereth was particularly bothered by the "homogeneity" of museum villages. He found that "villages are still largely populated by white, Angol-Saxon, nondenominational Protestant males." He suggested that museum curators become better historians. And Michael Wallace, recently writing in the *Radical History Review,* criticized "explana-

Fig. 6.1. Staff members at Old Sturbridge Village attempt to interpret one of history's most difficult and subtle subjects: attitudes and beliefs underlying politics—in this instance, the 1840 presidential campaign.—*Old Sturbridge Village, Sturbridge, Massachusetts. Photograph by Robert S. Arnold*

tions" of open-air history museums, arguing that although most museums had abandoned "the American Heritage" notion of history for a "more pluralistic conception of the U.S. past," still they "shied away from politics and struggle: slave culture was one thing, slave revolts another." Wallace also noted a failure of museums to "explore the ways the present evolved out of the past." Williamsburg, for example, failed to "explain the connections between eighteenth-century slavery and twentieth-century racism (or black nationalism). Admitting that the realities of ex-

ploitation contradicted the ideals of liberty was only a first step."[4]

Each of these informed students of the living-history museum believed that it was a powerful institution with a responsibility that it was sadly avoiding. Each echoed the earlier call of Theodore Blegen, the pioneer social historian, who, in his *Grass Roots History* (1947), related this story:

Soon after the liberation of Norway, I had a communication from one of the museum authorities in that country. The Nazis had seized the great folk museum of Norway, occupied its buildings, turned

Fig. 6.2. Nuances of cultural change are interpreted at Iowa Living History Farms: interpreter-farmers react skeptically to the sales pitch of a McCormick reaper dealer in the later 1840s. —*Iowa Living History Farms, Des Moines, Iowa*

Fig. 6.3. Sometimes the most effective argument is demonstration: here, the reaper scorned by the farmers in figure 6.2 shows its stuff. —*Iowa Living History Farms, Des Moines, Iowa*

them into factories and laboratories. But the museum did not quit. Its friends continued to sustain it, and in 1944 they celebrated the anniversary of its founding. With guards on watch to warn of a Gestapo raid, they held a secret meeting, at which speeches were delivered on the museum's future and Grieg music was played. And a gift of sixty thousand crowns, gathered by secret solicitation, was presented to the director. "The day's events," I was told, "merged with the life of hundreds of years that the museum itself illustrated in its buildings and exhibits." . . . This sidelight on the care for folk culture in another country set me to wondering about the cultivation of American folk-cultural interests. Do we care? Do we accept responsibility for interpreting the traditional beliefs, customs, folk arts, ideas and practices to help to explain what we are as a people?[5]

These calls for a clarification of purpose prompted many museums to question just what historical themes living-history programs were best able to address. At least four themes or aspects of history emerged that I believe many living history interpreters would feel comfortable focusing upon. They are a historical site's context, processes, folklife, and cultural differences from the

world of today.

The significance of a historical site's *context* often leaps out at you on a visit to a historic house, restored fortress, re-created village, or living historical farm. There are many fine examples, and a variety have already been discussed in this section: the John Ward house in Salem, Ford's Wayside Inn, Colonial Williamsburg, the National Park Service's Lee-Custis mansion, Pliny Freeman Farm at Old Sturbridge Village, Plimoth Plantation, any one of the farms at Iowa's Living History Farms, and of course both Louisbourg and Old Fort William.

The historical context at Plimoth is particularly evident. When you visit the plantation, you go, first, to a two-story blockhouse which served the Pilgrims as a lookout, fort, and meetinghouse. It sits atop a hill, overlooking the village below, and it looks somewhat like a medieval keep—creosoted, black, and foreboding. Looking over the parapet, you can see the entire village with its several dozen houses and outbuildings, fenced gardens, livestock pens, and rutted streets—all surrounded by a palisade fence in the form of

Fig. 6.4. Looking over the parapet of Plimoth Plantation's blockhouse, a visitor can see the entire village, with its thatch-roofed houses, rough-fenced gardens, livestock pens, and rutted streets—all surrounded by a wall of palisades.—*Plimoth Plantation, Inc., Plymouth, Massachusetts*

an elongated diamond or kite. Beyond the palisade are fields of corn and barley, rough meadows, patches of forest, and the sea. If you look carefully, you notice that the village is alive. People move, here and there: a woman hangs out her laundry on the front fence to dry; a young cooper adzes a stave; several children carry a wooden bucket of slops to some pigs; and the thatcher carries a shoulder-load of reeds to a roof comb he is repairing. Their activities weave a web, a context that gives meaning to each person, artifact, and activity. In the 1960s, we might have called this approach to Plimoth *ecological*. Seen in that way, the village is a pulsating web, filled with interrelated people, animals, plants, houses, barns, and so on. In Pilmoth's landscape, there is a "scheme of things" to be discerned: a field of barley, a brewhouse, a cooper's workshop, and several dozen thirsty Pilgrims—all are related, within Plimoth's ecological context. A living-history museum, in particular, has the potential to re-create a particular historical context and, if well interpreted, to convey its significance to the modern visitor, who is, in fact, a stranger from another time and place.

Recently a student of mine, Drew Beisswenger, provided an illustration of the second theme, the *process* of a historical site.

Beisswenger was serving a summer internship at the Tennessee Valley Authority's living historical farm, The Homeplace 1850, where life as it was in 1850 in western Kentucky and Tennessee is re-created. Drew phoned and asked what I thought about his staying on into the autumn season and returning to graduate school in the spring semester.

I asked him why, and he reasoned, "Well, I've planted and cultivated the tobacco crop, and I'd like to stick around for the harvest and curing."

"Do you want to work, eventually, in a living-history museum?" I asked.

"Yes," he said, "I'm convinced that this is the best way to teach people about traditional farming or, for that matter, any folklore, even shape-note singing."[6]

I couldn't agree more. A good living historical museum demonstrates life over time; it can convey the logic underlying work, the seasonal significance of custom, and the temporal dimension of everyday life.

When I was working at the Colonial Pennsylvania Plantation, a re-created 1770s Quaker farm outside Philadelphia, I was always fascinated by the popular appeal of butchering, especially with Boy Scout troops. Its visceral magnetism stemmed, in part, from the boys' desire to see exactly how you metamorphoze a four-hundred-pound sow into a steaming pile of hams, bacons, and sausage links. Living-history museums, and especially farms, specialize in providing visitors with an insight into preindustrial causality. In addition to providing a "geographic" context, they provide a temporal one.

Programs that interpret this historical site process aspect of life in the past often have great appeal. An excellent example occurred at Sleepy Hollow Restorations, a few years ago. In August 1981, an arsonist firebombed the colonial Dutch barn at Phillipsburg Manor in Tarrytown, New York. It was a tragic loss. In addition to demolishing the barn, the fire destoyed a flock of sheep, a cow, a barn cat, and a collection of farm implements.

There was no question about replacing the barn; it was needed to complete the manor's eighteenth-century living historical farm. There *was* a question about how to rebuild the structure. John Harbour, director of Sleepy Hollow Restorations, decided to hire Richard Babcock, a skilled builder of barns, to erect the new barn in a colonial manner, using the tools and technology of the eighteeth century.

In the spring of 1982, Babcock and his five sons, all dressed in period clothing, began to piece the massive barn together. When faced with difficult construction problems—such as raising anchor beams weighing better than two tons more than twenty feet into supporting vertical posts—Babcock experimented with traditional technology. To solve *that* problem, he used an antique windlass of the sort used to raise anchors on ships of the period. A few months after Babcock had begun, I visited the manor and asked him about the experiment. He said it had been a challenge mentally, as well as physically. The problem was to get inside the head of a colonial carpenter and see things his way. Given the specific jobs that had to be done and the tools and men at hand, what techniques would have been devised? Did visitors enjoy the scene of an old barn being reconstructed this way? "Oh, yes," Babcock said, "I see the same people coming back week after week. Many ask me how I finally solved this problem or that. You know, everyone is at heart a sidewalk superintendent."[7]

A third theme, *folklife*—or the everyday life of ordinary people—can be sensitively interpreted at living-history museums.[8] There is, perhaps, no better way to understand and appreciate the domestic routine of a Civil War soldier, a North Dakota bonanza wheat farmer, a Victorian servant girl, or an Acadian

Fig. 6.5. At Fort Mackinac, on Michigan's Upper Peninsula, the cacophony of flintlocks fired by military marksmen attracts the attention of a crowd of visitors.—*Mackinac Island State Park Commission, Lansing, Michigan*

Fig. 6.6. Visitors at Fort Mackinac are drawn to the drama of a courtmartial. Events such as these lend themselves superbly to living-history interpretation.—*Mackinac Island State Park Commission, Lansing, Michigan*

fisherman than to meet and talk with them on their home turf. Living history is humanistic to the core; it allows you to carry on a dialogue with the past. In that sense, it is the most democratic of interpretive modes; it allows the visitors to delve as deeply as they wish into the lives of their historical counterparts. That can be a liberating experience for both interpreter and guest.

One winter afternoon, in the meetinghouse at Old Sturbridge Village, I observed a perfect example of populist history at its best. The department of interpretation was rehearsing a dramatization of a New England town meeting. A variety of interpreters were on hand to represent the mixture of social classes, ethnic groups, and political parties that one might have found in an early nineteenth-century rural Massachusetts town: there were Yankee farmers, Whig businessmen, Presbyterian advocates of temperance, and a handful of rowdy types. Candles were lit, and a full agenda of town business addressed. There were questions of taxes, blue laws, relief for the poor, and upkeep of the roads. Although the "actors" were working from a rough script, they began to improvise. The debate became lively and took on a life of its own. Irish and English clashed, farmer and miller exchanged harsh words. There were flashes of wit and examples of rhetorical elegance. Visitor and interpreter alike were caught up in the play, and at its end we all joked about the power of Cilo, the muse of history, who whisked us back into another time and brought its social texture to life.[9]

I can remember other experiences with grass roots history on a human scale—salting down codfish at the Acadian Village in New Brunswick, watching a deserter being court-martialed at Fort Mackinac—but nothing captured the excitement of that historic town meeting that, seemingly, decided to reincarnate itself.

Last—living history, with its power to

Fig. 6.7. A young minister addresses his fellow townsmen at a re-enactment of an early nineteenth-century Thanksgiving service held in Old Sturbridge Village's meetinghouse. —*Old Sturbridge Village, Sturbridge, Massachusetts. Photograph by Robert S. Arnold*

transport a person vicariously from one time to another, inevitably invites us to *compare historical periods* in the past with our own and to confront the fundamental questions of why some things stay the same and others change.

That comparison can sometimes be painful. At Living History Farms, interpreters would often welcome visitors to the 1900 Farm—and then sadly watch, as older guests

Fig. 6.8. History on a human scale: Loyalist farmers, political refugees from the United States, harvest hay on their New Brunswick farm. Kings Landing tells the story of these dissenters, who were driven into exile in the years following the American Revolution. —*Kings Landing Historic Settlement, New Brunswick, Canada*

would break down and cry, suffering from nostalgia. The visitors would be invited to sit by the kitchen table, have a cup of coffee, and chat about old times.

Often, the conversation got around to changes that have occurred on Iowa farms during the twentieth century. Some changes were deemed good, others bad. Grandmothers would notice the intense heat of the 1900 kitchen, driven up into the nineties by the wood-fired range, and comment that the good old days weren't really ideally pleasant. Retired farmers would run their hands along

the familiar lines of an antique cultivator and ruminate about the drudgery of cultivating corn long into the summer evenings. Still, older couples would muse, far more families lived on the land, then, and many owned their own farms. There was such a thing as a rural community. Now, the Iowa landscape seems deserted, littered with the skeletons of family farms. A traditional way of life stretching back to biblical times seems to be disappearing. Where have all the farmers gone? Interpreters were familiar with these reflections, the result of spontaneous comparison of then and now. Visitors never needed to be led into a discussion of "significant historical themes." They were more than willing to provide their opinions about cultural change, albeit they seldom did so in the jargon of the social scientist or the academic historian.

The older the historical site, the more difficult it often is to draw a clear line of cause and effect between past and present. Plimoth Plantation often appears as exotic to visitors today as a South Sea island. A colleague of mine once confided that she didn't really enjoy the plantation: "Anything before the eighteenth century," she confessed, "is just too foreign for me." However, she appreciated the attempt by the interpreters there to humanize the legendary Pilgrims. "Once," she said, "I got into an argument with one of them about religion and realized that he was just like the born-again preachers you see on TV."[10] That interpreter had done his job well. As Freeman Tilden said, "The chief aim of interpretation is not instruction, but provocation."

The strength of large, complex living-historical sites such as Plimoth, Louisbourg, or The Homeplace 1850 is that they represent, through their context, processes, and folklife, a three-dimensional account of the past. They give one a lot to make comparisons with. Robert Ronsheim writes that

The past has a unity and needs to be considered as whole. This is something many historians who write books or give lectures have been able to avoid by dealing with specific portions of the past; most historical museums cannot avoid the issue.

A living history program is important, even an essential tool, to be used in capitalizing on that opportunity. Properly used, the interest and involvement it can generate can be used to aid the visitor to a clearer perception of the past.[11]

And, he might add, the present, as well.

NOTES

1. Cited in Cary Carson, "Living Museums of Everyman's History," *Harvard Magazine* 83 (July-August 1981): 82. See also Barbara Carson and Cary Carson's thoughtful "Things Unspoken: Learning Social History from Artifacts," in *Ordinary People and Everyday Life*, James Gardner and George Rollie Adams, eds., (Nashville: The American Association for State and Local History, 1983), pp. 181–203.

2. Robert Ronsheim, "Is the Past Dead?," *Museum News* 53:3 (November 1974): 62.

3. Thomas J. Schlereth, "It Wasn't That Simple," *Museum News* 56:1 (January-February 1978): 39–40.

4. Michael Wallace, "Visiting the Past: History Museums in the United States," *Radical History Review* 25 (1981): 86–87.

5. Theodore Blegen, *Grass Roots History* (Minneapolis: University of Minnesota Press, 1947), p. 3.

6. Drew Beisswenger, telephone conversation with author, August 8, 1983, in Bowling Green, Kentucky.

7. Richard Babcock, interview with author, May 22, 1982, at Philipsburg Manor, North Tarrytown, New York.

8. An excellent introduction to the relationship between folklife studies and open-air museums is J. Geraint Jenkins's "The Use of Artifacts and Folk Art in the Folk Museum," in Richard Dorson's *Folklore and Folklife: An Introduction* (Chicago: University of Chicago Press, 1972), pp. 497–516.

9. This experience took place on Friday, November 6, 1981, at Old Sturbridge Village, Sturbridge, Massachusetts.

10. Interview with a colleague who prefers anonymity, June 30, 1982, at Plimoth, Massachusetts.

11. Ronsheim, "Is the Past Dead?," p. 62.

Part 2
Time Bandits:
Living History as Research

7

The Taste of History

IN the spring of 1972, Roger Welsch and I went to Plimoth Plantation, not as interpreters or tourists, but as researchers.[1] We were both interested in traditional English food and drink and had always wanted to try out recipes from the Elizabethan period, using historically accurate ingredients, utensils, and facilities. Plimoth was the ideal historical laboratory, and Jim Deetz gave us permission to live in the William Brewster house for a couple of weeks in late March and early April. For the first half of our stay, the village was closed to the public, so we were isolated from virtually all twentieth-century intrusions: television, electric lights, phones, and the rest of it. However, during the second week, the museum began its spring season, so we were visited by a variety of early-bird tourists tough enough to come out in the late snow and damp cold of a New England March. Each week provided a different learning experience.

Our primary goal was to make Pilgrim beer. We had Elizabethan recipes that we wanted to test for malting and brewing. We had both done some work on traditional home-brewing and had a clear idea of the technology involved. Often, however, even the most complete recipes from seventeenth-century primary sources omit basic steps. By simulating the original processes in an accurate historical context, we hoped to fill in the gaps, rediscovering data that had been lost from traditional written and iconographic sources.

And, of course, we wanted to taste a really good simulation of the beer that Shakespeare, Raleigh, and the Pilgrims once drank. Each adult in the 1620s drank a gallon and a half of small beer or "weak" beer (about four percent alcohol) daily; it was their liquid bread and an integral part of their core diet. We were interested in gaining a better understanding of the beverage that was so important to them.

Roger and I were not particularly good scientists. We had anticipated that living and working in a re-created 1627 village would be an enlightening adventure, a pleasant background to our experiment. What we had *not* expected was the culture shock of living within a closed, gloomy (to us) village in a small peasant cottage for a fortnight. After a week of sleeping on an itchy, straw-filled mattress, of being chilled to the marrow by freezing nor'easters off Cape Cod Bay, and of unremitting hard physical work punctuated by meals of boiled salt fish and sour porridge, we were worn down in body and mind. It was obvious that neither of us was prepared, physically or mentally, for seventeenth-century frontier living. Our attention turned increasingly from the brewing experiment we had undertaken to the ways in which the realities of life had changed in three and a half centuries.

We had begun the project hoping to learn something about the Pilgrims—and we ended up discovering far more about ourselves, our own period of history, and the "cultural, temporal, and spatial" gulf between the first New Englanders and ourselves. At times, the problems of bridging that gulf intellectually seemed impossible.

There was, however, one moment when we felt really close to the Pilgrims. It was April 5. Roger later wrote of the "staggering despondency" we felt, as we "stood in the center of the dark, dreary village in a light snow, looking out on a stormy sea, listening to its roar, overcome by the realization that some 350 years before, the Pilgrim villagers had watched their last real contact with the world they had known, the *Mayflower*, sail eastward on this very night, leaving them alone—perhaps the word is *abandoned*—on these hostile shores."[2] That night was the closest we came to really traveling back in time and appreciating what the pilgrims must have felt.

Ironically, our beer provided us with a "taste" of history. When we finished brewing, we asked Jim Boggs, the village cooper and a native of East Anglia—the Pilgrims' English homeland—if he could make a barrel for us. He enthusiastically went to work; and a day later he rolled the barrel down the hill and helped us ladle into it all fifty-six gallons of the sweet, dark, highly hopped brew. We chatted as we worked, and Jim told us of his apprentice work in the great Bass Brewery at Burton-on-Trent. That was where he had learned his coopering, making beer barrels in the old way.[3] Jim also talked of his early days on an East Anglian farm and of his mother's home-brewing. She had made a traditional small beer for the farm workers during March and October and followed a family recipe. We

asked if he remembered it, and he said yes, for he had helped her with the brewing throughout his boyhood. The recipe he recited to us was virtually identical to the historical, late sixteenth-century one we had used. Ours, too, had come from an East Anglian family. We then asked Jim, somewhat hesitantly, whether he thought he could remember the *taste* of his childhood beer sufficiently well to compare it with our simulated brew. Again he said yes, for he had what "you might call a beer memory. Some people are good with teas, some with wines. My specialty is beer." I didn't think we could contain our excitement at this stroke of luck.

We waited for the beer to age one week, the normal period, then invited Jim down and tapped the barrel. He poured a little on his fingers, gauging its texture, inhaled its bitter aroma, and finally sipped a little. He paused, smiled, shook his head, and said, "Yes, that's it," and finished the mug with obvious satisfaction. If Jim was pleased, *we* were overjoyed at our success in getting as close as it was conceivably possible to get, in re-creating a historical taste. I remember Roger, after several pints, saying, "Now, *this* is what history is all about!"

Had we been better prepared, we might have documented our brewing experiment more carefully, for the data we generated—given Jim Boggs's fortuitous input—was unique. Several years later, I met Hans-Ole Hansen, the Danish experimental archaeologist, at Lejre, his Historical-Archaeological Research Center outside Copenhagen.[4] We discussed the brewing experiment and my problems with documentation, and he noted that an attempt at total simulation of life, such as our experiment, could be so traumatic that careful documentation was impossible. He preferred to concentrate on one experiment at a time. Hansen gave me a report he had written on the first ten years of the Lejre center, which contained this advice:

It is imperative that every single experiment should be observed and recorded to such a degree that it is possible for another researcher, without performing an extensive trial series, to use these results as a foundation for further research. . . . The need for the detailed recording of work processes might be surprising to some people: "But can't these work processes be obtained through still-living traditions?" The answer, unfortunately, is no. Very little of the information in ethnographic studies is sufficiently detailed to be used as work descriptions and as the basis for imitation of the work. Therefore, every notation about an almost extinct work process, a disappearing house-building technique, and other preindustrial skills, should be recorded from the viewpoint of the possibility of future imitation. . . . Imitative experiments may make an essential contribution to general anthropological research: the development of a way [of] describing [how] the work process [must be done] so that the process could be repeated not only by the observer but also by someone unfamiliar with the original work.[5]

Looking back, I console myself with the thought that we were newcomers to the field of "experimenal archaeology" and its "imitative experiments," and despite our failures in one area, we did succeed in others. In our first week at Pilmoth, we learned that one byproduct of simulated experiments can be a useful comparison between key aspects of historical and contemporary cultures, especially the activities of everyday life.

In our second week there, we learned another lesson, when visitors began to arrive and ask us what we were doing. We quickly discovered that they were fascinated by the idea of using the village as a historical laboratory. We discussed with them the methods of historical and archaeological research used by the museum in attempts to re-create Plimoth as accurately as possible. But the visitors seemed particularly interested in our attempt to corroborate written, iconographic, and material sources (probate court records, diaries, letters, paintings, and drawings from the period, surviving artifacts, etc.) with

experiments, such as our attempt to simulate the Pilgrims' brewing. A number of visitors wanted to know more about the use of "imitative experiments" or the use of simulation as a research tool. Their interest encouraged me to begin a more serious examination of the field of experimental archaeology and its leading figures, projects, and potential impact on our understanding of past cultures.[6]

John Coles, an archaeologist at Cambridge University, in his readable *Archaeology by Experiment* and *Experimental Archaeology*[7] has told the complete story; and J. A. Graham, R. F. Heizer, and T. R. Hester have compiled a comprehensive work, *Bibliography of Replicative Experiments in Archaeology*.[8] The picture that emerges from their work is one of literally hundreds of serious scholars who have, for the past century, been using simulation as a research tool. Coles has written:

One way in which archaeology can reach back and experience some parts of ancient life is through attempts to reproduce former conditions and circumstances. By trying to make and use some of the weapons and tools of the past, we can often gain an insight into the importance of these objects to their original inventors and owners. By building copies of houses, palisades, and fortresses, we can appreciate better the scale of ancient enterprise, and the organizations of labour required. By constructing and using replicas of boats and wagons we can understand the problems of communication and colonization in early times. And by trying to actually live as our ancestors did, by experiencing the concerns of the past, we may become aware of our prehistory, of past problems concerned with wood supplies and shelter, and the inventive nature of man. . . . Experimental archaeology [is] a study designed to look at ancient man as an inventor, a technician, a craftsman, an artist, and a human being. By reproducing his actions, archaeologists can better understand not only his technical abilities but also his reasons for choosing one course of action rather than another. This is the kind of information which all archaeologists seek, the meaning behind the surviving relics.[9]

Experimental archaeology was developed in the late nineteenth century, at roughly the same time that Hazelius was establishing Skansen. Archaeologists saw in experimentation a means of practically testing theories of past cultural behavior, especially technological processes involving the use of tools, and a method for obtaining data not readily available from more traditional artifactual analysis and historical research. The resulting data could then be used to formulate new theories about historic economic and cultural systems. Because the archaeologist or researcher sought to "imitate" or "replicate" the original process as nearly as possible, the method has often been termed "imitative" archaeology.

Coles, in his two books, describes more than three hundred experimental projects. they include experiments with prehistoric and historic forest clearing; plowing, crop-planting, harvesting, and storage; cooking; housebuilding and usage; natural and accidental destruction of structures; construction of earthworks and roads; boat-building and navigation; stone work and woodworking; manufacture of weapons, tools, and musical instruments; antler and bone craft; ore smelting and smithing; leather-working; textile production; pottery, paint, and paper manufacturing; and animal- and plant-breeding.

In short, there is almost no aspect of prehistoric or early historic life that researchers have not investigated, using imitative experiments. Some projects simply strive to make a simulated copy of an original artifact, often using modern materials and methods. Others go a step further, as Welsch and I did at Plimoth, and try to make a simulated copy using historically accurate raw materials and production methods. Other experimenters go even further and put the simulated object to use in an attempt to understand its original function better than before. If Welsch and I had actually worked a full Pilgrim's day— fishing, farming, doing chores, etc.—and

eaten a daily menu of Pilgrim dishes, including a gallon and a half of beer, we would have taken our experiment to this stage. We didn't; but we subsequently wished that we had carried our project to its logical conclusion. Understandably, because of the cost in time, labor, and materials, and the lack of complete re-created environments, the number of complex functional projects are fewer than experiments that simulate and test specific objects and processes.

While all imitative experiments utilize a vicarious form of time traveling, it is the complex functional projects that use the time-machine model. Examples include the fabrication and operation of boats, ships, farms, villages, and cultural landscapes. Most complex projects have occurred after World War II and were influenced by the highly publicized work of Thor Heyerdahl.

Heyerdahl was born in 1914 in Larvik, Norway.[10] His father was a wealthy businessman, his mother a free-thinking Social Darwinist. They decided to educate Thor in a manner similar to that chosen by Hazelius's parents for their son, Artur—with heavy emphasis on the social sciences and including years spent in the backcountry on the Swedish border, about a hundred miles from Dalecarlia, where—fifty years earlier—Artur Hazelius had done *his* fieldwork. One of Thor's boyhood friends, Arnold Jacoby, described Heyerdahl as fascinated with the "differences between modern and primitive life."[11] The freedom Heyerdahl had experienced, living in the remote regions of central Norway, combined with a "half-religious worship of nature, caused him to doubt whether civilization was a blessing to mankind." Jacoby writes of his friend's youthful questioning in the early 1930s:

What was a worthy form of life? This question became at last the most important of all problems for him. He talked continually of returning to nature. Modern man, he said, had his brains stuffed full, not so much of his own experience as of opinions and impressions derived from books, newspapers, magazines, radio, and motion pictures. The result was an over-loaded brain and reduced powers of observation. . . . The drawbacks of civilization were not discernible unless seen from the outside. . . . Civilization might be compared with a house full of people who had never been outside the building. None of them knew what their house looked like, although they lived in it. It was necessary to go outside to see the house as it really was. This was precisely what he wanted to do.[12]

For the next fifty years, Heyerdahl looked at contemporary civilization from the perspective of the prehistoric world. In 1937, he set off for the South Seas with his wife, Liv. For a year they lived the primitive life in the Marquesas island of Fatu-Hiva. Two years later, with the modest proceeds from his account of their adventure, *In Search of Paradise*,[13] they lived in the remote mountain area of British Columbia. While there, Heyerdahl published an article in the *National Georgraphic*, "Turning Back Time in the South Seas,"[14] and gathered material for his theory on North and South American influences on Polynesian culture. Heyerdahl argued that there might have been two separate migrations by sea from the American mainland to Polynesia: the first from Peru, via Easter Island; and the second through Hawaii, from British Columbia. In 1970, Heyerdahl sailed across the Atlantic Ocean in *Ra II*, a papyrus boat; and in 1977, he sailed a similar reed boat, *Tigris*, from the mouth of the Tigris and Euphrates rivers, in Iraq, well into the Arabian Sea to Djibouti.[15] It was the 1947 *Kon-Tiki* expedition, however, that established him as the best-known of the experimental archaeologists. After the *Kon-Tiki's* voyage, simulation became a more acceptable research tool.

Heyerdahl sought to prove that people could have sailed the four thousand miles between South America and the Polynesian Islands, transplanting themselves and their culture, before A.D. 1100. He did not claim that they actually did make the voyage; he

only proposed to generate new data that would prove that such a voyage was feasible and therefore must be considered as evidence in all further considerations of the cultural history of South America and the Pacific. His experiment attained its goal.

The best accounts of the *Kon-Tiki* were written by Heyerdahl himself. In addition to his *The Kon-Tiki Expedition: Across the Pacific by Raft*,[16] written for the layman, Heyerdahl presented detailed academic accounts of his voyage, for scholars, in a number of other books and articles published in the 1950s.

Kon-Tiki was a model project in experimental archaeology. Heyerdahl carefully reviewed the historical records from the west coast of South America—especially reports by early Spanish sailors and missionaries—of indigenous Peruvian balsa rafts that Indians used to transport cargo along the coast in the 1500s. Following descriptions in this historical material, Heyerdahl built a raft in the spring of 1947. Since he had no archaeological survivals to copy, the *Kon-Tiki* had to be a total re-creation, in much the same manner as Plimoth Plantation was. However, it was as historically accurate as Heyerdahl was able to make it. He used only locally available materials: balsa for the raft's logs, hemp ropes, bamboo cross beams and deck, a mangrove-wood mast, and reed and banana leaves for the cabin. When the raft was completed, it looked totally unseaworthy, and both his friends and his advisers speculated on which disaster would end the voyage first. Virtually no one outside of the crew thought they had a chance. On April 28, 1947, the *Kon-Tiki* set sail from the Peruvian port of Callao. One hundred and one days later, ship and crew reached the Tuamotu Islands, after a voyage of more than four thousand miles. They averaged more than forty miles a day and encountered a variety of weather conditions. Later, Heyerdahl wrote of their feelings at night, before they fully understood just how seaworthy the *Kon-Tiki* was:

Fig. 7.1. Thor Heyerdahl's *Kon-Tiki,* en route from Chile to the Tuamotu Islands, a voyage of more than four thousand miles. In the middle of the Pacific Ocean, Heyerdahl muses, A.D. 1947 often seemed like 1947 B.C. —*Reprinted from* Kon-Tiki, *by Thor Heyerdahl (Chicago, Ill.: Rand McNally & Co., 1950)*

When swallowed up by the darkness, we heard the general noise from the sea around us suddenly deafened by the hiss of a roller close by and saw a white crest come groping toward us on a level with the cabin roof, we held tight and waited uneasily to feel the masses of water smash down over us and the raft.

But every time there was the same surprise and relief. The *Kon-Tiki* calmly swung up her stern and rose skyward unperturbed, while the masses of water rolled along her sides. Then we sank down again into the trough of waves and waited for the next big sea.[17]

Heyerdahl and his five crewmen tested the raft thoroughly and carried out numerous experiments with navigation equipment. They were unable to tack into the wind, a serious problem that Heyerdahl later solved with a series of less-publicized and shorter trips along the coast in the mid-1950s. They were able to solve a variety of smaller problems and, in the end, became adept sailors of the raft. They did not simulate ancient Peruvian life aboard the raft; they didn't eat a traditional diet or wear native clothes. That was not their purpose, although Heyerdahl later wrote that they could have survived on the fish that were constantly streaming by the raft. He called dolphins "our daily bread," and described them as the "best eating imaginable."

At times, they broke the time barrier and entered the world of the ancient Peruvians. They would take a rubber dinghy out, look back at the solitary raft, and contemplate.

Coal-black seas towered up on all sides, and a glittering myriad of tropical stars drew a faint reflection from plankton in the water. The world was simple—stars in the darkness. Whether it was 1947 B.C. or A.D. suddenly became of no significance. We lived, and that we felt, with alert intensity. We realized that life had been full for men before the technological age also—in fact, fuller and richer in many ways than the life of modern man. Time and evolution somehow ceased to exist; all that was real and that mattered were the same today as they had always been and would always be. We were swallowed up in the absolute common measure of history—endless unbroken darkness under a swarm of stars.[18]

This timeless point of view enabled the crew the better to "see in our mind's eye the whole flotilla of such vessels, spread in a fan formation beyond the horizon. . . . When we jumped on board the raft again, we often sat down in a circle round the paraffin lamp in the bamboo deck and talked of the seafarers from Peru who had all these same experiences fifteen hundred years before us."[19]

The raft became for the crew an extraordinary time machine. For the next generation of experimental archaeologists the *Kon-Tiki* was an inspiration and a model to follow, on both land and sea.

NOTES

1. Roger Welsch, "Very Didactic Simulation," *The History Teacher* 7:3 (May 1974): 356–364.
2. Welsch, "Very Didactic Simulation," p. 358.
3. The experience of men like Jim Boggs has been described by George Ewart Evans in *Tools of Their Trades: An Oral History of Men at Work c. 1900* ((New York: Taplinger Publishing Company, 1970).
4. Hans-Ole Hansen, interview with author, August 22, 1973, at Lejre, Roskilda, Denmark.
5. Hans-Ole Hansen, *Some Main Trends in the Development of the Lejre Center* (Roskilda, Denmark: Lejre Historical and Archaeological Research Center, 1973), pp.11–12.
6. A good introduction to the field is found in Robert Asher's "Experimental Archaeology," *American Anthropologist* 63 (1961): 793–816.
7. John Coles, *Archaeology by Experiment* (London: Hutchinson, 1973); John Coles, *Experimental Archaeology* (London: Academic Press, 1979).
8. J. A. Graham, R. F. Heizer, and T. R. Hester, *A Bibliography of Replicative Experiments in Archaeology* (Berkeley: Department of Archeology, 1972).
9. Coles, *Experimental Archaeology,* pp. 1–2.
10. Arnold Jacoby has written a biography of Thor Heyerdahl, his boyhood friend: *Señor Kon-Tiki* (Chicago: Rand McNally & Company, 1967).
11. Jacoby, *Señor Kon-Tiki,* pp.38–40.
12. Jacoby, *Señor Kon-Tiki,* p. 39.
13. Thor Heyerdahl, *Fatu-Hiva: Back to Nature* (New York: Doubleday & Company, Inc., 1975).
14. Thor Heyerdahl, "Turning Back Time in the South Seas," *National Geographic* 79:1 (January 1941): 109–136.
15. Thor Heyerdahl, *The Tigris Expedition* (New York: Doubleday & Company, Inc., 1980).
16. Thor Heyerdahl, *The Kon-Tiki Expedition: Across the Pacific by Raft* (Chicago: Rand McNally & Company, 1950).
17. Heyerdahl, *Kon-Tiki,* p. 104.
18. Heyerdahl, *Kon-Tiki,* p. 173.
19. Heyerdahl, *Kon-Tiki,* p. 173.

8

I Built a Stone Age House

L ESS than ten years after Thor Heyerdahl set sail on the *Kon-Tiki,* another Scandinavian, Hans-Ole Hansen, was beninning a series of archaeological experiments that would result in the establishment of a major experimental institution, the Historical-Archaeological Research Center at Lejre, in Denmark. The center began very humbly, when the seventeen-year-old Hansen built his first "Stone Age" house in 1956. With the help of teen-age friends, Hansen recreated not only a wattle-and-daub longhouse, fifteen meters long by six meters wide, but also a semicircular house and a work shed. His dozen helpers took ten days and used nine tons of clay for the daub, two thousand willow and hazel rods for the wattle, seventy-two poles for uprights and rafters, two hundred and twenty bundles of reeds and rushes for thatching, and a hundred laths for the roof. They used elm bark strips to tie everything together and a cartload of hay and stone for flooring and hearth. Throughout the experiment, they avoided modern tools and methods.

Hansen lived in the smaller shed, from time to time, to study it from the inside out. He was careful, however, not to assume that his modern living habits and use of the interior space duplicated those of his prehistoric forebears. After several years, the longhouse accidentally burned down, allowing Hansen to study its remains and compare them with those of actual archaeological sites of ancient houses. He wrote up his early experiences in *Undommelige Oldtidhuse* (1961), which was translated into English and published as *I Built a Stone Age House* a year later.[1] The book is charmingly youthful and full of enthusiasm, but also characterized by an attention to detail, clear thinking, curiosity, and modesty.

In 1962, Hansen was "discovered" by Danish television promoters, who persuaded him to build a simulation of an Iron Age house excavated in 1937, and then burn it. Hansen this time carefully monitored his house's destruction with temperature gauges and marked its timbers with metal tags. Later, he "excavated" his copy and was able to compare its remains with those of the original Stone Age house.[2]

Hansen's enthusiasm for imitative experimentation grew; and in 1964, he leased fifty acres on a large estate in Lejre, just outside Copenhagen, and with the help of eighty volunteers from throughout Europe, began the Historical-Archaeological Research Center. They built, during the following two years, ten different prehistoric historic houses, some based on actual archaeological sites from various parts of Denmark and representing different periods and others constructed solely to test architectural theories. Some were later burned, and others were allowed to weather naturally. On occasion, Hansen and members of the center's staff occupied the houses, to see whether experimentally-built-in elements such as smoke holes, windows, sleeping platforms, hearths, and screens separating human living space from animal stalls really worked. These "live-ins" provided the staff with what they call a "whiff of the past" and drew much public attention. In 1968, the Danish Ministry of Education agreed to provide the center with operating funds to augment the seed capital originally granted by the Carlsberg Foundation. Lejre's future life as a viable Danish research and education institution was assured.[3]

I first visited Lejre in the summer of 1974. I was on the way back from a conference in Finland and stopped off in Copenhagen to see Grithe Lerche, an archaeologist who specializes in prehistoric agriculture and foodways. When I mentioned my work at Plimoth, she said, "You must meet Hans-Ole; he is at the center of experimental archaeology." Grithe and Hans-Ole, it turned out, had been students together working with Professor Axel Steensberg, who had done a variety of experiments with early farming tools during the 1940s. Grithe called Hans-Ole, and he agreed to talk about Lejre the next day.

The Historical-Archaeological Research Center is an hour's drive west of Copenhagen, and the landscape along the way is rural and very European. To my American eyes, the countryside was overtidy, parceled out into neat villages, farms, and forests. The center, however, was a kaleidoscope of activity, verging on confusion.

Before meeting Hansen, I spent half a day walking around the center's fifty acres of gentle hills and woods. I had expected an open-air museum, something like the Frilandsmuseet, the Danish national folk

museum, also near Copenhagen. There was no resemblance. Lejre contained an odd mixture of preindustrial buildings, scattered about in clusters. There was an "Iron Age Village" with nine large houses at one end of the center and a group of tile, pottery, iron, textile, and wood workshops at the other. In between were A-frame laboratories and several eighteenth- and nineteenth-century houses that had been relocated or re-created. Fields seemed everywhere, along with meadows for grazing and woods of oak, beech, ash, and willow. Cattle, horses, and sheep wandered freely, and there were pens for goats and swine. Staff members and students in blue jeans, jerseys, and sandals or sneakers also seemed everywhere, busy with experiments. Frequently, there was a sign at the entrance of a building, "KUN FOR KURSES" —"Class in Progress." As living museums go, Lejre was bursting with energy.

Hans-Ole was quick to point out that Lejre was only superficially like a museum.[4] Its purpose was not to collect and preserve old artifacts, but to study preindustrial life by "reinventing and perpetuating" traditional tools, technological processes, farming methods, arts, and crafts. The method he and others had developed for doing those things was the "imitative experiment."

There were essentially two kinds of experiments done. The simpler involved testing archaeological theories by using simulated copies. For example, since there are no Iron Age houses surviving, and what you have to work with are only archaeological clues such as patterns of post holes, can you design and build a structure that will stand by using these patterns as hypothetical floor plans? Or, to give a few simpler illustrations, how does a flint knife really cut meat, a stone axe chop down a tree, a prehistoric oven bake bread, a clay pot boil porridge?

The second, more complicated experiment tries to determine the nature of preindustrial work and everyday life. For example, the

Fig. 8.1. Overlooking the Historical-Archaeological Research Center at Lejre, in Denmark, is the hide of a sacrificial horse, head still attached, placed there by the center's staff members, who sought an archaic symbol to emphasize the spiritual aspects of prehistoric life.—*Lejre Historical-Archaeological Research Center, Denmark. Photograph by the author*

Lejre staff knows the type of wheat that Danes grew in the Neolithic period, as well as the implements used to till and harvest it. What was the yield per acre that a farmer could expect? How many acres would it take to feed a family of six—or eight—or ten? How much grain could one safely store? How long does it take to mill a pound of wheat using a hand-turned stone quern and how long must you boil it over an open fire? And so on.

Hansen pointed out that there were some things about prehistoric life that we will never know, and that was the reason for one particular "exhibit" at Lejre. Overlooking the entire center, at the edge of a forest of old oak and beech, was the head and skin of a sacrificed horse, impaled by Hansen on a long pole thrust into the earth at a slant, so that the legs and feet of the skin hang perpendicular to the ground. This archaic symbol signified, for the staff, the spiritual aspects of ancient life that no experimentation with material culture would ever shed light upon.

Hansen also stressed the center's concern with subjectivity. It was all too easy to imagine that, just because you felt scared, or dirty, or tired, or pleased while doing an "imitative experiment," your prehistoric ancestor must have felt the same way. Not so: feelings are not objective, or measurable, and care must be taken not to "live back," or project our cultural relativism onto earlier ways of life. This, Hansen said, was one reason why his staff seldom dressed in simulations of prehistoric clothing: it was too easy to slip into an essentially false frame of mind and to begin believing that, just because one was "dressed for the part," one was a Viking. *Bad science*, that. Generally, the only time the center staff wore facsimiles of ancient clothing was to test such garments for warmth, practicality, and wear patterns. Hansen even noted that, when he and others lived in the re-created houses, it was to test the houses, not themselves—how can you really know how a house functions in winter if you don't warm it with the appropriate human and animal bodies?

As I think back on our long conversation of almost ten years ago, what stands out is how well the staff at Lejre was able to travel successfully back in time and try out prehistoric living from the point of view of the people who lived in Stone Age, Bronze Age, and Iron Age Denmark. While the Lejre researchers certainly didn't act like preindustrial farmers and craftsmen, and while they surrounded themselves with a wide variety of modern scientific measuring and and documenting devices—still, the staff really seemed to be able to adopt an ancient perspective, enabling them successfully to "reinvent and perpetuate" long-lost traditions. By 1974, ten years after Lejre's inception, the staff had already conducted experiments with upright warp-weighted looms; textiles and tailoring; pottery; pit- and kiln-baked earthenware; bog-iron smelting; smithing; neolithic and postmedieval house

Fig. 8.2. One of the Lejre Research Center's imitative experiments: clay furnaces, built for smelting bog-iron. Only the technological past is simulated in the Lejre project.—*Lejre Historical-Archaeological Research Center, Denmark*

Fig. 8.3. A researcher at Lejre carries out two experiments at once: she both cooks and dresses in neolithic fashion.—*Lejre Historical-Archaeological Research Center, Denmark*

usage; animal breeding; slash-and-burn agriculture; plowing; food processing, preservation, and storage; hand tool construction; saddle and horse gear; and household and domestic activities. And they were more than willing to interpret their successes and failures with both enthusiasm and humility. More than a half million visitors had walked around the center's craft workshops, Iron Age houses, and neolitihic fields. Its staff had given courses in simulation to more than a thousand teachers, and well over ten thousand students had participated in workshops. Lejre's impact on Danish education was considerable. Hansen was also having an influence on other European experimental archaeologists.

Across the North Sea from Denmark, on the south coast of England, another very different research center was also taking shape in the 1970s. Peter Reynolds, its founder, called it the Butser Ancient Farm Research Project. He set the project up in 1972, with the goal of reconstructing an Iron Age farm as it would have actually existed about 300 B.C. The farm was named *Butser Hill* after the hill

where the project was carried out. One interesting feature of Butser Hill, beside its being one of the highest elevations in southern England, was its use, during the Iron Age, as the site for a Celtic farm. It was on this exact site that Reynolds wanted to reconstruct his farm. Needless to say, before he began work, he meticulously re-excavated the site and pored over early archaeological reports.

When I visited Butser Farm in the late summer of 1977, I expected a second Lejre. Reynolds had earlier spoken to me of Hansen's work and of his regard for what the Danes were doing.[5] On the surface, Butser Farm looked completely different from Lejre; but in reality, the spirit of both projects was the same. To get to Butser Farm, I climbed over the 750-foot Butser Hill, through the wild grass and grazing sheep. Once on the summit, you could look thirty miles in any direction. The thought certainly crossed my mind that, from here, you could easily see an invading force of Romans or even Danish Vikings.

The farm is actually located on a northern spur, known locally as Little Butser, and look-

Fig. 8.4. To protect the delicate archaeological site at the Butser Ancient Farm Research Project, in England, its founder, Peter Reynolds, closed the farm to an understanding public, who could visit his nearby educational farm.—*Butser Ancient Farm Research Project, England. Photograph by the author*

Fig. 8.5. One of the Iron Age Butser Farm's experimental round-houses.—*Butser Ancient Farm Research Project, England. Photograph by the author*

ing something like a gigantic tadpole swimming away from the hill but still connected to it by its tail. As I walked down to the "tail," I was not welcomed by a sign, as one is at Lejre, inviting one in; rather I was greeted by a fence and a small historical marker that politely said, essentially, "This farm is off-limited to the public." At one time, in August 1975, Reynolds did open the farm, for a few days, to visitors, but the damage to the delicate site was so great that he had to close the project down to all but a few chosen guests. Still, even from the distance of the restraining fence, I could tell there was a farm below, albeit a highly unusual one.

When Reynolds began Butser Farm, with the help of a few friends, his specific objectives were:

. . . to construct three or four round-houses with barns, byres, etc., as the nucleus of the farmstead. A ditch and bank with a palisade fence was to be built around these buildings, and radiating from the farmstead would be a number of fields and paddocks with associated tracks and fences. Crops, the prehistoric varieties or the nearest equivalent, were to be grown in the fields, and the

appropriate livestock would be brought in to complete the range of activities. Everything had to be accomplished within the strictest scientific limits possible and correlated directly to archaeological evidence. All the round-houses, for example, had to be constructed according to specific excavated house plans. In fact, all buildings of whatever kind which were constructed at the Ancient Farm are based directly upon scientific archaeological evidence. This allows a clear focus upon the excavated detail and reminds us that excavation is not simply the collection of artifacts for museums and art historians, but an attempt to understand how people of the past lived and worked.[6]

Within five years—and on a minuscule budget—Reynolds had completed the farm. He modestly said that it was at best a "simple reconstruction," the "physical realization of one possible interpretation" of the site's archaeological history. In fact, it was as "pre"-historically accurate as Louisbourg or the Governor's Palace in Williamsburg, similar reconstructions on original sites. The comparison with these giants is deliberate and relevant: the Butser Ancient Farm Research Project is one of Europe's and the world's major efforts in experimental archaeology.

Reynolds's goal was not just to re-create a farm, but to use the project area as "a huge open-air scientific research laboratory," where "detailed and precise field experiments could be conducted into prehistoric agriculture, industry and buildings." He also wanted to "devise improved systems of archaeological data retrieval and recording."[7] By 1979, Reynolds had already accumulated enough new data to command a reappraisal of the life and work of English farmers at the time of the Roman conquest. His *Iron-Age Farm: The Butser Experiment* (1979) is a remarkable report that draws the serious scholar into the everyday life of the Iron Age by a careful re-examination of the ordinary farmer's home, outbuildings, livestock, crops, crafts, food, and especially seasonal work patterns.

But the process of re-creating and operating the farm was both intellectually and physically demanding. Reynolds likened it to having "a huge, three-dimensional jigsaw puzzle, some pieces clearly seen, others not yet imagined or even suspected. Which pieces should one create first? What scale of priorities to adopt?"[8] When I visited him, Reynolds was taking "inventory" of a field of Emmer wheat.[9] He had a light wooden frame a meter square and was moving from one part of the golden field to another, following a mental grid. He would stop, lay the square down, hand-pick every bearded head of wheat within the square, and put each in a numbered plastic bag so that he could later count and weigh the exact yield of wheat per square meter. We talked about the sheer hard tedious work of documenting farm practices, whether prehistoric or historic; and later in his report, Reynolds wrote about the problems of just re-creating a field:

In effect, it is quite simple, if extremely arduous, to construct a field. Once that field has been planted with a crop, a process has been started. Unfortunately, on a field which is not treated with the modern pesticides and herbicides it is not just the planted crop which grows. A profusion of weeds and grasses suddenly appear, and if allowed to flourish unchecked will severely restrict if not completely destroy the planted crop . . . Inevitably, therefore, weeding either by hoe or hand becomes necessary. The time spent in maintaining a crop becomes an important factor in the general farm management. Reaping the harvest and its subsequent analysis also take their appropriate portion of time and at the end, after many long hours of effort, all that is left is a field. The three-dimensional jigsaw puzzle inevitably involves the fourth dimension of time.[10]

By 1979, Reynolds had constructed two large roundhouses, five fields, and a paddock system for a flock of twenty Soay sheep and a small herd of long-legged Dexter cattle, two of which were trained as a working pair to pull his plow, a replica of an ard. Reynolds had also acquired an Exmoor pony, goats, and various domestic fowl and was able to study the "interaction of all these different elements" through the "experiencing of controlling, training, and maintaining the livestock and managing the crop programme."[11]

Reynolds's ability to organize the various elements of his project was formidable. I remember his carrying a small pocket tape recorder around the farm at all times, to help him make "verbal notes" as he observed the effects of a heavy rain on the thatch roof of one of his houses, the rooting pattern of his "ancient pigs" (a cross between a European wild boar and a Tamworth), the extent of Fat Hen (pigweed) in the wheat field, or reconsidering another possible function for the chalk pits that dotted the farmscape beside storing fodder, salting meat, holding water, or working potter's clay.

Still, the general atmosphere of the farm was quiet, almost ghostly. There was little human activity, none of the buzz of Lejre; only a solitary archaeologist-farmer working very hard and thinking even harder. But on the basis of his experiments, simulating life and work in the Iron Age, Reynolds had already postulated new theories on population density, settlement patterns, land use,

Fig. 8.6. Peter Reynolds of Butser Farm, taking inventory of his crop of Emmer wheat.—*Butser Ancient Farm Research Project, England. Photograph by the author*

agriculture, food storage, vernacular architecture, and other aspects of neolithic culture.

Many of these suppositions quietly undermine the popular stereotypes of premedieval England. For example, because of new data yielded by experiments with old wheat varieties, plows, and chalk-pit storage, Reynolds has suggested that far more land was under cultivation along the Southern coast of England far earlier than had been previously thought, that storage facilities had been perfected to preserve the additional wheat, beans, vetches, and flax grown, that the rural population of England was considerably larger than generally believed, and that the Romans invaded Britain, not out of a love of conquest, but because England was a potential breadbasket for their western empire. Reynolds, however, is cautious and careful not to claim too much for experimental archaeology. "Perhaps the story of Iron Age farming as told in this book [*Farming in the Iron Age*] is almost right, perhaps it is largely wrong. As more excavations take place and more evidence is discovered, we shall need to revise the story in places. In ten years' time

we may even have to rewrite the whole story."[12]

For experimental researchers such as Reynolds and Hansen, time is another dimension, and simulation a useful tool for exploring it.

NOTES

1. Hans-Ole Hansen, *I Built a Stone Age House* (New York: The John Day Company, 1964). An English edition appeared in 1962.

2. *The Prehistoric Village at Lejre* (Roskilde, Denmark: The Historical-Archaeological Research Center, 1977), p. 12.

3. *Prehistoric Village*, p. 14.

4. Hans-Ole Hansen, interview with author, August 22, 1973, at Lejre, Roskilde, Denmark.

5. Peter Reynolds visited the Colonial Pennsylvania Plantation in the fall of 1976. I returned the visit and interviewed him on the bank holiday weekend of September 2–4, 1977.

6. Peter Reynolds, *Iron-Age Farm—the Butser Experiment* (London: The British Museum, 1979), pp. 21–22.

7. Reynolds, *Iron-Age Farm*, p. 23.

8. Reynolds, *Iron-Age Farm*, p. 26.

9. Peter Reynolds, interview with author, September 4, 1977, at Butser Hill.

10. Reynolds, *Iron-Age Farm*, p. 26.

11. Reynolds, *Iron-Age Farm*, p. 28.

12. Peter Reynolds, *Farming in the Iron Age* (Cambridge: Cambridge University Press, 1976), p. 4.

9
Museums in the Making

THOR Heyerdahl's book *Kon-Tiki* provoked scholars and fascinated armchair adventurers. To the archaeologist and the historian, the voyage of the *Kon-Tiki* served as a challenge. Heyerdahl had dared to apply the guiding principle of science—that theory should be checked by experiment—to a historical problem. To the layman, however, Heyerdahl was a Nordic Galahad, a daring young scholar-hero on a quest, undaunted by either the Pacific or public opinion. In the 1950s and 1960s, Heyerdahl found himself a celebrity, and the experimental method he popularized became a regular feature for cultural journalists. Month after month, articles on experimental archaeology appeared in the *National Geographic, Natural History,* the *Smithsonian,* and the travel section of the Sunday *New York Times.* Their leads often suggested the notion of time travel, as in Geoffrey Bibby's article on Lejre in the 1970 *Horizon:* "An Experiment with Time: At a new Danish research center, archaeologists—and a multitude of others—are learning how life really was lived two thousand years ago."[1]

Experimental projects were soon undertaken by scholars concerned with interpreting the new methods of imitative research to a growing audience whose interest had been kindled by researchers like Thor Heyerdahl.

It was as if the researchers had thrown open their labs and invited the public in to see them at work. The new methods of experimental historical research were pointed out, and staff people were careful to emphasize questions, not answers. There was an obvious and welcomed humility to this approach: "experts" were admitting that they did not, in fact, know all the answers, but did have interesting new methods that might solve some equally fascinating questions.

One of the first and most intriguing of these innovative research and educational projects, with which I was fortunate to be involved, was the Colonial Pennsylvania Plantation. I was a founder (1972) and first president (1972-1974) of the Bishop's Mill Historical Institute and the first director of the Colonial Pennsylvania Plantation (1972-1976), the BMHI's major project. The plantation was a cross between Butser Hill and Lejre. Located fifteen miles from Philadelphia, the site had once been a real farm, founded around 1710 by a Quaker family who lived and worked on it for more than a century. Some of the original buildings still stood in the early 1970s, along with a few stone walls and mature shade trees. Still visible were the outlines of a colonial field system and a system of farm lanes. Underground, of course, there was a wealth of artifacts waiting to be excavated. In this sense, the plantation resembled Butser Hill. In fact, when Peter Reynolds visited the Colonial Pennsylvania Plantation in 1976, he felt right at home.

Anyone familiar with Lejre would have also noticed similarities to the Danish project. The plantation was a beehive of activity, with historical and archaeological research of all kinds continually going on in full view of visitors. There were traditional archaeological excavations to be seen. Grids were laid out all over the plantation grounds, and you could see, on a given day, a well, a springhouse floor, or a root cellar being excavated. Artifacts were processed on site, and there was a current exhibit of the artifacts that were turning up—pottery, bones, clay pipestems, coins, nails, old farm tools, and so on.

Side by side with the archaeologists were architectural historians, busy studying—then restoring—the major farm buildings: a large stone house, springhouse and dairy, servants' cottage, and barn. Much of the restoration work was also done on site, by house carpenters and cabinetmakers using traditional tools and methods.

Several rooms of the farmhouse had been turned into a research library, and visitors could chat with staff historians poring over old probate court records, diaries, account books, and early census data. Posted at the front gate were weekly diary entries from the daybook of a Quaker farmer, Benjamin Hawley, who had lived nearby in the 1750s, 1760s, and 1770s, and recorded his daily comings and goings.[2] The entries were changed every week, allowing a visitor who came, for example, during the week of April 21, 1974, to read about what Hawley was doing the same week, two hundred years earlier.

Finally, there were always a number of "interpreter-researchers" dressed in period clothing and using reproduction tools and utensils, attempting to "rediscover" accurately or to test traditional ways to plow a field, turn over a garden, cheddar a cheese,

Fig. 9.1. At Colonial Pennsylvania Plantation, living history was used as a research tool. One project documented the life history of a colonial shirt, seen here in middle age.—*Colonial Pennsylvania Plantation, Delaware County, Pennsylvania. Photograph by the author*

or cook a meal. "Living history" simulations, experiments in colonial folklife, were perhaps the most popular of the plantation's "living exhibits," although most visitors readily grasped that the plantation was, in essence, a "museum in the making," and historiography in all its varied forms was on display.

To some, the project seemed confusing. A well-known agricultural historian and museum curator visited Colonial Pennsylvania Plantation in 1976 and asked, "Why are you opening before you're ready?" Another

Fig. 9.2. The rather comical early stages of a plow experiment at Colonial Pennsylvania Plantation. For modern farmers, the Jeep was easier to handle than the plantation's plow-horses.—*Colonial Pennsylvania Plantation, Delaware County, Pennsylvania. Photograph by the author*

Fig. 9.3. Colonial Pennsylvania Plantation's plow experiment in its more serious later phase (see figure 9.2). One result of this test was the discovery that plows with wooden moldboards had about 25 percent more friction than plows with cast-iron moldboards.—*Colonial Pennsylvania Plantation, Delaware County, Pennsylvania. Photograph by the author*

pioneer of "pure" living-history interpretation was bothered by the "modern intrusion" of archaeologists and historians working next to costumed interpreters. To him, the historical atmosphere was ruined.

However, ctitics were in the minority. By and large, visitors readily grasped the concept of the plantation as a 120-acre historic laboratory where they could see a variety of research methods, including imitative experiments, under way. Most were familiar with the idea behind *Kon-Tiki* and could easily equate that experimental voyage with the plantation's trip into the past. And they appreciated the curiosity of the staff, which coincided with their own.[3]

The plantation's research director was Donald Callender, Jr., an archaeologist who had previously worked at the Maya site in Tikal, Guatemala. In Guatemala, Callender had become particularly interested in experimental research, so the plantation offered him the opportunity to test his ideas. In 1976, Callender described the project in an article called "Reliving the Past: Experimental Archaeology in Pennsylvania":

The Plantation is not conceived as an open-air museum (such as Colonial Williamsburg, Old Sturbridge Village, or Plimoth Plantation), but as a laboratory in which serious investigators are testing their understanding of a colonial farm by seeking to re-create its original environment. . . . Using the kinds of tools and techniques that were standard in the eighteenth century [we] are doing many of the daily tasks which were performed by colonial husbandmen. . . . In many cases this leads to more questions than answers.[4]

Callender went on to report on a number of experiments: analysis of the modern "colonial" garbage accumulated in the farm's trash pits over a two-year period; comparison of a modern iron plow with a replica of a colonial wooden one; and reconstruction of an outbuilding with timbers made on the farm. The last was particularly popular with visitors, and Callender's description is worth repeating:

Fig. 9.4. An attempt was made to document as many phases of colonial life as possible at Colonial Pennsylvania Plantation. Here, adzing comes in for close attention.—*Colonial Pennsylvania Plantation, Delaware County, Pennsylvania. Photograph by the author*

In the process of reconstructing an eighteenth-century springhouse, preliminary exploration showed that the large roof beams known as plates had been cut from felled trees, hewn with a broadax and then pit-sawn to the correct size. Evidently, the other timbers used in the structure had been sawn in the mill, probably a local water-powered one known to be operational at the time. We then reconstructed the springhouse using the processes and materials indicated by the architectural features. It soon became apparent why the plate beams had not been sawn in a mill. Their weight, four hundred pounds, and their size, ten inches by ten inches, by twenty-five feet, prohibited their being transported any great distance. The rough-hewn logs which supplied these beams weighed three quarters of a ton. When they were hoisted into position on the sawing platform, smoke could be seen coming from the block and tackle, a clear indication of the stress of the load. The smaller roof rafters, flooring, and framing could have been moved by cart or wagon down the muddy roads, but the larger timber would have had to be made on the plantation by hand.[5]

Callender, who was also a fine sailor, affectionately used to call the plantation his "land ship." Heyerdahl was one of Callender's mentors, and although he admitted that the plantation was not as "spectacular or controversial as the *Kon-Tiki*," still, it enabled tens of thousands of visitors to share in the attempt to "relive the past."

The effect of the Colonial Pennsylvania Plantation's interpretive programs stressing historical methodology was startling. Visitors were delighted with this "treasure hunt" philosophy and with a staff that invited them to become colonial "sidewalk superintendents." The plantation's approach was well publicized as a model Bicentennial project.[6] On Friday, August 22, 1975, Peter Tonge, the science correspondent of the *Christian Science Monitor*, visited the project with his family and, after a day of working together with the staff, summed up his experience and the special attitude that made the plantation unique:

Several blasts on a cow horn summoned us from the fields for a midday meal of boiled summer squash and onions, cabbage and cucumber, cheese, and hot sourdough biscuits washed down with springwater, mint tea, or raw milk, as you wished. For dessert, we had a bowl of wild blackberries picked fresh that morning.

It was a wonderful way to savor the life of the 18th-century American farmers, for that is what the Colonial Pennsylvania Plantation is all about.

We had looked forward to that meal, for we had scythed a good deal that morning, stacking the grass for hay. It was a hot day, and our loose-fitting linen shirts were sweat-soaked. But Ross Fullam, the only man among us who could mow an acre in a day, was the wettest of all. He had put his scythe through a hornets' nest and could escape the angry insects only by diving into the creek.

Ross Fullam accepted the dunking philosophically. After all, it was part of the unique experiment here to rediscover and record what it was probably like to be an American farmer 200 years ago. And says farmer Fullam, "they [the early colonial farmers] presumably danced to the hornets' tune on occasions, too."[7]

Peter Reynolds, working independently in England, discovered the same public interest in living history experimentation that characterized the Colonial Pennsylvania Plantation.

As the Ancient Farm slowly took shape on Little Butser, its popularity grew. From the very beginning the concept captured the imagination of both

Fig. 9.5. Staff members and volunteers at Colonial Pennsylvania Plantation kept diaries of their daily "discoveries." Learning by doing was the project philosophy and main interpretive theme. — *Colonial Pennsylvania Plantation, Delaware County, Pennsylvania. Photograph by the author*

professionals and laymen. . . . More and more parties wanted to visit the site, to see for themselves the experiments, the houses, the crops, which were fundamentally revising the old accepted theories. This pressure became so severe that there was a distinct risk that it would introduce a further and unacceptable variable to the experimental work.[8]

In 1976, Reynolds decided to make the transition (as he put it) from "laboratory to living museum." He accepted the offer of the Hamshire Count Council of a five-acre site just off the main London-to-Portsmith highway and began constructing a "demonstration" farm. Here, in a facsimile of the actual Ancient Farm, Reynolds and his staff could interpret Iron Age buildings, tools,

crops, livestock, farming methods, and other day-to-day activities. The project was popular with the general public from the start, attracting many of Britain's archaeological buffs. In August 1976, Queen Elizabeth II visited the Demonstration Farm and lent her support to its work.[9]

No counterpart of either the Colonial Pennsylvania Plantation or Peter Reynolds's Demonstration Farm exists in North America at present. Instead, individual living-history museums such as Old Sturbridge Village and Fort Michilimackinac have begun interpreting specific research projects. Sturbridge regularly puts on "exhibit" the construction of period buildings using historical tools and methods, and in the center of Michilimackinac, operating archaeological excavations have been interpreted to visitors since 1959.[10] Both exhibits are reminders that our knowledge of life in the past is never complete and that even the best of museums are always "in the making."

NOTES

1. Geoffrey Bibby, "An Experiment with Time," *Horizon* 12 (1970): 96–101.

2. Benjamin Hawley's diary is in the Chester County Historical Society, West Chester, Pennsylvania.

3. One of the first scholars to realize the significance of the plantation was Edward Hawes, a professor of history at Sangamon State University in Springfield, Illinois. See his thoughtful "The Living History Farm: New Directions in Research and Interpretation," *ALHFAM Annual* 2 (1976): 41–60.

4. Donald Callender, Jr., "Reliving the Past: Experimental Archaeology in Pennsylvania," *Archaeology* 29:3 (July 1976): 174.

5. Callender, "Reliving the Past," p. 176.

6. As one of the major Bicentennial projects of the state of Pennsylvania, the plantation attracted national attention. See "Living History Farms Stir New Look at Old Life-Styles," *Bicentennial Times* 3 (February 1976): 2.

7. *Christian Science Monitor*, Friday, August 22, 1975.

8. Reynolds, *Iron Age Farm*, p. 93.

9. Reynolds, *Iron Age Farm*, p. 108.

10. David Armour, assistant superintendent of the Mackinac Island State Park Commission and a boyhood friend of the author, interview with the author, July 28 and 29, 1983, at Fort Mackinac, Mackinac Island.

10

All at Sea

WHILE Hans-Ole Hansen and Peter Reynolds were slogging around in neolithic mud and Ross Fullam was drying off from his colonial dunking, scores of other researchers were taking to sea. Thor Heyerdahl's example had been a heady one, and literally scores of experimental voyages were made in the following three decades. In his *Early Man and the Ocean*, Heyerdahl pointed out the obvious but often overlooked importance of sea travel: "Man hoisted sail before he saddled a horse. He poled and paddled along rivers and navigated the open seas before he traveled on wheels along a road. Water-craft were the first of all vehicles [and] man's first tool for his conquest of the world."[1] In the preindustrial world, sailors visited virtually all the world's continents and islands in a variety of ships and boats. They were capable of long sea-going voyages and had developed the technology to build, sail, and navigate complex vessels. As John Coles has put it: "The basic archaeological problem is not *if* man could travel long distances in prehistoric times, but *how* he actually did travel."[2] That was the challenge for experimental archaeologists after Heyerdahl: to design, operate, and test re-creations of man's earliest ships.

Actually, there was a significant experimental voyage made more than fifty years before the sailing of the *Kon-Tiki,* and it set high standards for voyages that followed, including Heyerdahl's. In 1880, a Viking ship was excavated on the western shore of Oslo Fjord in Norway. The ship was at least a thousand years old. It had been buried at Gokstad as a funeral vessel and had survived in excellent condition.

Thirteen years later, a replica facsimile of the Gokstad ship was built by Magnus Andersen, a sailor and editor, who wanted to sail it across the North Atlantic as Norway's contribution to the 1893 Great Exhibition in Chicago, commemorating the four-hundredth anniversary of Christopher Columbus's "discovery" of America. Andersen appreciated the inherent irony of his project and knew that others would, as well—if he were successful. The ship Andersen built was twenty-four meters long, five meters wide, and weighed over twenty tons. It carried a large single sail and sixteen pairs of oars. The replica set sail from Bergen on April 30, 1893, and arrived safely in Newfoundland twenty-seven days later. It had encountered severe storms along the way, but had no difficulties, due in large part to the ship's design. Andersen noted that the ship's "elasticity, combined with the fine lines naturally made for speed, and we often had the pleasure of darting through the water at speeds of ten, and sometimes even eleven knots."[3]

Captain Andersen sailed his Gokstad ship up the Great Lakes and arrived at Chicago in the summer of 1893, to a rousing welcome. He had proved conclusively that the Vikings could have reached America at least five hundred years before Columbus. A half-century later, the Viking landfall of L'Anse aux Meadows in northern Newfoundland, dated c. A.D. 1,000, was discovered, validating Andersen's theory. His voyage was a superb example of experimental archaeology. He had meticulously built a simulated copy of an original artifact, avoided modern materials and processes in its production, and sailed it in a traditional manner, thereby gaining a visceral feeling for the way the original ship actually functioned. The voyage also had another characteristic of later experiments—it was daring, dangerous, highly publicized, and fascinating to both academic and lay audiences. To the public, it represented a voyage into the mysterious past. Had H. G. Wells's *Time Machine* been published two years earlier, Andersen's ship no doubt would have been called a "time machine."

One of the advantages of ships as a medium for experimental archaeology was their capability of sailing into the open sea, well out of sight of land, thereby becoming free of virtually all modern intrusions and interference. Outside variables could be almost eliminated, leaving the crew as the only real contemporary factor to be reckoned with. That was a major concern of archaeologists who had evolved a set of ground rules for imitative experiments. John Coles reviewed them in *Experimental Archaeology* and noted that these rules were "observed in most experiments, although they may be unacknowledged as such, because they are basically common sense."[4] They include analyzing the scope of the experiment beforehand, thereby keeping the number of variable factors to a minimum; using only

historically accurate materials and methods; limiting modern technology so as not to interfere with the experiment's results; documenting the process carefully enough so that it could be repeated later by another researcher; improvising new methods if feasible; assessing the experiment in terms of its reliability; and never claiming absolute proof, stating the degree of probability only that the process is indeed historically accurate.

Of the many simulated voyages that seriously tried to stay within these unofficial guidelines, two types can be identified: long ocean-going trips like that of the *Kon-Tiki*, which test theories of major migrations; and shorter coastal and river voyages that are more concerned with the nature of early commerce.

Both experiments can generate useful data, but the former, longer trips, because of their drama and inherent danger, have eclipsed the latter in the public eye. Tim Severin, who has successfully carried out both types of voyages and written eloquently of his work, is an ideal representative of those who have taken experimental archaeology to sea.[5]

A geographer and medieval scholar, Severin was educated at Oxford and Harvard. As an Irishman, he was particularly interested in the legendary voyages of Irish monks who, after the collapse of the Roman Empire, spread Celtic Christianity throughout northern Europe. By A.D. 800, Irish missionaries had established colonies in Scotland; in the Orkney, Shetland, and Faroe islands; in Iceland; and even in Greenland. In fact, when the Vikings reached Greenland about A.D. 980, they found relics left there by Irish monks—foundations of buildings, stone implements, and the remains of oxhide boats.

Severin was particularly interested in the voyages of Saint Brendan (c. A.D. 484-577). Stories of Brendan's trips across the north Atlantic to Newfoundland and *back* circulated in oral tradition for three centuries after his death, until they were written down in a chronicle called *Navigatio Sancti Brendani*. What interested Severin was not the claim that Brendan and his crew had crossed the Atlantic well before the Vikings or Columbus, but the boat he was supposed to have sailed in: a large leather sailing curragh made of hides stretched over a wooden frame.

In 1973, Severin began carefully to build a reconstruction of the type of boat described in the *Navigatio*. The vessel was constructed in Ireland of forty-nine ox hides tanned with oak bark, double-stitched with waxed cord, stretched over a frame of greased oak and ash. The frame itself was lashed together with leather thongs. The boat had two ash masts and two sails—at first made of leather but later replaced with Irish linen. The *Brendan*, as Severin called his curragh, was about thirty-five feet long and seven feet across, displaced about five tons, and carried a crew of five. As was the case with the *Kon-Tiki*, few beside the crew of the *Brendan* actually believed the little ship could make it across the Atlantic.

On May 17, 1976, Severin and his crew sailed her up the Irish and Scottish coasts to the Faroes, then on to Iceland, where they wintered. The following May, they set out again and miraculously reached Newfoundland in late June. They had sailed 4,200 kilometers in fifty sailing days, encountering strong headwinds, ice packs, and a gale off Greenland. Robert Radcliff of the National Geographic Society's news service describes the landfall:

At first you could just make it out as our Boston whaler crashed through the four-foot Atlantic chop. Newfoundland's coastline thinned behind us, and to the northeast a brown smudge bumped the horizon. It wasn't one of the whales we'd been seeing for the last hour, spouting and flaunting their flukes free of the waves. It was the *Brendan*, growing into a small sail, which gradually swelled to show its red Celtic cross. Even under full canvas, the *Brendan* seemed to be taking her ease, just idling along out of the past, reaching for the New

World almost tentatively. We had a fleeting feeling that, for St. Brendan and his curragh full of missionary monks, it might have been like this in the 6th century—as the old legend now seemed to shout.[6]

Although Severin did not prove that Saint Brendan had actually once sailed to America, he did strengthen the argument that the voyage once could have been made. Severin also learned a great deal about *how* such voyages in the Celtic period would have been accomplished. He wrote:

Brendan had demonstrated that the voyage could be done with medieval material and medieval technology. . . . Timber, leather, and flax proved to be more durable in many instances than metal, plastic, and nylon; and certainly the former were much easier to work with and could be adapted for day-to-day requirements. This was vitally important when, aboard our small craft, we were only able to carry a few hand tools and a very limited stock of spares. The modern equipment worked better, until it broke, but then the traditional gear, clumsy and inefficient though it was, managed to survive the adverse conditions and that was what mattered. . . . Apart from modern waterproof outer clothing, the medieval sailor was better clad in his woollen trousers, shirt, and cloak than in garments of synthetic fibres. And when he embarked on a cold, wet voyage in an open boat, his diet of dried meats and fish, oats, fruits and nuts, was unsurpassed. It was more nutritious and palatable, and lasted better than the dehydrated packaged foods of today.[7]

Just four years later, Tim Severin undertook another voyage, inspired by another medieval collection of stories, *The Thousand and One Nights*. His interest here was in the legend of Sinbad the Sailor, who was reputed to have sailed from the Arabian Peninsula to China during the Caliphate of Haroun al Rashid, around A.D. 786 to A.D. 809. After exhaustive research on both the stories of Sinbad and the nature of medieval Arab ship design and navigational principles, Severin began building a replica of a kind of Arab craft nonexistent—or at least not seen—for centuries. Not a single nail was used in the craft's construction. Rather, the ship's hull was made of fitted planks sewn together with four hundred miles of coconut rope. He named it the *Sohar*, after the Omani city said to have been Sinbad's birthplace. The ship was eighty feet long, twenty feet wide, drew just six feet, had three masts and two decks, and carried a crew of twenty. Sohar set sail from Oman on November 23, 1980, and reached Canton, China, on July 11, 1981. In seven and a half months, the *Sohar* had sailed more than six thousand miles, across the Arabian Sea, around India, through the Bay of Bengal, and up the South China Sea. Despite very heavy weather off Vietnam, the *Sohar* behaved well, and Severin later wrote that, "With a new set of sails she could have turned around and set out for Muscat at the start of the next northeast monsoon in China."[8]

Severin had gone against the advice of Marco Polo, who, in *The Book of Marco Polo*, describing his thirteenth-century travels in China, Southeast Asia, Persia, and the Arab world, had warned his fellow mariners about the Arab ships:

Their ships are very bad, and many of them founder, because they are not fastened with iron nails but stitched together with threads made of coconut husks. They soak the husk until it assumes the texture of horse hair; then they make it into thread and stitch their ships. . . . This makes it a risky undertaking to sail in these ships. And you can take my word that many of them sink, because the Indian Ocean is often very stormy.[9]

Severin had also disregarded the advice of modern naval historians, preferring instead to delve into the surviving folklore of Arab shipwrights and the knowledge that a flourishing Arab trade with the Orient had once existed and could—and should—be better understood. Experimental archaeology was the means he selected to realize that goal.

In *The Sinbad Voyage* (1983), Severin documents, step by step, every stage of the *Sohar*

project: design, construction, operation, and function. He stays well within the "rules of the experimental archaeology game," although he is obviously a humanist concerned with not only the technical aspect of the ship but also its culture, the difficult-to-describe patterns of traditional activities that enabled its crew of twenty to bond together and sail halfway across the world. Except for emergency safety equipment (life rafts, life jackets, flares, etc.), the voyage was carried out entirely with traditional medieval equipment, supplies, and food. The crew for the most part even wore traditional clothing.

What emerges from Severin's story of the *Sohar* is a portrait of a time machine, a floating laboratory that enabled him to explore the everyday life and work of a ship as it was experienced a millennium earlier. Especially fascinating are his descriptions of the *Sohar's* smells, sounds, appearance, and "feel":

It was romantic to the eye, but the nose gave quite a different impression. *Sohar* stank. . . .

The sounds aboard a medieval Arab sailing ship are unique. The groaning and creaking of timber and rope . . . the high-pitched creak of the coconut fibre ropes holding the mast . . . the soft, regular thump of the tiller . . .

Night was a good time aboard *Sohar*. Occasionally we had a blood-red moonrise as the moon rose slowly through the layers of desert dust that lay behind us toward Arabia. As the light faded, the colours of the night became silver and black. The crimson emblem of the Sultanate on the sail turned to the colour of dried blood in the moonlight, and the curves of the sails arranged themselves into graceful patterns and intricate relationships.

We were becoming virtual extensions of the ship herself, responsive to her movements and moods. When *Sohar* lolled, becalmed in yet another interval of light airs, we too would laze and doze. But when the wind strengthened and the ship started to hurry forward through the water, we responded in kind: a sense of activity and urgency filled the ship. There was a controlled excitement at the thought of yet another few miles passing beneath her keel.[10]

For Severin, the sensual experiences of his crew are significant clues in the elusive search for a more complete understanding of the many real sailors whose true adventures were commemorated in the Sinbad stories.

Tim Severin is only one of scores of experimental researchers who took to the sea in the wake of the *Kon-Tiki*. Heyerdahl himself sailed across the Atlantic on *Ra I* and *Ra II*, twice risking his life in an attempt to prove that ancient Egyptians may have settled central America. Later he constructed another, far larger reed boat, the *Tigris*, and tested the theory that Sumerians might have established a trading network that tied India to Arabia. Even more activity took place in the Pacific. Several dozen voyages have been made since Heyerdahl's pioneering effort. Balsa rafts have even made the voyage from Peru to Australia, and one raft captain, Vitale Alsar, has logged more than twenty thousand miles—more than the circumference of the earth.[11]

Perhaps the most significant voyage was made by the *Hokule'a*, a re-created Polynesian two-masted double canoe, which in 1975–76 navigated from Hawaii to Tahiti and back, navigated from Hawaii to Tahiti and back, demonstrating that extensive open-sea voyages across the Pacific in both directions were possible. Will experimental voyages such as these continue? John Coles thinks so and wryly suggests that soon someone may attempt to reconstruct Western man's most famous ship, Noah's Ark.[12]

NOTES

1. Thor Heyerdahl, *Early Man and the Ocean* (London: Allen and Unwin, 1978), p. 19.

2. John Coles, *Experimental Archaeology*, p. 50.

3. Coles, *Experimental Archaeology*, pp.25–26, 76–79.

4. Coles, *Experimental Archaeology*, pp. 46–48; and John Coles, *Archaeology by Experiment*, p. 15.

5. Tim Severin, *The Brendan Voyage* (London: Hutchinson, 1978); Tim Severin, *The Sinbad Voyage* (New York: G. P. Putnam's Sons, 1982).

6. Cited in Sean White's "The Impossible Voyage," *Ireland* 27:6 (November-December 1978): 31.

7. White, "Impossible Voyage," p. 31.

8. Severin, *Sinbad*, p. 239.

9. Cited in Severin, *Sinbad*, p. 20.

10. Severin, *Sinbad*, pp. 79, 95, 97–98, 182.

11. Coles, *Experimental Archaeology*, p. 63.

12. Coles, *Experimental Archaeology*, pp. 64–69, 88–89.

11

A Life on the Ocean Wave

AT the time Tim Severin was testing the seaworthiness of prehistoric ships, a number of historic voyages were being re-enacted by researchers who were delighted to interpret their experiments to national and international audiences. Many of the voyages were sponsored by museums as novel exhibits—like Plimoth Plantation's *Mayflower II.* Often, professional photographers and writers were included on the crews.

Unlike the prehistoric simulations of Heyerdahl, Severin, and others, which were based on only the slimmest of evidence, historical re-enactments were generally well documented. Sir Francis Drake, Christopher Columbus, and Father Jacques Marquette each left logs of their expeditions that proved invaluable to the re-enactors. Nevertheless, building and sailing copies of the *Niña,* the *Golden Hind,* the *Mayflower,* or even the *voyageur* canoes of Pére Marquette and Louis Jolliet presented real research problems for modern shipwrights and sailors. Often, they had to rely on imitative experiments to fill in the gaps in the historical record. For the researchers, as well as the public, the "learning-by-doing" aspect of these trips often provided the most interesting stories. In the end, then, it's often difficult to tell whether the prime motivation for these voyages is research or interpretation. Not that it really matters; re-enactments like that of *Mayflower II* can be considered worthwhile for any number of reasons. Three voyages, a decade apart, are representative of projects that mix research and interpretation.

In 1949, Plimoth Plantation asked a naval architect and historian, William Baker, to draw up plans for a replica of the first *Mayflower.* They wanted it as much like the original as possible, absolutely "100 percent right in rig, in hull form, in lines, in manner of working and sailing, and everything else."[1] After two years of research, Baker concluded that the original ship had been a square-rigged trading barque, typical of the late sixteenth and early seventeenth centuries. Alan Villiers, the experienced Australian sailor who captained *Mayflower II,* wrote that "She was just some wandering little sailor that the Pilgrim Fathers could hire cheap, and nobody paid any attention to her then. We know she must have been old because one of her main timbers broke while she was in a storm. . . . She was only about 180 tons, which is less than the size of many tugs."[2]

No exact description or plans of the ubiquitous *Mayflower* survived, so Baker had to design a reasonable facsimile of the original. That was not so difficult as building the ship, a job that fell to Stuart Upham, whose family had been constructing wooden ships in Devon, England, for more than two centuries.

The keel was laid on July 4, 1955. Upham was determined to build her as authentically as possible, and older "chippies" (experienced shipwrights) were hired for the project. Only authentic raw materials were used, and most of the technology employed was traditional hand work. Upham later recorded his experience in *The Illustrated Story of How the* Mayflower II *Was Built* (1960). It makes fascinating reading, with its accounts of "tree-nails" (wooden pegs) made from century-old cider vats, hemp from old mail bags teased into calking oakum, and sails handwoven of Scottish flax.

Captain Villiers wanted authenticity in diet, also. He researched the Jacobean sailor's diet and tried to come close to it.

Getting the right sort of provisions was a problem. Our ship has no refrigeration, and so the food has to be old sailing-ship style, whether we like it or not. That means lots of salt beef and salt pork, which is carried in barrels. But nobody packs that kind of meat anymore, for there has been no demand for it for years. Even the Grand Banks cod-fishing schooners have refrigeration.

We tried every ship chandler in England. It was always the same story: no old sailing-ship salt beef or pork. So we have had to commission the oldest ship's butcher we could find to have beasts specially slaughtered and salted down in the approved manner. Just ordinary corned beef won't keep for months at sea. There are very few butchers left who even remember how to prepare the meat for rough sea salting.[3]

Villiers also noted that the "old-time sailors ate a lot of cheese and drank a lot of beer." He decided to keep the cheese but not the beer, as the allotted allowance in the early 1600s was a gallon a day. *Mayflower II's* sailors drank water—and, in accordance with Admiralty policy, lime juice.

Alan Villiers, who had sailed in windjammers twice across the Atlantic and once

around the world, handpicked a crew of thirty-three, and after brief sailing trials, the *Mayflower II* set sail from Plymouth, England, on April 20, 1957. Fifty-four days and fifty-five hundred miles later, they reached Nantucket. The crossing had actually taken thirteen days fewer than the Pilgrims had needed in 1620, but the modern voyage was just as traumatic as the first one.[4] Villiers was forced to take a longer southern route around the Sargasso Sea, because of a delay in the ship's launching. He later wrote that it was go south or be de-masted by northern gales.[5] He chose survival over historical accuracy, at least as far as the route was concerned. In all other ways, "This lively little ship is altogether too historically correct for my liking," her first mate told Villiers.

Mayflower II was light and top-heavy; she "rolled violently, like the pendulum of a clock," leaked badly, and had no headroom between decks. She was also short, less then ninety feet long, and "so she pitched into the short steep seas and jumped and leapt and cavorted all over them. She was like a wild little bronco constantly taking an uneven series of high fences and rolling and all but falling over as she came to each one."[6] And everyone was seasick, even the hardiest old salts.

Sometimes Villiers would take the ship's small launch out and look back at the ship.

Her colorful hull, gaily painted in patterns of browns and reds and greens and blues, looked at its best in the light of the later afternoon sky, and the view from her quarter was superb. She looked like an outsize museum model come to life. . . . I would hardly believe that my ship was real.[7]

At other times he would walk the high poop deck and think of Columbus, whose *Santa Maria* was little different from the *Mayflower.*

Sometimes there were extraordinary sunsets, brooding, melancholy goings-down of the burning sun that seemed to have a threat in them, as if the sun were telling us that it would not be back again. . . . These helped me imagine the forebodings of Columbus's distraught crews. *Go back, go back*, the dark and threatening skies seemed to be saying; *you are sailing to the edge of the world!* But they went on, and so did I.[8]

The moment of truth for the *Mayflower II* came in a gale off the Carolinas. Villiers remembered a passage in William Bradford's account of the first *Mayflower's* voyage, describing the way Captain Jones, when faced with high winds, "took in all sail, and the ship lay—as he put it—a hull, just left to herself in the raging waters." Villiers had often talked with the crew of trying out this maneuver if conditions were right, and "Now, it looked as if we had them." After the perilous task of taking in the sails, they hove to and waited anxiously. Villiers remembers:

We need not have feared. She came up, shoulder to the sea, lying safely and quietly with an easy motion, falling off a little and then coming up again, like a duck with its head under its wing asleep on a turbulent lake. . . . Indeed it was amazing. I reflected that the Pilgrim Fathers, who tossed through many such a wild night in Atlantic storms, at least knew tranquility in great gales.[9]

Villiers's fine book is full of "re-discoveries," and this is one of the appeals of the voyage of the *Mayflower II*. It allowed modern men to experience a way of life and work that had virtually died out after the advent of the age of steam.

The voyage of the *Mayflower II* was followed by a number of long sea voyages, some historically accurate, others less concerned with authenticity.

One of the most daring of the former types was that of the *Niña II*.[10] A Spanish naval lieutenant, Carlos Etayo Elizondo, received a modest inheritance in 1957, took a leave of absence from his military duties, and began a reconstruction of Columbus's caravel, the *Niña*. In January 1962, he laid the keel, in the ancient shipyard of Pasajes, the seaport of San Sebastian. The ship was historically accurate in every detail, constructed of oak and pine from the Pyrenees and hand-built with wooden pegs and wrought-iron spikes. By June, Elizondo had completed the hull, launched her, and was working on *Niña II's* masts and rigging. He was joined by the twenty-nine-year-old American underwater archaeologist Robert Marx, who persuaded him to "go exactly the way Columbus did, eat the same chow, wear the same clothing, use the same arms, and navigate by the same methods." Marx signed on as pilot and navigator and set out to collect facsimile sixteenth-century costumes, cannon, swords, and sailing gear. They recruited a crew of seven other men, some of whom had never been to sea, and carried out sea trials in the summer of 1962.

On September 19, they set sail from Palos, Columbus's home port, bound for the Canary Islands a thousand miles away. They had "no motor, no radio, no modern lifesaving equipment, no provisions except roughly the same as Columbus had carried." Their only anachronistic concession was to allow the crew a ration of tobacco. The *Niña II* almost immediately ran into a thirty-hour storm and began leaking like "an old washtub." It also heeled dangerously, and Marx, hanging over the port railing, could see the "keel knifing up out of the foaming water." The main cabin filled with water, and the hold was a shambles. "Jugs containing water, wine, vinegar, and brandy were broken." Containers for rice, flour, and beans were shattered, and olive oil made everything slick. The crew had lost half its food and three-quarters of its water. Marx also lost his fifteenth-century hourglasses, which he was using for navigation. Incredibly, on October 3, they reached the Canaries, and their priest, Father Sagaseta, said a mass of thanksgiving for them in the same church that Columbus had visited nearly five centuries earlier.

A week later, on October 10, the *Niña II* and crew left from Los Polmas, bound for San Salvador in the Bahamas, more than three thousand miles away. The second leg of their voyage was literally a life-and-death adventure. Two major problems faced them. First, they were hit by a storm that blew them badly off course and becalmed them far to the south within "insect range of the African coast." Second, they rapidly ran out of food. Their water barrels leaked, and after just five days at sea, half their supply of fresh fruit and vegetables—melons, bananas, oranges, and so on, had rotted. The crew was forced to eat shark meat and uncooked tortillas. Two weeks out, their remaining water was undrinkable. Marx wrote that "It [the water] had turned a horrible shade of brown . . . was full of living creatures and smelled worse than gall." They were forced to drink sour wine cut with seawater.

Elizondo and Marx decided, on the seventeenth day, to reveal to the crew their desperate situation. Whereas Columbus, on his seventeenth day out, was already halfway across the Atlantic, the *Niña II* had barely started and was seriously short of provisions. The crew discussed their predicament and voted to proceed. The next day the winds picked up, and they were soon averaging forty-five miles a day. Despite a series of storms and near starvation, they continued. On November 30, fifty-two days out, the *Niña II* was spotted by a U.S. Navy hurricane hunter that dropped them a life raft and an emergency radio. They asked the navy to drop them water and tobacco, but refused any other aid. Marx explained their philosophy in a *Saturday Evening Post* cover story:

To the world outside our small ship, this must seem a foolish dedication to the ideal of authenticity. But to the crew of the *Niña II* it was important. We had endured great peril for a historical principle. It would have been a serious matter to forfeit it all in a moment of physical weakness. We knew full well that we still belonged to the 20th century; three times during the last phase of our trip we had seen the awesome spectacle of great rockets rising silently into the skies above distant Cape Canaveral. But we were also members of that ageless fraternity of seamen, each of whom owed a debt of gratitude to all the great explorers of the past.[11]

On Christmas Day, after seventy-seven days of struggle, the *Niña II* reached San Salvador. The crew gathered on deck, sang the "Salve Regina," and fell to their knees. Marx wrote that he had "at least a small idea of how Columbus must have felt on October 12, 1492," Although it had taken the *Niña II* more than twice the thirty-six sailing days Columbus used, still the crew had followed as nearly as they could the "historic wake of the great explorer. In the end, that was worth the strain and the terror, the doubts and the endless labor against the sea."[12]

Ten years after the voyage of the *Niña II*, another more interpretive type of re-enactment was undertaken by Reid Lewis and seven other fresh-water sailors. During the summer of 1973, they re-created, day by day, the voyage of Father Jacques Marquette and Louis Jolliet in 1673. Their primary goal was to celebrate the Tricentennial of the original voyage.

Setting out from St. Ignace, on the Upper Peninsula of Michigan, they retraced the three-thousand-mile route through the Great Lakes, down the Mississippi River, and back. Lewis was resolved to "bring living history to the people of the Midwest," hoping to make "Midwesterners conscious of the history of their region. With this pride would come, it was hoped, an interest in preserving the natural and man-made vestiges of the past." Great care was taken in selecting interpreters, since the voyage was planned as an "educational device" in which all the participants would portray Marquette and Jolliet's actual *voyageurs* and "be proficient in interpreting and communicating their observations and experiences" to the thousands of well-wishers along the way. A Jesuit historian, Father Joseph P. Donnelly, developed a day-by-day itinerary, duplicating the original voyage for them and for a year briefed them on the folklife of the period. Each of the interpreters began a rigorous physical fitness program over the winter of 1972 and each studied the historical material available about the character he was to portray. Together, they practiced paddling their canoes and even tested their endurance by going up the Illinois River in a snowstorm. On May 17, 1973, they set out, following the north shore of Lake Michigan. Reid Lewis, a high school French teacher and scholar of the *voyageur* period, later wrote that "We felt a sense of invigoration and freedom that must have approximated the experience of the original explorers. Beautiful white sand beaches backed by dark pine forests evoked [in us] the fleeting impressions of being the first white men to pass that way."[13]

The crew was able to carry our a number of informal "imitative experiments," especially during the early stage of the voyage along the sparsely populated Upper Peninsula. For example, they tried out primitive sails, resembling those used by Jolliet and Marquette. H. Dean Campbell, in his published diary of the voyage, *A Second Impression*, described this experience:

Having no rudder, we ride the waves in a roller-coaster fashion along their five- and six-foot crests. Bill Dweyer, as forward paddle, is stroking furiously to hold the canoe into the waves. A very real possibility of upsetting exists. Once again we silently remember the Coast Guard warning. ["If you should turn over, you have exactly seven minutes to survive in the numbing waters of Lake Michigan."] My fingers turn white under the increasing pressure on the sail ropes. . . . We are now riding waves as much as two hundred feet at a stretch. For me it is perhaps the most thrilling day of the entire voyage. (Friday, May 18th)[14]

When both canoes finally reached Hog Island and all were safely on shore, "the relieved *voyageurs* hugged each other in giddy jubilation, ecstatic just to be alive."

Later, their sense of reliving the original voyage began to wane. Lewis wrote that "Raw sewage in the water and an occasional junked car on the bank were grim reminders that we were back in civilization."[15] The continual demonstrations and lectures in each town along the way drained their energy. Ultimately, they gave more than 160 presentations, often cutting into their evenings and leaving them only five hours of sleep a night. Interpreting became almost more tiring than paddling fifty-seven strokes a minute, 3,420 strokes per hour. Yet, in the final week of their trip, Campbell mused on how difficult it would be to re-enter the modern world.

We are within our final week, our emotions are many. I believe we will all be happy to complete our journey; we are physically and mentally tired. But, there will be losses too. A spirit of freedom is born from these past four months. Daily combat with wind, rain, waves, sun and frost creates an independence that can tolerate rooms for only short periods of time.[16]

On September 19, 1973, one hundred and twenty-six days after it began, the voyage ended. Campbell, assessing its results, noted that "the primary reason for celebrating the Tricentennial was to cause French colonial history to come alive, to become meaningful to these people along our route of travel."[17] Lewis, Campbell, and the other crew members felt that the re-enactment had been a success. More than 300,000 people viewed their passing. Campbell wrote that "Many were convinced that we were actually French or French-Canadian. Small children inquired of their mothers, 'Are they real?' Slightly older children were confused, not knowing how we could be three hundred years old."[18] However, the crew also learned important lessons. As they paddled through Lake Michigan, Green Bay, and the Fox, Wisconsin, Illinois, and Mississippi rivers, they "de-mythed" history and began to "accurately imagine the daily life style of the past," growing closer to the original *voyageurs* with whom they identified. In the process they "re-invented" the techniques of sailing and paddling large canoes over immense distances. Perhaps more significant, the new *voyageurs* began to understand the functional importance of a "feeling of brotherhood," especially with the other members of their crew. For the re-enactors and their audience, it was this appreciation for an earlier form of social bonding that became the surprise "lesson" of the project.

Campbell later touched on a theme that runs through the writings of Villiers, Marx, and other researchers who were concerned with interpretation:

A frequent question asked by persons along the route of our expedition was: "I'd give an arm to go on such a voyage; are you going to write a book?" I understood this question to be a request by some to share in the experiences encountered.

With the encouragement of friends I have attempted to place on paper a factual account of my impressions of this historic re-enactment. To some, my writing may deflate a common but erroneous concept of mystery or romanticism associated with such ventures. To still others I hope to make human those explorers of the past by recounting some of the everyday happenings that must have been a part of their exploits also.[19]

This goal of totally submerging oneself in the stream of life at some point in the past has characterized many recent experimental and interpretive projects. There is an attempt to go beyond the replication of technology and get at the thoughts and feelings of people of another time, whether they be famous or forgotten, and somehow vicariously to re-live their everyday lives. And there is an implicit need to share that experience with others, through living exhibits, as in the case of Plimoth's *Mayflower II*, or by well-written books or articles such as Marx's "We Sailed the Columbus Ship."

NOTES

1. Stuart Upham, *The Illustrated Story of How Mayflower II Was Built* (Plymouth, Massachusetts: Plimoth Plantation, 1960).

2. Cited in Jean Colby's *Plimoth Plantation: Then and Now* (New York: Hastings House, 1970), p. 100. See also Alan Villiers's *The New Mayflower* (New York: Scribners, 1958).

3. Alan Villiers, "We're Coming Over on the *Mayflower*," *National Geographic* CX 1:5 (May 1957): 727.

4. Alan Villiers, "How We Sailed the New *Mayflower* to America," *National Geographic* CXII:5 (November 1957): 639.

5. Villiers, "How We Sailed," pp. 635–636.

6. Villiers, "How We Sailed," p. 655.

7. Villiers, "How We Sailed," pp. 655–656.

8. Villiers, "How We Sailed," p. 667.

9. Robert Marx, "We Sailed The Columbus Ship," *Saturday Evening Post*, January 26, 1963, pp. 26–36.

10. Marx, "Columbus Ship," p. 35.

11. H. Dean Campbell, *A Second Impression* (Privately Printed, 1974); Reid Lewis, "Three Hundred Years Later," *Historic Preservation* 26:4 (July-September 1974).

12. Marx, "Columbus Ship," p. 36.

13. Lewis, "Three Hundred Years," p. 7.

14. Campbell, *A Second Impression*, pp. 9–10.

15. Lewis, "Three Hundred Years," p. 9.

16. Campbell, *A Second Impression*, p. 88.

17. Campbell, *A Second Impression*, "Prologue," pp. 1–3.

18. Campbell, *A Second Impression*, "Prologue," p. 3.

19. Campbell, *A Second Impression*, pp. 89–90.

Fig. 11.1 Following the example of Plimoth Plantation's *Mayflower II,* the staff at Fort Michilimackinac, on Michigan's Upper Peninsula, build a replica of the *Welcome,* a colonial sailing vessel that plied the Straits of Mackinac in the late 1700s. —*Mackinac Island State Park Commission, Lansing, Michigan*

Fig. 11.2. The anachronistic launching of the colonial vessel *Welcome* was a major regional media event.—*Mackinac Island State Park Commission, Lansing, Michigan*

Fig. 11.3. The *Welcome* on one of its periodic cruises around Mackinac Island. —*Mackinac Island State Park Commission, Lansing, Michigan*

12
Homecoming

HJEMKOMST in Norwegian means "homecoming." It is the name given a re-created Viking ship that, in the summer of 1982, sailed to Norway from Duluth, Minnesota.[1] Robert Asp, who had built the ship by hand, wanted its voyage to symbolize the emigrant's desire to return home. Tragically, Asp died of leukemia in 1980 and never made the crossing home to Norway. It was left to his three sons and a daughter to make the voyage in his stead.

As I listened to their story, one hot summer day at Vesterheim, the Norwegian American museum in Decorah, Iowa, *hjemkomst* seemed an apt caption for a number of recent projects that have attempted to re-create totally everyday life in the past. For researchers in Virginia, Holland, and England, the goal was not to build Stone Age houses following the model of Hans-Ole Hansen, but to re-create functioning homes and, with them, a facsimile of domestic life as it was in an earlier time. They wanted to use experiments with material culture to help them move into the far more elusive realm of culture itself.

The most serious of these projects, from a professional archaeological point of view, were undertaken by Errett Callahan, a professor at Virginia Commonwealth University in Richmond, Virginia. I first heard of Callahan's work from Hans-Ole Hansen, who had read the professor's *Old Rag Report: A Practical Guide to Living Archaeology* and had used it as a training tool at Lejre.[2] Hansen had great respect for Callahan, who, in the summer of 1973, had built with his students a "prehistoric" camp in Coconino, Arizona.

The purpose of this experiment was to re-create a prehistoric stone tool workshop. Callahan and his students studied the prehistoric site carefully, in much the same way Reynolds had researched the Butser Hill area. They then made replicas of the many original stone tools they had excavated and used these copies to maintain a hunter-gatherer type of summer encampment.

During their stay in Arizona, Callahan carefully trained his students in Stone Age technology, pottery, basketry, and primitive foodways. Each student prepared his own tools, bedding, dried-food supply, and other equipment. They lived in rough shelters made of juniper branches and low trees. Despite the heat, the lack of potable water, the unusual terrain, and unusual foods, the nine team members not only survived, but actually began to enjoy the routine of Stone Age life. They tried out a number of experiments with tool-making, hunting and gathering wild food, cooking in rock pools with hot stones, and various crafts. Many of the team members actually felt a culture shock

123

when they returned, at summer's end, to "civilization."

In his report on the experiment, *The Wagner Basalt Quarries: A Preliminary Report,* Callahan noted that it was almost impossible to re-create a prehistoric people's total culture.[3] The best an experimenter could do was to concentrate on certain basic aspects of material life such as food, clothing, and shelter, and hope to surmise an understanding of the more subtle aspects of life, such as social behavior and daily patterns of work and play. Callahan felt that a really valid project had to be a long-term effort.

To go out for a few days, knowing that one can return to comfort it things don't work out—and to make generalizations from the experiences learned thereby—is to fall victim to deceptively convincing but incredibly naive cliches. One must stay with the land long enough to wash out his old systems (both physical and cultural) in order to fall into the rhythm of the natural. This, I believe, cannot be done in less than a two-week period, and I am coming increasingly to suspect that a full year cycle may be necessary to arrive at "complete" breakthrough. The ultimate test of experimental or living archaeology must await such a thorough investigation.[4]

In the following two summers, 1974 and 1975, Callahan carried out his Pamunkey Project, re-creating a Middle Woodland period Indian site, ca. A.D. 1,000. Callahan was clear in what he and his students were *not* trying to accomplish; in his *Old Rag Report,* he set out his goals for the Pamunkey Project:

We had no interest whatsoever in simply "playing Indian" or "survival," as some have accused us. Yes, we did live like Indians; and yes, we did manage to survive, and rather well, at that, under Indianlike conditions. But we were careful not to allow ourselves to think that we really were living in the past or that we were . . . resurrecting the past.[5]

During the first summer, eight researchers lived beside the Pamunkey River in eastern Virginia for a month. They had all been well trained by Callahan in the technology of the period. The Pamunkey site was ideal, a forest of beech trees near open meadows, swampland, and the river itself, whose tidal waters rose about three feet a day. The natural environment was rich in wild plants, animals, shellfood, and fish. The students rapidly "washed out" their modern "physical and cultural systems" and set about building a home of sweetgum wood and hickory bark. They used local clay to make pots for stewing and ovens for baking. They gathered a surprising variety of edible roots, tubers, nuts, berries, leaves, and flowers; collected shellfish and eggs; and caught frogs, turtles, and snakes. They failed to kill any larger animals, although they became fairly proficient with facsimile bows and arrows. Most important, the students kept detailed records of virtually all of their daily activities, including the construction of a large thatched shelter, the cooking of black-snake stew, and the making and using of almost seven hundred stone tools. They also recorded social behavior patterns, often revealing very twentieth-century points of view:

During work, some of our women tended to communicate verbally with one another without ceasing and to laugh a lot. Both are necessary to congenial social interaction, of course—at least among the participating group. But these very actions tended to reduce concentration and to lower the rate of production.[6]

During the winter of 1974–75, Callahan returned to the site three times to record changes that had occurred since its abandonment. The following summer, seven students again lived there, including two hold-overs from the previous years. They repaired the main house and set about living. they planted a garden of gourds and corn, built a woven fish weir, and cleared paths. Food procurement took about three to four hours a day; the remaining time was spent making tools, cooking and eating, and documenting everyday life. The Pamunkey Project established a model for subsequent experiments in re-creating the folklife of a prehistoric people. It is no surprise that Hans-Ole Hansen used the record of this project as a primer at Lejre.

Callahan returned to the Pamunkey camp a year later and ironically described its conversion—into a modern American subdivision:

Houses erected over site. . . . Front yard, formerly the heart of our camp, now leveled and ready to grow grass. Lumber, trash, and other "improvements" all about. But to the knowing eye, a few evidences of our occupation are seen: our shell midden, some potsherds, our trail to the dish-washing area with sherds in the mud beneath, the remains of our fish weir in the lagoon. . . . All in all, the new owners have been quite successful in erasing any sign that we ever had been there. The wonder of modern technology.[7]

In January 1976, Callahan visited Colonial Pennsylvania Plantation. We had read with care his reports on the Arizona and Virginia projects and were greatly impressed with his work. Callahan spent a leisurely winter day at the farm. He was physically imposing, but gentle in manner. As I watched him walk around our fields and gardens, I kept imagining him as a time traveler, moving comfortably from prehistoric to colonial times, from Indian camp to Quaker farm. He was, of course, nothing of the sort. Callahan was a pioneer experimental archaeologist with a superb ability to fit into an alien natural or cultural environment and catch its rhythm. As the afternoon waned, he joked with us about the differences between our eighteenth-century implements—plows, hoes, harrows, etc.—and the Stone Age tools with which he was more familiar. We asked him for a demonstration, and he took out an atlatl and spear and nailed a target thirty yards away.

Callahan also influenced a Dutch biologist, R. Horreus de Haas, who, with his son, had been planning since 1973 a project similar to the Pamunkey experiments.[8] The elder de Haas was seventy-one when he participated in the Pamunkey camp. He returned to Hol-

Fig. 12.1. Grinding grain by pounding it between two stones, at the Polder Project, in Holland. The goal of the Dutch experimenters was to explore the elusive realms of Stone Age culture.—*Polder Project, Bilthoven, the Netherlands*

land enthusiastic about the potential for experimental archaeology and joined his son in recruiting a suitable team of volunteers and clarifying their project's goals. In *Living a Stone Age Life: Report of a Creative Game*, a collective record of the experiment, they explained that "The participants with whom this report is concerned have only wanted to play a challenging game. They wanted to find out if it is still possible for Western Man of today to live under the same circumstances as did their predecessors."[9]

At first, the Dutch group considered really getting away and living on an uninhabited island in Denmark or Norway, in the wilds of Exmore in England, or within the fens of Calangues in southern France. Eventually, they were offered a ten-hectare (twenty-five acre) plot in a Dutch *polder*, swampy land recently reclaimed from the North Sea. It was attractive for three reasons: it was free, convenient, and near a neolithic archaeological site dating about 3,000 B.C. Since this was the period of prehistory that they wanted to sim-

Fig. 12.2. The Polder Project Staff, feasting on a porridge of whole grains and wild fruits. — *Polder Project, Bilthoven, the Netherlands*

ulate, the *polder* site was ideal. Eventually, ten "grown-ups" and four children joined in the game. They included, besides the de Haas family, a chemist, two housewives, and four college students specializing in medicine, agriculture, cultural anthropology, cinematography, and forestry.

Despite the collective lack of advanced archaeological experience, the "Polder Project" was well planned. From October 1973, the team met every two or three months in Bilthoven in a "prehistoric school," where they studied subsistence technologies and experimental archaeological methods. They also worked out four rules for their game:

1. Only a few exisiting paths within our lot are used. This is to keep the landscape as untouched as possible, [so as] not to frighten the animals and to minimize the risk of discovery by the outside world.

2. All the ground, the food, and the big house are common property. The small huts and their inventory are private property. Of the main food (wheat) everyone is allowed to take as much as they need. Food gathered is divided equally among the group. Valuable things such as milk, honey, and nuts are

Fig. 12.3. Polder Project staff members fabricating an experimental wattle-and-daub "private" house. Most of the project's structures weathered well.—*Polder Project, Bilthoven, the Netherlands*

rationed in accordance with the size of the family.

3. Spare time is a costly thing, to which everyone has an equal right. The group is to decide to what extent this is possible.

4. Tools should not be borrowed from others. This is to prevent frustration. In case [a borrowed tool is broken], the owner, who knows what an effort it has been to make the object, will be sad, whereas the user will feel guilty. This rule should be an incitement to everyone to have his own tools in order. Of course everyone will always be ready to help when this is necessary.[10]

The basic rules were more than adequate and helped establish a framework within which the various individuals could work together harmoniously.

In the autumn of 1975, they began serious work on the site. Six different "private" huts were built for practice before the "big house" was attempted. The "big house" eventually took three hundred man-hours to construct, but it was so sturdy that, four years later, it was still in excellent condition. They also worked on a storehouse, a well, a shed and enclosure for goats, beehives, and a series of

Fig. 12.4. Constructing a coracle with skin-and-wicker frame at the Polder Project. The little craft would be used in navigating the nearby North Sea estuaries and marshes.—*Polder Project, Bilthoven, the Netherlands*

small fields. They then made up their individual and family inventories of clothes; stone, wood, and bone tools; various utensils, such as baskets and cooking pots; and sleeping mats and blankets. By July 1976, everyone was prepared, the site was complete, and they were ready to begin.

From the start, the "game" was a great success. For three weeks they lived a Stone Age life: cultivating their fields, tending goats, grinding wheat for porridge, cooking and eating together, digging clay and making pots, cutting reeds and wood, and even relaxing a little. They found that they didn't miss the modern world. Quite the contrary, they enjoyed life under simulated neolithic conditions and felt that they all gained a better understanding of their predecessors and their natural and cultural Stone Age environment. The group enjoyed "re-inventing" ancient skills and learning to co-operate in order to survive. The lack of outside pressures gave them a "sense of peace," and their activities improved their physical fitness.

Fig. 12.5. As the Polder Project progressed, the staff became more skilled. Here they construct a large community "long house." The structure, once completed, has served as their project home since 1977.—*Polder Project, Bilthoven, the Netherlands*

Fig. 12.6. The Dutch experimenters at the Polder Project carried back to the modern world a better understanding of their Stone Age past and a deeper appreciation of the culture of our ancient counterparts.—*Polder Project, Bilthoven, the Netherlands*

After the three weeks were over, they decided to continue the experiment. In 1977, they built a "long house" and used it as a base for subsequent short-term occupations. As of today, 1984, the "game" continues, quietly and without publicity. John Coles has called it "an excellent example of a small experiment, asking no more than to see how things would work out, and how people would respond [under Stone Age conditions]. That all found it satisfying, and that all gained some understanding of the past, and appreciation of the environment, is sufficient."[11]

As the Dutch "Polder Project" drifted quietly along, the British Broadcasting Corporation was mounting a far more widely publicized operation.[12] The BBC decided to document a "year in the life" of an Iron Age village. The project was conceived by John

Percival, a television producer and amateur archaeologist. After a visit to Lejre, Percival returned to England enthusiastic about producing a documentary that would show more than the usual "backsides of diggers and chattering archaeologists." The result was a twelve-part series of half-hour color films called "Living in the Past." The series followed the agricultural calendar month by month, with the first film focusing on March and covering the project's philosophy, selection and training of "Celtic" volunteers, building of the Iron Age settlement, and arrival of their "back-bred" stock. This film, and the series as a whole, elicited widespread comment from archaeologists, television critics, and interested laymen. It was also a popular success.

The BBC Iron Age village was created on a

private estate in Wiltshire, isolated in thirty-five acres of forest, surrounded by fifteen acres of arable field. It was cut off from all twentieth-century contacts, with the exception of the BBC television crew who visited the settlement twice a week to film and a local doctor who was called in four times to handle emergencies. The "settlers," six couples and three children, were selected from a pool of over more than a thousand volunteers. They were a mixed lot: three teachers, two students, a hairdresser, a nurse, a doctor, a social worker, a union official, a mathematician, and a builder. The team was trained in "proper Iron Age" life during the winter of 1976–77, taking classes in traditional carpentry, pottery, metalwork, and weaving. Survival experts also coached them on the hazards of long-term exposure and the use of natural foods. The BBC prepared the site by digging a well, building a boundary wall of earth, and clearing out a patch of woods for the settlement. They also provided the volunteers with a basic inventory of Iron Age tools (replicas), crop seed, and basic livestock: three cows, four pigs, nine goats, twenty-five sheep, forty chickens, and bees.

In March 1977, the modern "Celts" set to work building a large round house, similar in design to Peter Reynold's prototype at nearby Butser Hill. It took them three and a half months to finish it, much longer than expected. However, the completed house more than provided warmth and comfort during the bitterly cold winter of 1978, when Britain endured a series of heavy blizzards. In the spring, the participants sowed their crops—wheat, barley, oats, peas, and tick-beans—began lambing, and cut three and a half tons of hay with long-handled reaping hooks. During the summer, they finally succeeded in making pottery, after many trial-and-error experiments, built a forge for shaping iron, and tended their flocks. In autumn, the team began preparations for winter: harvesting grain, gathering wild fruit and mushrooms, butchering surplus animals, and making clothes and footwear. Finally, during January and February, they rested from their long year's labor, sitting around the hearth fire, singing, telling stories, and drinking homemade brews such as mead, elderberry wine, and a primitive beer. The mead, made from honey, was the most potable, and they fermented and eagerly drank more than twenty gallons. Everyday life took on a slow rhythm, and John Rockcliff, who had been a builder before joining the project, said that they "almost hibernated and felt tired without twelve hours' sleep."

Despite the total absence of modern conveniences—electricity, plumbing, newspapers, radio, tobacco, and soap—everyday life for the team was both full and comfortable. The only modern devices they insisted on were sanitary napkins and contraceptives. They were frustrated, however, by the realization that they didn't have the basic skills of the Celts. Peter Little, who was an accomplished craftsman, said that "We could probably equal their skills in ten years, but in one year we were only just getting the hang of it."[13] He was ready to take on a second year, but money ran out.

Assessing the project as a serious exercise in experimental archaeology, John Coles had grave doubts. He concluded that life in the BBC village fell far short of an accurate simulation of life in the Iron Age. But Barry Cunliffe, and archaeological professor at Oxford, liked the project. He found it "absolutely fascinating."

It makes marvelous television, and I welcome it for that. But also, when I visited the site, I was very intrigued by walking around and examining the effect that these villagers had had on their environment. Just looking at their rubbish heaps, the paths they had worn, the effect on the soil, told me a lot about Iron Age sites that I have dug.[14]

When the experiment ended in February 1978, there was a general sadness at the thought of having to return to the present—a time trip of some 2,300 years. But the group left with a sense of satisfaction at having lived as nearly in the Celtic style as they had, growing their own crops, tending their flocks, making needed tools, clothing, and containers, and evolving a folklore to enrich their everyday lives. And the BBC was pleased with its success at having interpreted a major archaeological experiment to an audience of millions around the world.

These three projects, all carried out within the last ten years, illustrate living history's potential as an experimental research tool. Each had a distinct and unique basis.

Callahan's Arizona and Virginia projects were carefully controlled archaeological experiments—pure research. Callahan has never sought publicity; in fact, the projects' only record is in the form of technical field reports, privately printed and difficult to obtain.

The BBC Iron Age settlement, on the other hand, served primarily as an interpretive project and can be seen as a "living history" museum that reached its audiences through film. BBC planners never intended to match the level of scholarship found at Butser Hill or Lejre.

Finally, the Polder Project was carried out almost in a spirit of fun. The Dutch volunteers came across as "buffs," using living history as a form of serious recreation. J. and R. Horreus de Haas's 1982 book *Als in Het Stenen*

Tijdperk (As In the Stone Age) is enthusiastic in tone, popular in style, and an invitation to other modern nonspecialists to attempt this envigorating form of time travel.

NOTES

1. Mrs. Robert Asp, interview with author, July 30, 1983, at the Norwegian American Museum in Decorah, Iowa.

2. Errett Callahan, *The Old Rag Report: A Practical Guide to Living Archaeology* (Richmond, Virginia: Department of Sociology and Anthropology, Virginia Commonwealth University, 1973).

3. Errett Callahan, *The Wagner Basalt Quarries: A Preliminary Report. The Ape. Experimental Archaeology Papers*, 3 vols. (Richmond, Virginia: Virginia Commonwealth University, 1974), vol. 3.

4. Callahan, *Old Rag Report*, p. 48.

5. Callahan, *Old Rag Report*, p. 4.

6. Cited in John Coles, *Experimental Archaeology*, p. 216.

7. Errett Callahan, *The Pamunkey Project, Phase I & II. The Ape. Experimental Archaeology Papers*, 4 vols. (Richmond, Virginia: Virginia Commonwealth University, 1976):4:255.

8. This "Polder Project" is still continuing, and I have carried on a modest correspondence with R. Horreus de Haas during 1983.

9. R. Horreus de Haas, *Living a Stone Age Life: Report of a Creative Game* (Bilthoven, Netherlands: Werkplaats-Kindergemeenschap, 1978).

10. Horreus de Haas, *Living a Stone Age Life*, p. 7.

11. Coles, *Experimental Archaeology*, p. 227.

12. Correspondence with John B. Yater, Public Relations Officer with the BBC; Timothy Green's "Modern Britons Try the Iron Age, Find They Like it," *Smithsonian* 9:3 (June 1978):80–87; "Reliving the Iron Age in Britain," *Time*, March 13, 1978, pp. 68–69.

13. Green, "Britons," p. 86.

14. Green, "Britons," p. 86.

Part 3
Doin' the Time Warp:
Living History as Play

13

Black Powder

AS Philadelphia's 1876 Centennial Exposition drew to a close, a band of history buffs put on a show that drew 60,000 spectators.[1] On October 19, 1876—Virginia Day—the Southern states re-enacted a medieval tournament. There were fifteen knights, representing the thirteen original states, the Union, and the Centennial; and the "day's work before them was to ride over a given course, thrust their spears though diminutive rings and enjoy the plaudits of the multitude." Five thousand Virginians "rendezvoused" on the Centennial grounds to cheer their champion on; only one other "state" day, Pennsylvania's, drew more people to the Exposition. The tournament re-enactment provided a reporter from the *Philadelphia Times* with "a novel sight . . . the like of it was never seen in Philadelphia before." He noted that it had been organized by "men who first saw light below Mason and Dixon's line" and was a great success. One highlight for the *Times* reporter occurred early on:

North Carolina's representative, handsomely equipped with a suit of golden armor, and looking every inch a knight—a fearless and accomplished rider, and all over a man—a native of the State he represented, dashed up to the first arch with such speed that he carried away the rod from which the ring was suspended. But not dismayed by this, he kept up his speed and laid before the judges the two remaining rings. He asked, with apparent justice, that he might to allowed a trial at one more ring, to atone for the breaking of the arch, and the judges replied that he should have dropped his lance when the ring came down. "It is not knightly to drop your spear," the knight replied, and the crowd heard him and cheered him.[2]

The tournament ended that evening with the "crowning of the Queen of Love and Beauty." A hall had been "handsomely decorated, a throne having been erected on the south side, the platform brilliantly illuminated with candelabra, upheld by bronze figures of knights and pages, and bordered by pyramids of rare exotics." The hall was packed when the queen and her attendants, glowing in medieval gowns of white satin, arrived, their faces shining in the "rays of calcium light, and beaming with joyous anticipation." They walked slowly to the throne surrounded by "fair ladies, gallant knights, heralds, pages, and marshals, [and] presented a picture of rare magnificence."[3]

These knights and their ladies were not simulating the more dramatic and colorful side of medieval life for the sake of research. And they weren't particularly interested in interpreting its folkloristic nuances for general audiences. Rather, they were time-traveling for fun, donning armor and practicing martial and courtly arts in a spirit of play. At home in nearby Maryland, Delaware, Virginia, and the Carolinas, tournaments were considered holidays, festivals, a time to relax, eat a little barbecue, and enjoy competing with kinsfolk and friends in an archaic sport that had long since entered the realm of folklore.

Similar medieval re-enactments have been revived in the last decade, in the form of madrigal feasts, revels, and tournaments of the Society for Creative Anachronism. But during the 1930s, it was the muzzle loading rifle, not the lance and sword, that became the central motif of the living-history buffs' movement. And for those smitten with black powder, the key organization has always been the National Muzzle Loading Rifle Association.

The National Muzzle Loading Rifle Association (NMLRA) had its genesis on February 22, 1931, in Portsmith, Ohio.[4] At a rifle and revolver club sponsored by the Norfolk and Western Railway's YMCA, a debate on the accuracy of the muzzle-loading rifle versus modern guns provoked Oscar Smith, the club's secretary, to suggest a match. Sixty-seven riflemen came, with their old family heirlooms. In all, seventy rifles were used, "the youngest of the lot dating back to 1880" and fired by the man who had made it.[5] Bill Large, an NMLRA founding member, recalled,

At the first match we held in Ohio, many old match shooters were there. However, most did not shoot. It wasn't that the weather was so bad, it was just everyone being there. It was a celebration of accomplishing something we had set out to do. I can still see the snow falling and everyone standing around the campfires looking around and talking—might say, as happy as a bunch of kids at Christmastime.

Yessireeee! There was a 100 percent cry at that first shoot to keep it (NMLRA) going. "Where's the next shoot?" "When can we plan another one?" That was a GREAT DAY.[6]

Bill Large had been inspired as a boy by Bill Cody, who brought his Wild West show to

Ironton, Large's home, in 1916. During a parade, Large said, Cody "stopped his hoss in front of where I stood, as close as I could get; I touched his foot, right front. Bill Cody said 'Son, you will be a great shot.' " Large later learned to shoot in the same manner as most of the other competitors—by following the example of his father and grandfather. The founders of the NMLRA were reviving an indigenous tradition.[7]

The second match, held a year later, brought out a number of old gunsmiths; and in 1933, more than 260 contestants and more than 2,000 spectators came to Friendship, Indiana—many from great distances. Walter Cline, another charter member who, Large said, always "wanted everything absolutely authentic,"[8] remembered one Tennessee rifleman saying, of the event, "Nine hundred miles—to shoot five holes in a piece of paper."[9] But that sharpshooter and most others came back, year after year, to Friendship, the National Muzzle Loading Rifle Association's national headquarters.

By 1939, the NMLRA, officially founded in 1933, had grown large enough to publish a magazine, *Muzzle Blasts,* a modest four-page affair. The fiftieth-anniversary issue, in February 1983, ran to sixty-four pages and was distributed to the association's now nearly 25,000 members. While an interest in old rifles is the chief characteristic of both the NMLRA and its magazine, there had been, almost from the start, a concurrent enthusiasm for the folklife of the pioneers and soldiers who once used these rifles. *Muzzle Blasts* articles increasingly dealt with the lore of early marksmen, from the eighteenth-century Kentucky long hunter to the Civil War sharpshooter. Photographs of members in early issues of *Muzzle Blasts* and in Walter Cline's 1941 informal history of the NMLRA, *The Muzzle-Loading Rifle: Then and Now,* often show them in buckskins and homespun clothing.[10] Early in Cline's book, for example, is an action photo of the author in a buckskin shirt and a fur cap, firing a "beloved flint-lock." Later, there are portraits of Les FitzGerald, who "dresses and hunts as did our pioneers," with his trophy deer brought down with a flintlock rifle; and Bud Sackett, clad in moccasins, buckskins, and raccoon cap, in the role of Daniel Boone. Many members had no trouble reconciling twin interests in old guns and in the people who once used them. Both constituted, in NMLRA's terms, "an experience in heritage." The association officially expressed this historical sensitivity:

Each NMLRA member holds within himself the responsibility to the supreme heritage tendered him by his forefathers. Just as they were trappers, militiamen, tradesmen, businessmen, farmers, and adventurers—so it is today. . . . We reflect a living past into a special "way of life" using the arms and methods of the early pioneers.[11]

Within the NMLRA, however, three groups were gradually evolving.[12] Some members preferred to concentrate on the rifles themselves and felt that target-shooting and hunting gave them more than enough activity. They were not particularly interested in experiencing the clothing and life style of a historical group or period. However, others were fascinated by the "primitive" culture of the early long hunters, *coureurs de bois, voyageurs,* frontier settlers, mountain men, and Indians. They instituted "primitive" camps during the association's annual matches at Friendship, began to form offshoot organizations, and started referring to themselves as "buckskinners."

A third group took up the Civil War. In 1949, friendly matches between buffs interested in experiencing military shooting were held at Berwyn Rod and Gun Club in eastern Maryland. These competitions attracted the attention of some Southern riflemen from Norfolk, Virginia; and in May of 1950, the Norfolk Long Rifles (later the First Regiment, Virginia Volunteers) met the Washington Blue Rifles for a weekend match.[13] The

Fig. 13.1. Hughie ("Poor Devil") Newman, an experienced member of the American Mountain Men, attempts to teach a "pilgrim" the first steps in firing a flintlock.—*Photograph by Todd Buchanan*

weather was drizzly, but the competition wasn't. Each unit had scoured antique shops and searched collectors' shelves for months before the match and turned out as authentically attired and equipped as it was possible to be on short notice. Several hundred spectators gathered to witness what was to be a historic event for buffs. From this modest match, between two fledgling units, would come scores of battle re-enactments during the Civil War Centennial (1961–65) and American Revolution Bicentennial (1975–83). Within twenty years, buffs interested in military history would number in the tens of thousands.

The Confederates won the first "battle." After both units had marched onto the field to the strains of "Dixie," they fired at balloons from a range of twenty-five yards and later, after a "cease fire," at standard match targets from fifty yards. Firing and loading as fast as possible as part of a unit was a new experience for many of the men. They were fascinated with the firing line, with its pungent smells of gunsmoke, cacophony of drum and rifle, powder-flashes of red and smudges of gold amid the wash of blue, gray, and butternut brown. On the second day of the match, a drill and manual-of-arms demonstration took place, awards were given out, and the concept of a North-South Skirmish Association formed. Enthusiasm ran high. When the match ended, many problems were raised about the nature of military tactics and safety. It was obvious that, if further matches were to take place, organization was necessary. Rules had to be worked out and policies formulated.

In the following years, initial rules and regulations were agreed upon; and in 1958, the North-South Skirmish Association (N-SSA) was incorporated, thus making it one of the first *organized* groups of living-history buffs. Unlike the National Muzzle-Loading Rifle Association, there were no individual memberships in the N-SSA; only *units*, authen-

Fig. 13.2. A primitive member of the National Muzzle Loading Rifle Association relaxes after a day's target-shooting. — *Photograph by Ken Grissom*

tically attired and equipped, could belong, and then only if they had first been "inspected" by the national commander and looked over by other older units at the National Skirmish. Units had to consist of at least a company of eight trained men, and no one could hold a rank higher than sergeant. Each unit was to follow the loading drill and the manual of arms used by the regular state troops or militia of the United States or Confederate armies during the Civil War. There was a dual emphasis placed on rifle or artillery marksmanship and on the camp "culture" of the period. For that reason, the N-SSA attracted, from the start, academic and lay historians and antique collectors. Following the lead of the NMLRA, a magazine called *The Skirmish Line* began publication in 1955, and its articles and advertisements provide a clear record of the N-SSA's history during the last quarter-century.

By 1983, the association had reached a membership of just under two hundred units, consisting of more than three thousand buffs. It had also purchased, in 1963, a three-hundred-acre farm, near Winchester, Virginia, for its national headquarters. Named Fort Shenandoah, the site has served as the location for national skirmishes in the spring and fall, echoing the roar of musket, hand gun, carbine, and cannon during the day, and the more pacific sounds of dance tune and campfire song at night.[14]

The most traumatic period in the young organization's life came during the Civil War Centennial, when it became obvious that North-South Skirmish Association members constituted the only organized body capable of accurately simulating Civil War military life in camp and on the battlefield. Members realized that, although their original reason for forming the N-SSA had been to further a hobby that provided them with both recreation and an outlet for their deep interest in history, they soon would be called upon to perform for the nation. As a result, the years before the "war" saw an increase in membership, research, and concern with interpretation. But their Centennial experience would prove a great deal more complex than that of their "medieval" counterparts in Philadelphia eighty-five years earlier.

NOTES

1. McCabe, *Centennial History,* pp. 269–273. See also Rollin Gusta Osterweis, *Romanticism and Nationalism in the Old South* (New Haven: Yale University Press, 1949).
2. McCabe, *Centennial History,* p. 271.
3. McCabe, *Centennial History,* p. 271.
4. Walter M. Cline, *The Muzzle-Loading Rifle: Then and Now* (1942; reprint, Friendship, Indiana: NMLRA, 1981), p. 118.
5. Cline, *Muzzle-Loading Rifle,* p. 119.
6. Bill Large, "This Was the Place—the N & W YMCA, Portsmouth, Ohio," *Muzzle Blasts* 44:6 (February 1983): 26.
7. Bill Large, "A Letter," *Muzzle Blasts* 43:4 (December 1981): 15–16.
8. Large, "This Was the Place," p. 26.
9. Cline, *Muzzle-Loading Rifle,* p. 26.
10. Cline, *Muzzle-Loading Rifle,* Plates 5 and 6, between pp. 24 and 25.
11. National Muzzle-Loading Rifle Association brochure, 1983.
12. A survey of the forty-five years of *Muzzle Blasts* illustrates this trend.
13. John Abel, "The Story of the North-South Skirmish Association," *Gun World* (April 1972). Reprinted by the N-SSA for its press kit.
14. Dale Jones, my graduate assistant at Western Kentucky University for the years 1982–1984, and I interviewed more than fifty "buffs" for this book. One of the most helpful representatives of the N-SSA was John Sharrett III, interviewed by phone on December 9, 1982. Sharrett provided an insider's view of the N-SSA's early history.

14

Civil Wars

ON May 15, 1965, near Brownsville, Texas, eleven Confederate buffs attacked a single Yankee, armed only with fireworks.[1] After seventeen minutes of Rebel yells and cherry bombs, the soldiers went home, along with a thousand disappointed spectators. The Battle of Palmito Hill, the last battle of the Civil War Centennial, had been re-enacted. The original battle, fought five weeks after Appomattox, had pitted four hundred Southerners against five hundred Union troops for three bloody days. Because of a breakdown in communication, the men involved were unaware that the war had ended. Ironically, at the re-enactment, more traffic-directing policemen showed up than soldiers. The Palmito Hill part of the Centennial observance ended not with a bang, but with a firecracker's pop.

Such anticlimactic fiascos as the re-enactment of the Battle of Palmito Hill couldn't take away from thousands of buffs the attachment they had developed during the four years of dramatic simulations of battlefield, parade, firing line, and campfire. Instead of depressing buffs, inaccurate re-enactments seemed rather, to instill in them the desire to become even more authentic, to eliminate the polyester uniform and the chrome bayonet, and to discourage the gun-happy, hard-drinking "cowboys"—or "farbs," as the

pseudo-buffs were called. Serious buffs took control of their battle re-enactments, skirmishes, and weekend bivouacs. In a way, the recreational side of living history came of age during the Civil War Centennial.

Before the "war" even got started, a groundswell of support for re-enactments was evident. Karl Betts, executive director of the Civil War Centennial Commission, the co-ordinating agency responsible for the celebration, testified before a House Appropriations Committee, in April 1961, that local organizations were determined to re-enact Civil War battles and historical incidents:

We have done a great deal to discourage re-enactments on many, many occasions. But the local people want to do it, and there is very little you can do to prevent that. The urge to stage battles had reached such proportions that, in the South, for example, they are commemorating their defeats as well as their victories.[2]

Eventually, scores of re-enactments took place. "President Lincoln" was "inaugurated" on the steps of the Capitol on March 4, 1961—six weeks after John Fitzgerald Kennedy really did become president there. Ironically, twice as many people—twenty thousand—turned out for the re-enactment as there had been for the original 1861 ceremony. A college speech professor portrayed Lincoln, and the

Fig. 14.1. As the Civil War Centennial progressed, the authenticity of many units improved. The artillery company of Fort Niagara, New York, illustrates.—*Old Fort Niagara, Youngstown, New York. Niagara Gazette photograph by Andrew J. Susty*

poet and Lincoln biographer Carl Sandburg interpreted the event for the audience. The *New York Times* notes that:

After the ceremony, the official party, guarded by troops wearing blue uniforms that are now familiar only from textbooks and motion pictures, went to lunch at Willard's (now the Willard Hotel) as Lincoln had done.

There they ate the same meal that he ate: mock turtle soup, corned beef and cabbage, and blackberry pie. Later there was an Inaugural Ball.[3]

The battle re-enactments that followed were far more controversial. A week later, Fort Sumter was bombarded. Charlestonians "cheered each time geysers of flame, indicating a direct hit, shot up from the fort three miles down the harbor."[4] But in June 1961, "a band of Confederate soldiers was chased out of Philippi, West Virginia, commemorating the first land battle in the war."[5] To many observers, the Philippi battle came close to duplicating the original one, but with a few differences: the re-enactment lasted longer, and several hundred people lined the town's main street to watch the Southerners' retreat.

Otherwise, the uniforms, "equipment, muskets, sidearms, bayonets, and other paraphernalia of war" were authentic. Members of the North-South Skirmish Association had done their homework. The same could also be said of the battle of Manassas or Bull Run, re-enacted on July 22.[6] Three thousand soldiers, about half from the N-SSA and half from the National Guard, refought the battle before a crowd of thirty-five thousand people.

The action, accurate as to sequence and detail, was a sort of dramatic resume of the battle's highlights, displaying the broad outlines of strategy and the most interesting or critical turns. A narrator using loudspeakers described the moves on the field, spanned gaps in the action, and touched on events at remote points.

A large statue of General [Stonewall] Jackson on horseback near the middle of the action had been covered with netting and foliage because it was considered a hazard to illusion.[7]

The day was hot, and ninety soldiers collapsed among the numerous stuffed dummies strewn around the field to represent casualties. One Union soldier, Fred Kaiser, of Detroit, suffered first-degree burns on his chest when a cannon was accidentally discharged as he was running by; and a Confederate, Sam Haywood, of Arlington, Virginia, was knocked over when he was hit above the heart by "a piece of lead that a Yankee skirmisher had apparently failed to clear from his gun barrel before taking the field."[8] The lead pierced his uniform, but only bruised his chest. That kind of accident bothered many buffs. A close friend of mine, who was fighting in a Pennsylvania unit, returned from the battle wary of participating in further re-enactments. Many of the men on both sides, he said, seemed bent on refighting the war, and he was afraid that some "drunken hothead would decide to really let fly with a Minié ball."

His sentiments were echoed by officials of the Civil War Centennial Commission, and on December 4, 1961, Allan Nevins, the historian, replaced Maj. Gen. Ulysses S. Grant III, who had resigned as head of the Commission in August. Nevins announced that battle re-enactment would be de-emphasized. "Our central theme will be unity, not division. . . . We shall allow the just pride of no national group to be belittled or besmirched."[9] However, after it was learned that "Among President Kennedy's varied cultural tastes, it now develops, is one for sham battles," the Commission quietly reversed its policy. The *New York Times* noted that Nevins had gone to the White House to report on the Commission's work.

"When are you going to put on another sham battle?" President Kennedy asked.

The chairman said none was being planned.

"That's a pity," Mr. Kennedy mused, "I like sham battles."[10]

Thereafter, the flash of musketry and the roar of cannons resounded over the battlefields of Antietam, New Market, Perryville, Gettysburg, and dozens of other lesser engagements, including Palmito Hill. By war's end, John F. Kennedy had been assassinated, and many Civil War buffs had been burned out by what seemed to them an enforced role in a very controversial spectator sport. The National Park Service had ruled its battlefields out of bounds for re-enactors, many of whom, devoted buffs admitted, were only interested in beery "farbfests." For many, the Civil War Centennial had become a lost cause that could be redeemed only by a return to the basic philosophy of the North-South Skirmish Association, which stressed historical accuracy and safety.[11] Fortunately, the Bicentennial of the American Revolution offered serious buffs a second chance.

In the late 1960s and early 1970s, the living-history movement matured, as preparations for the bicentennial began.[12] During most of the Civil War Centennial, I had been out of the country in Scotland and Uganda. One

Fig. 14.2. Members of the Colonial Pennsylvania Plantation Militia during a winter bivouac near Valley Forge. —*Colonial Pennsylvania Plantation, Delaware County, Pennsylvania*

evening in 1972, I got together with four buffs who had been long active in re-enactments. All were members of the National Muzzle Loading Rifle Association and the North-South Skirmish Association and had "fought" in many of the larger battle re-enactments—Manassas, Antietam, Gettysburg, etc. They had marched down Pennsylvania Avenue in the "Grand Review," and two of them had seen Henry Fonda play Lincoln at the Second Inaugural. They agreed on a number of points. There had been too much shooting, too many "Cowboys and Indians," not enough authenticity, and an over-emphasis on pleasing the crowd. Although

they had all found the "spectacle of the battlefield" awesome, they preferred the quiet of the camp, when buffs could relax, talk shop, and compare uniforms and equipment. They also enjoyed the long marches, especially through quiet farm country.

Looking ahead, each of these four buffs wanted to enjoy the Bicentennial fully, but on his own terms. One wanted to get together with other buffs and re-enact some of the war's famous marches, such as Benedict Arnold's Quebec campaign across New England in the winter of 1775–76, and George Rogers Clark's 1778 successful attack on the forts at Kaskaskia, Cahokia, and Vincennes.

Fig. 14.3. The 78th Fraser Highlanders, of St. Helen's Island, Montreal—a superb example of a Brigade of the American Revolution "reactivated" unit.—*The Fraser Highlanders, St. Helen's Island Museum, Montreal, Canada*

Another decided to concentrate on historical clothing; he hoped to gain real understanding of the craft of eighteenth-century tailoring, and he showed me a copy of Robert Klinger and Richard Wilder's *Sketch Book 76* (1967) that he felt was a model for future handbooks. Two other buffs wanted to stay close to home and form a really authentic militia unit that would muster regularly and "drill for their own pleasure." They all hoped to do far more research on all aspects of the folklife of the 1770s, seeking to understand the cultural roots of the common people who were caught up in what was America's first "civil war." They were also interested in the neglected Quakers, Indians, Tories, and British, as well as the more popular Continental armies of Washington. And—most surprisingly, to me—they seemed to have lost the sexual myopia of an earlier age and wanted to include wives and companions in their activities. Living history had entered the modern world.

An umbrella organization that these buffs found much to their liking was the Brigade of the American Revolution (BAR), founded in the early 1960s by serious buffs. Similar in organization to the North-South Skirmish Association, the brigade placed extraordinary emphasis on authenticity and safety. Made up of autonomous "reactivated" British and American regiments, the Brigade of the American Revolution soon set the highest possible standards for historical accuracy. George Newmann, one of the BAR's founders, told me that their goal was military units that fit together like "grandma's quilt." Newmann, a Connecticut businessman, cited a number of reasons for the brigade's success. Every unit "coming in" was rigorously inspected. It had to adopt as its model a specific historic regiment or unit and then become the mirror image of that unit. No modern compromises were allowed. For example, "regimental belt buckles had to be made from historic molds, and only real flints were used in rifles." American units followed Baron von Steuben's manual, thereby insuring uniformity on the field, and many soldiers decided to carry only authentic articles in their packs. BAR members were encouraged to become totally familiar with eighteenth-century life, and women were invited to participate fully. Women often brought to the BAR units a knowledge of crafts, spinning and weaving, and everyday open-fire cooking. "It's not unusual to see them going about camp with their bare feet, smoking clay pipes." The bottom line for the BAR, Newmann said, was authenticity. "If you're not correct, you'll be pulled off."[13]

The impact of the brigade on the living-history movement during the Bicentennial was considerable. Its publication, *The Dispatch,* was widely read, its encampments visited, and its drills closely watched. The brigade set up an annual spring "School of the Soldier" at its Connecticut cantonment in New Windsor and established a policy for sanctioning regional encampments, some of which welcomed visitors and became virtual "extension" schools for other buffs. The BAR's presence at battle re-enactments lent an extra measure of authenticity. Events re-enacted at White Plains, Brandywine, Saratoga, Monmouth, and especially Yorktown achieved

Fig. 14.4. A regimental surgeon sets up his tent at Fort Ligonier, Pennsylvania. Encampments often feature the less martial aspects of eighteenth-century military life.—*The 18th-Century Society, New Alexandria, Pennsylvania*

new heights of verisimilitude.

Two years went into the planning of the Yorktown re-enactment. Tom Deakin, overall commander for the re-created armies, took a year's leave of absence from his job, and Bill Brown of the National Park Service spent months inspecting potential units. They had to be the "cream of the cream," said George Newmann, who himself led a contingent of twenty-four New England regiments. All the participating units had a particular patina achieved through the effects of a decade of battles and encampments. "Uniforms were beginning to get worn; the sheen was gone."[14] Eventually, twenty-five hundred soldiers representing more than a hundred French, British, and Revolutionary units were selected, and during the third week of October 1981, they simulated what many connoisseurs of living history believe was the movement's finest "moment in time." *Time's* reporter Kurt Anderson wrote:

Behind a bulletproof plastic shield, like travelers in a time machine, a jubilant Ronald Reagan and his guest, French President Francois Mitterrand,

Fig. 14.5. Changing the guard at Old Fort Niagara, near Buffalo, New York.—*New York State Department of Commerce*

watched the Bicentennial celebration of the transatlantic partnership that brought independence to the thirteen colonies. . . .

The centerpiece of the celebration was the reenactment of the Battle of Yorktown, which was planned long before either President had been elected. The troops, volunteers from twenty-three states who brought their own period equipment, came with 1,000 wives and children (also decked out in period clothing); the lot of them camped in a period tent bivouac for five days. All weekend long, 180,000 tourists reveled in the show: attacks on British redoubts, demonstrations of colonial battlefield surgery and finally, the white handkerchief of surrender waved by the English. Afterward, a Massachusetts colonial and his camp follower were married, *vraiment*, in an 18th-century ceremony, and dancers, jousters and drummers roamed the field. Occasionally time seemed out of joint, as when, in a surreal moment, 21 F-15 jets blasted out of the blue over a parade of musket-bearing troops across the ancient greensward. Now, as then, it was fire support the colonials did not need.[15]

In the ranks, the mood at the surrender was poignant. "To see the flags covered, to hear the drums muffled, was strangely affecting," recalled Barbara Deloury, a member of a British artillery unit. "We had thought that they would taunt us or yell insults, but instead there was this eerie silence. When the men went to lay down their weapons, a few of them began singing 'God Save the King.' My teen-age daughter turned to me with tears in her eyes, and said, 'Why are they doing that? They shouldn't have to give up their guns!' Then I understood what it must have meant to those British women, standing in almost the same spot, exactly two hundred year ago." She went on. "For those moments—all the pain in my feet and legs from the hours of standing, all the money we have spent, and all the days, months, and even years of work and research—for those moments, I'd do it all again."[16]

NOTES

1. *New York Times*, May 16, 1965, 29:4.
2. *New York Times*, April 14, 1961, 28:5.
3. *New York Times*, March 5, 1961, 1:3.
4. *New York Times*, April 13, 1961, 1:6.
5. *New York Times*, May 7, 1961, 15:1.
6. *New York Times*, June 4, 1961, 23:1.
7. *New York Times*, July 24, 1961, 8:1.
8. *New York Times*, July 22, 1961, 12:4.
9. *New York Times*, December 5, 1961, 31:2.
10. *New York Times*, May 7, 1962, 22:3.
11. John Sharrett III, phone interview with author, December 9, 1982.
12. Interview in Philadelphia, on August 26, 1972, with four colleagues whose anonymity I wish to preserve.
13. Dale Jones and I interviewed a number of BAR members who were active from the brigrade's inception. I would particularly like to acknowledge the help of Larry Bradbury, George Newmann, Tom Deakin, Bill Brown, G. Godney Godwin, and R. H. Griffiths. The latter spelled out his thoughts in a five-page, typed letter, which was of great assistance. See also Peggy Thomson's "Realistic Garb for 1976 Versions of Revolution," *Smithsonian* 6:12 (March 1976): 40–47.
14. George Newmann, phone interview with author, November 29, 1982.
15. Kurt Anderson, "A Last Bicentennial Bash," *Time*, November 2, 1981, p. 31. See also Del Marth's "A Bicentennial Finale," *Nation's Business* (September 1981): 81–83.
16. "Behind the Lines," *Americana* 9 (January-February 1982): 56.

15

Weekend Warriors

THE re-enactment of military history did not end with Yorktown. Military history is one of the most vital areas for living-history buffs today. In May 1983, I spoke about the future of re-enactment groups with a friend whose family is in the business of making military clothing.[1] For more than thirty years, they have been providing uniforms for the most demanding of history buffs. He was now spending most of his time doing research, since customers were increasingly knowledgeable and easily spotted the most minute inaccuracies.

With the Civil War Centennial and the celebration of the Bicentennial of the American Revolution now over, I asked, was their market holding up?

"Absolutely," he replied, although the big demand was now for U.S. Cavalry uniforms from the Indian Wars period, especially the 1880s. Orders were coming in from the Dakotas, Colorado, Texas, and overseas—especially Sweden and Germany. Weekend warriors, he mused, had also added recent wars, including World Wars I and II, to their repertory. But he felt that the Civil War would continue to provide his firm with orders, since buffs interested in this conflict are so numerous. He concluded that the Revolutionary War had been dragged out by the Bicentennial and was now almost dead, but

many of the Brigade of the American Revolution units had moved over to the French and Indian War and the earlier periods of the eighteenth century.

In short, I observed, American living-history buffs were currently re-enacting just about every military aspect of American history with the exception of Vietnam.

"Yes," he replied, "and for us, that means good business."

Leaders in the military re-enactment field estimate the number of active buffs at more than fifty thousand. The dedication of these "weekend warriors" to historical accuracy is strong. In large measure, this level of authenticity is due to the growth of a "cottage industry" of sutlers that has sprung up to equip the armies of buffs with their uniforms, weapons, and equipment. The military living-history movement has many of the characteristics of a "little tradition," flourishing outside the mainstream of academic and public history.

Insiders in buff circles are in touch with what is going on, in large part because the movement has a predilection for publications, and every unit, regiment, brigade, and army seems to have its own newsletter, magazine, or dispatch. Reading these is akin to listening in on a party line. Publications are colloquial, earthy, and informative.

Figs. 15.1. and 15.2. The number of units "reactivated" by buffs numbers in the many hundreds. These men portray Indian warriors who formed independent units and supported the British forces during the French and Indian Wars.—*The 18th-Century Society, New Alexandria, Pennsylvania*

A good example is the *F&I War,* a new magazine for "French and Indian War Associators for Re-enactments." Based in Pennsylvania, it started publication in 1982. The editor, Ray Washlaski, an experienced buff,[2] announced in the premier issue:

Now it's here—the newest magazine for the 18th century with emphasis on the French & Indian War. Additional articles on cooking, clothing, weapons, how-to's, patterns, fact, fiction, as well as schedules of events from units throughout the eastern and midwestern United States, plus advertisements introducing you to suppliers of

18th-century equipment and reproductions necessary for your re-enactment groups.[3]

The following issues of *F&I War* validated Washlaski's claims and constitute a clearinghouse of information on the craft of recreating the 1750–1763 period.

In the third issue, Washlaski included a list of all the serious units he could discover actively re-enacting America's first "world war."[4] There were 136 in all. The British forces included 18 regular regiments—heavy on grenadiers and Highlanders; 16 independent companies—mostly Rogers' Rangers; 5 surgeons (3 of whom were women); and 6 allied Indian units. The French army consisted of 6 regular regiments, including a *"corp royal de l'artillerie* and *canoniers-bombardiers,"* and 46 assorted *compagnies, gens du bois, malice,* and *partisans* from the Department Marine.

Geographically, the forces ranged from Maine to Florida, Maryland to Ontario, with the heaviest concentration in New York, Pennsylvania, and the Midwest.

I asked Washlaski if the list was definitive. He said, no, it had to be constantly brought up to date, since new units were forming all the time. He found it difficult to estimate the number of individuals involved—perhaps four or five thousand, if one included camp followers. "It's a great hobby, you know."

Each issue of *F&I War* also included an annotated schedule of re-enactments and events. These ranged from a "liberty-pole capping" in Massachusetts to a "cessation of arms" in Annapolis, Maryland, and a "disbanding of Washington's army" in New York. There were also musters, firelock matches, *voyageur* rendezvous, a colonial "rout" or dessert party, assorted battles, encampments and sieges, several seminars, a number of workshops, period Scottish games, the king's birthday—open to "British, Loyalist, and German troops only," concerts of eighteenth-century military band music, religious services, and one "fleatique." Quite a few events were open to participants only. A number of historic sites friendly to living history sponsored re-enactments. These events included encampments and tactical drills at Tippecanoe Battlefield, firelock matches at the Boone Homestead, and rendezvous at several dozen period forts operated by state historical societies in Pennsylvania, Michigan, Illinois, and the New England states.

F&I War's articles and advertisements were also imaginatively varied and illustrated the serious buff's concern with authenticity and the growing number of sutlers interested in

Fig. 15.3. A French dandy and his lady at a French and Indian War rendezvous at Old Fort Niagara. During the 1970s, women became active in the buffs' movement in increasing numbers.—*The 18th-Century Society, New Alexandria, Pennsylvania*

purveying the right stuff. There were scholarly features on a rich variety of topics: men's everyday dress of the 1750s; rifle slings; firearms; wounds; footwear; a French tent called the *"belles de armes"*; ways of interpreting history to encampment visitors; leggings; leather breeches; historical archaeology at Fort Michilimackinac; sack posset and other eighteenth-century drinks; Montreal's *Musee Militaire*; the journals of Asa Clapp (a member of Rogers' Raiders); and French raiding-party tactics.

Fig. 15.4. Peter McNutt, a leather worker, plying his craft at the Old Fort Niagara rendezvous. — *The 18th-Century Society, New Alexandria, Pennsylvania*

Fig. 15.5. Private Dave and Ensign Ray Washlaski: like father, like son. Re-enacting has become a family recreation for many buffs. — *The 18th-Century Society, New Alexandria, Pennsylvania*

Washlaski included in the magazine book and record reviews, a list of forty-six French and Indian War sites and museum, and short pieces on particular units, such as Frazer's Highlanders. Each issue also contained a question-and-answer column on authenticity. Advertisements ran the gamut, from full-page invitations to visit Colonial Williamsburg to smaller suggestions to "Relive a part of history at Fort Ligonier." Sutlers promoted their "museum-quality accoutrements," sketchbooks on colonial French dress, reprints of court histories, custom-made leather work, and engraved powder horns. Professional

researchers ran price lists for their services (a county-wide tax lists search, three dollars per surname per year, etc.), and smaller organizations promoted their newsletters (North American Voyageur Conference's *Newsletter for Voyageurs*). There was also a *Sutlers' Gazette* listing seventy-four forges, artificers, trading posts, booksellers, tailors, and assorted merchants and stating, matter-of-factly, "This Sutlers' Gazette is published here solely as a source listing. The publisher assumes no responsibility for the authenticity of items sold, nor guarantees all items appropriate for the French & Indian War Period."[5] All this in a heavily illustrated issue that runs about a hundred pages and costs two dollars and a half.

F&I War is not unique; its significance lies in its representativeness. I could have inventoried half a dozen comparable journals. Some, such as Bill Keitz's *Camp Chase Gazette*, have been around for awhile. Keitz established it in September of 1972 and devoted it to the "American Civil War and those who study it, collect its artifacts, re-create it and try to preserve its battlefields as well as support the memorials dedicated to that conflict. The time frame/span covered is from 1846 through 1876."[6] Substitute *Civil War* for *French and Indian War* in the previous four paragraphs, and you have a fair picture of the *Gazette*. More recent is Neal Blair's *Post Dispatch*, a "magazine of living history of the Indian Wars period," which dates from September 1980. Published in Cheyenne, Wyoming, its focus is on the West, especially its parent organization, the General Miles Marching and Chowder Society (GMMCS), with whom a recruit might share the experience of a "two-to-five-day campaign, eating, sleeping, and living in the boondocks as our forefathers a century ago did." The GMMCS also provides "days of garrison duty at old military historic sites: military balls in full dress uniforms; dedications and grand openings at museums or historic sites; officiating at Memorial Day firing squad ceremonies and some recruiting duty, just to name a few."[7] Interestingly, the *Post Dispatch* gives frontier women and Indians their due, in the form of special issues. Blair also recently included a lengthy article on "Boots and Saddles Down Under," a review of Australian living-history activities during the last two decades.[8]

Perhaps the most thought-provoking of the newer living-history military organizations is the World War II Historical Re-enactment Society, which was founded in the early 1970s.[9] It began publishing *The Point* in 1974 and has the unusual policy of giving each

unit up to a page of space every other month. Reading *The Point* is a very democratic experience. By 1983, the society had forty-five units—sixteen American, two Russian, six British, and twenty-one German—organized in seven regional chapters. The society maintains ties with a similar re-enactment group in England, which seems to have a strong interest in simulating "Yanks." (The American and British groups had hoped to re-enact D-Day in France in 1984, but Tom Stubblefield, a leader in the World War II field, reported in *The Point* that that possibility was in doubt "due to the French attitude to (A) militaria, (B) guns, (C) German uniforms. As I understand it, all of Europe is 'death' on SS uniforms. They [the British] think that a military vehicle convoy will be about all that may be allowed."[10]) However, in 1982, the HRS successfully re-enacted major battles that had taken place on the Russian Front (Tennessee), in Yugoslavia (Ohio), Poland (Missouri), Germany (Kentucky), and the Ardennes Forest of Belgium (Oklahoma). A related east coast group, the World War II Historical Re-enactment Federation, also re-enacted a D-Day invasion of France, staged on the shores of Virginia Beach.

Fig. 15.6. Re-enacting a World War II battle—a "closed" event, limited to members of the World War II Historical Re-enactment Society.—*Allen Fishbeck, World War II Historical Re-enactment Society*

Fig. 15.7. World War II Allied troops storm a wurst factory in an isolated park re-enactment outside of St. Louis, Missouri.—*Allen Fishbeck, World War II Historical Re-enactment Society*

Both the World War II Historical Re-enactment Society and the Federation are difficult to join. More than 90 percent of the present membership—a thousand active buffs—have had extensive re-enactment experience in the North-South Skirmish Association and similar groups. Since all World War II battles are "closed" to spectators and are often held on remote, deactivated U.S. Army bases, members join up and fight for very personal reasons. High standards of authenticity are considered crucial, and *The Point* echoes with harsh evaluations of units that came to battles unprepared or incorrectly equipped. Conversely, the folklore of the society is filled with stories of units that entered the "time warp" and did a particularly good job of evoking the past.

I heard from several unit commanders the story of British paratroopers who drove twenty-four hours straight from St. Louis to Fort Story, Virginia Beach, where a D-Day re-enactment was scheduled to take place. Because of a heavy rain, the landing was delayed, so the paratroops sat for three hours in the dawn, singing regimental songs and waiting patiently for orders. "They just took a piece of history and wouldn't let go." The same British airborne division is famous for its ability to leap totally into role. "They use

Fig. 15.8. Absolute authenticity is a primary goal of World War II re-enactors. —*Joe Kalal, St. Louis, Missouri. Photograph by K. Nicholas Thoman*

the right accents, march everywhere in formation, listen to Glenn Miller, and even go drinking in pubs the night before the battle." One admirer said that "They will pore over historic photographs with a microscope, looking for details. You know, these Brits were once photographed during a mock battle, and when the prints were shown to a real World War II veteran, he looked at them and said, 'I remember that place. I was there with them.' He was amazed to later find out that they weren't actual World War II photos."[11]

In fact, the photos that heavily illustrate *The Point* reflect a sense of realism that is both materially and psychologically correct. These latter-day Willies and Joes slouch in just the right manner and often look as if they are waiting for Bill Mauldin to happen by and sketch them.

One of the most active World War II buffs, Tom Sullivan, a "paratrooper" from California, summed up the W.W. II Historical Re-enactment Society's attitude in particular and the feeling of weekend warriors in general:

You want to be able to put yourself in a situation that looks like World War II. It's like stepping into a movie and then saying to yourself, "It's happening. I'm really there." It's fun to put in a good hard day of doing it right. After that, you feel for what soldiers had to go through. Good weather or not, you go through with it. You really learn what it meant for them to joke about death. You don't relax during a battle because you're trying not to get killed. If you've been tramping about all day, you try to stay alive. You never know what's going to happen. It's quite an education. One thing, though: you've got to be pretty stable not to get re-enacting and real life confused.[12]

NOTES

1. Telephone interview, May 11, 1983, with a businessman who wishes to remain anonymous.

2. Like many other buffs, Ray Washlaski has been very helpful. On half-a-dozen occasions, he has taken time off from his work to answer my questions about the "weekend warriors."

3. *F & I War* 1:1 (Spring 1982): 5.

4. *F & I War* 1:3 (Fall 1982): 48–53.

5. *F & I War* 1:1 (Spring 1982): 51–53.

6. *Camp Chase Gazette* 10:9 (July 1983): 3.

7. *The Post Dispatch* 1:1 (September 1980): 1–2.

8. The ladies' issue was 3:6 (June 1982); Indian editions were 3:1 (January 1982) and 4:1 (January-February 1983); and the Australian article appeared in 3:10 (November 1982) as "U.S. Cavalry Down Under,": 5–11.

9. All the buffs' groups with whom I was in contact, including the HRS, sent me a representative selection of their publications and were more than willing to comment on their editorial philosophy, goals, etc. My thanks to Diana Lampe, co-editor of *The Point*.

10. *The Point* 9:1 (January/February 1983): 3.

11. Many HRS members willingly shared their thoughts and feelings about re-enacting. Special thanks to Diana Lampe, Dave Berry, Tom Stubblefield, Buz Broach, and Victor Sarno.

12. Tom Sullivan, telephone interview with author, October 29, 1982.

16
Rendezvous

ON the same February weekend that a mixed company of Russian guards and partisans was noisily re-enacting the storming of a wurst factory held by the Germans' 38th Jager Regiment in a park outside St. Louis, Hughie ("Poor Devil") Newman was nervously hosting his first winter rendezvous in a remote forest in western Kentucky.[1] Hughie was slowly working his way up the ladder in the American Mountain Men (AMM), the national organization of buffs interested in simulating the 1800–1840 period. He had started as a "pilgrim," advanced to "bossloper," and now was working on becoming a "hiverano." *Hiverano* is the Hispanic version of the French word *hivernant*, or "winter resident," and was used in the period of the fur trade to denote a man who lived year-round in the Rocky Mountains, co-ordinating the fur trade there.[2] One of the skills Hughie had to demonstrate to his peers was the ability to organize a successful winter rendezvous. So here he sat, on the edge of a Kentucky woods, waiting to see how many mountain men would show up. Dressed in a fringed jacket and pants made of buckskin that he himself had "brain-tanned," in the Indian manner, Hughie now and then sipped the homemade contents of a jug, a good-luck present from a friend, a "Grey Beard" who had reached AMM's highest rank.

Hughie was anxious but hopeful, for he had planned carefully. A month earlier, he had sent out a broadside:

TRADEWATER FREE TRAPPER
Is going to have a Rondezvous for AMM Brothers That Would Like to Make This Meet;

It Will Be On The Week-end of Feb. 18, 19, 20 at *"Beulah Cave Hollow"* !

Hope Yea Can Make It. The Location is: 12 mi. West of Madisonville, KY, 9 mi. South of Providence, KY, 7 mi. North of Dawson Springs, KY, and 21 mi. East of Fredonia, KY.

FOR MORE INFO CONTACT
Hughie ("Poor Devil") Newman

"Keep Yea Nose To The Wind!"

February 1983 was balmy in Kentucky, and the lure of Beulah Cave Hollow, a wooded valley honeycombed with sandstone caves and a bucolic waterfall, was too much for the mountain men to resist. By Saturday morning, sixty of them had driven in from Tennessee, Missouri, Indiana, Illinois, Ohio, and Kentucky. There was Dennis ("Dude") Tapp, Russell ("Two Shadows") McGuire, Ralph

Fig. 16.1. Hughie ("Poor Devil") Newman uses flint and steel in dry moss to start a spark for a fire, near Beulah Cave Hollow in western Kentucky. An experienced Mountain Man, Newman took less than half a minute to generate a flame.—*Photograph by Todd Buchanan*

Fig. 16.2. One of the main attractions of buckskinning is the chance to escape from the hectic chaos of twentieth-century life. Here two Texas buckskinners rest on the way into the wilderness.—*Photograph by Ken Grissom*

("Two Shoots") Marcum, Mike ("Medicine Man") Caudill, and others. In modern life they were coal miners, computer programmers, farmers, lawyers, teachers, school administrators, and contractors. Here, in the atmosphere of the 1830s, however, they were all buckskinners. "On the rendezvous, we're all equals," one older *hiverano* told me. "There's no asking how much money you make each year. We're back to basics here. You make it with your hands and your ingenuity. Care for some venison? I shot it myself." Hughie had attracted a hospitable crowd.[3]

Campsites were strung out along one side of the hollow. Two or three men shared a spot, usually at the mouth of one of the many caves eroded out of the rock bluff. Each camp had a small fire upon which was simmering a game stew made of rabbit, squirrel, or venison. Beds were cedar boughs covered with moss and Hudson's Bay blankets or dark-brown buffalo skins. Hanging nearby were *capotes*, coats made from blankets. Most were a brilliant red with broad black stripes, but a few were Kelly green, and one was gray with a black stripe. "Is that blanket authentic?" I asked. "Yes, it's a Whitney. They've been making them that color since 1669."

Many of the bearded, long-haired men rested against their packs. They smoked a pungent tobacco in clay pipes and busied themselves with the details of camp life: cleaning their long rifles, repairing moc-

Fig. 16.3. For many of its devotees, buckskinning is a fascinating respite from city life. The question often heard around remote campfires tended by buckskinners today is not why *some* people dress up in buckskins and take to the woods, but why *everyone* doesn't. The author (second from right) absorbs a good story at the Beulah Cave Hollow winter rendezvous. — *Photograph by Todd Buchanan*

casins, checking the contents of their "possible bags"—flint and steel, tinder, jerky, and so on. Each man also had a bullet pouch, shooting bag, and Green River knife, and a number had tomahawks. Powder horns were often scrimshawed, several with historically questionable erotic scenes. This shooting paraphernalia was hung from the limbs of trees before each campsite, in the manner of a medieval knight's shield and lance.

The atmosphere was pastoral. Everyone spoke softly, almost in a whisper, and the natural music of the hollow could be clearly heard: water pooling, squirrels scampering,

and the rustle of oak leaves. A few heads rose when a pack pony came up the trail. Otherwise, all was very quiet. Steve Laughbaum, a free-lance artist and designer from Nashville, shared his feelings about the rendezvous. "It's a great respite from city life. When I first heard about living history, I thought, why would anybody want to dress up in buckskins and camp out in the woods? Now I wonder why everybody doesn't do it. Just look around; isn't it perfect?"[4]

Two unscheduled activities momentarily interrupted the quiet. Early Saturday afternoon, everyone walked down to an abandoned cornfield for a shooting match. The targets were playing cards, candles, and a sapling; the distances twenty-five, fifty, and a hundred paces. The marksmanship was incredibly good. Using a variety of flintlocks, many handmade by their owners, these marksmen split the cards in half—shooting at the edges, rather than the card face; they snuffed out candles; and they cut the sapling down, one bullet at a time. Talk was lively, with a lot of kidding and side bets.

Later that evening, someone suggested building a sweat lodge. Word of the project moved quickly up the hollow, and in less time than it took to smoke a pipe, the men had constructed a Kentucky sauna by the waterfall. Stones were heated, and a dry heat of at least two hundred degrees attained. About a third of the men took part in the stimulation of the sweat lodge and the chilling stream. The conversation was nostalgic; other rendezvous were remembered, evaluated, and compared with Hughie's. Beulah Cave Hollow was judged a success, and "Poor Devil" was encouraged to keep on working toward his *hiverano* degree. It would take a while longer, Hughie told me, since there were twenty requirements in all, including a five-day trip under primitive conditions by foot, snowshoe, canoe, and/or horseback; skinning an animal and preparing the skin or hide for market; carrying on a conversation using Plains Indian hand talk; demonstrating an ability to use traps and snares made from natural material found in the area; preparing a report on the life style of the mountain man, frontiersman, or American Indian before 1840; and tracking a man or an animal under natural wilderness conditions. He was looking forward to the challenge. Often, when Hughie was down in the coal mines, he dreamed of days he would spend in the woods, a comforting thought.

The American Mountain Men was organized in 1968 by Walter ("Griz") Hayward in San Diego, California.[5] Early members were

both history buffs and wilderness survival experts. The movement spread east, attracting new members from the growing segment of the National Muzzle Loading Rifle Association who were not content just to participate in match shooting. They drew up a list of tough requirements for membership. The AMM wanted "men who are willing to step back in time, to attempt, for a short time, at least, to live life as man was meant to live it, a Free Individual, a true Son of the Wilderness."[6] By the 1980s, the association had attracted about a thousand serious members. But the American Mountain Men, like the Brigade of the American Revolution and the World War II Historical Re-enactment Society, was not greatly concerned with body counts. They consider themselves to be the hard core of a larger fraternity of living-history buffs who are interested in simulating the folklife of the Fur Trade era. The Mountain Men's motivation remains a mix of historical curiosity and interest in attempting to live the "natural life."

In 1983, Ken ("Cripple Creek") Grissom, outdoor writer for the *Houston Post* and a highly regarded buckskinner with three decades of experience as an NMLRA primitive, wrote *Buckskins and Black Powder: A Mountain Man's Guide to Muzzleloading*, which should remain the definitive handbook for purists for many decades to come.[7] Grissom's book compliments *The Buckskin Report*, the basic magazine for buckskinners that John Baird has been publishing in Montana since 1972. The *Report* is the counterpart of *F&I War, Camp Chase Gazette*, and other period publications for the serious buff.

There is, however, another branch of the buckskinners' movement that is characterized by a commitment to interpretation in addition to research and recreation. And it has developed its own form of rendezvous, which is not at all a quiet, peaceful affair. Its roots lie in William F. ("Buffalo Bill") Cody's popular Wild West shows that captivated

Fig. 16.4. Ken ("Cripple Creek") Grissom, author of *Buckskins and Black Powder,* the definitive handbook of buckskinners. — *Photograph courtesy of Ken Grissom*

rural and urban audiences from 1882 to 1916.[8] Simulations of the more dramatic incidents in Western history, especially in the late nineteenth century, were a feature of these shows. In 1907, for instance, Cody re-enacted the Battle of Summit Springs, casting himself as the killer of Tall Bull.

The earlier history of the West, however—the era of the fur trade, the rendezvous, and the mountain man—was first successfully interpreted, not by Cody, but by buffs in the Green River Valley of Wyoming, on July 25, 1936. The Sublette County Historical Association sponsored the pageant, which commemorated the original 1836 rendezvous when two hundred mountain men and more than two thousand Indians met to exchange furs for clothing, staples, and whisky.[9] The 1836 rendezvous was the first time that trappers from throughout the West had relaxed together and celebrated. The 1936 pageant featured ten historical scenes (including the "arrival of the first white women who had successfully crossed the Rockies"), as well as a country dance, picnic, and a competition for "the best costumes depicting the dress and manner of 1836."

Today, the Green River Rendezvous is still being re-enacted at Pinedale, complete with a pageant, parade, barbecue, dance, beard-cutting, and exhibit at the nearby Museum of the Mountain Man. It is now, however, only one of hundreds of similar festivals, fairs, feasts, demonstrations, "living displays," and re-enactments commemorating the era of the buckskinner. For many buffs, these events have become a significant mode of interpretation, through which they can reach a wide audience, as well as a good opportunity to "rendezvous" after hours with other re-enactors and "living historians."

A good example of this new multifunctional event is the Feast of the Hunter's Moon held every October near West Lafayette, Indiana.[10] The city lies in the valley of the Wabash River, quintessential *voyageur* country. This is fur trade territory, too, but quite different from the Green River Valley, Old Fort William, or the Fortress of Louisbourg.

The landscape along the meandering Wabash is characterized by heavily forested hills. The feast takes place in a wooded, twenty-five-acre park, just a mile downstream from the actual site of Fort Ouiatenon, a French trading post and fortified village founded in 1717. Ouiatenon was the first European settlement in what is now Indiana, and it had a stormy history. Built by the French, captured successively by the British in 1761, by Ottawa Chief Pontiac in 1763, by George Rogers Clark in 1778, and by the Miamis in 1783, the fort was finally destroyed

Fig. 16.5. Primitive members of the National Muzzle Loading Rifle Association zestfully chew the fat as sourdough biscuits bake and venison stew bubbles in a slow simmer on the fire.—*Photograph by Ken Grissom*

on the orders of President Washington in 1791, to prevent its continued use as a staging area for Indian raids into Kentucky.

The natural and historical context for the Feast of the Hunter's Moon is ideal. "Ouiatenon," a mountain man from Tennessee told me, "has very good vibes. The Feast is too busy. Except at night, you can hardly move. But I still like to go."

Begun in 1968 as a modest weekend outing for nine hundred Tippecanoe County Historical Association members and friends, the feast grew rapidly. During the 1970s, the association capitalized on the growth of, and pub-

lic interest in, living history. In 1982, the feast attracted more than four thousand buffs and sixty thousand tourists. Buffs bivouacked in three separate camps—Indian, *Voyageur,* and Military—each about four acres and teeming with life. Evenings, there was the sound of bagpipes, Indian drums, fiddles, and Quebecoise folk songs. The aroma of fry bread mixed with the smells of onion and pea soup, black powder, strong tobacco, and many campfires. Ottawa Indians, *coureurs de bois,* kilted highlanders from the Black Watch, and Jesuit missionaries lolled together under the oaks. And overlying all was the hum of

Fig. 16.6. Setting up a primitive camp. This scene occurs thousands of times yearly in all parts of North America.—*Photograph by Ken Grissom*

adult conversations mixed with the squeals of children playing Indian, *habitant,* soldier, or wolf. For buffs, the Ouiatenon camps at night were extraordinarily realistic. Ties with the modern world were cut, and the texture and rhythms of the rendezvous were quintessential eighteenth-century. The feast *did* have "very good vibes."

During the day, the Feast of the Hunter's Moon was a carnival. Busloads of tourists poured in from Chicago, Cincinnati, Indianapolis, and a thousand Midwestern small towns and suburbs. They gawked at the mountain men, Indians, *voyageurs,* and sol-

diers, who, in turn, gawked back. Two centuries met—uncomfortably, at first—and then more easily, as questions and dollars were exchanged. Every buff became an expert, and quite a few laid out blankets and displayed their treasures: Indian beadwork, intricate trade silver, polished dulcimers, and multicolored *voyageur* sashes—all for sale or barter, of course. Lines formed for a taste of rabbit stew, parched corn, croquinolles, meat pies, buffalo jerky, and several dozen other exotic victuals. And more than fifty traditional crafts were demonstrated, including paddle-carving, rush-weaving, cordwaining,

Fig. 16.7. Learning by word of mouth, by example, and by the time-honored method of trial and error. This young American version of Rousseau's natural man practices ramming home a charge.—*Photograph by Ken Grissom*

Fig. 16.8. Like mother, like daughter: the relaxation and disengagement of life as a buckskinner is increasingly attractive to members of both sexes and all ages.—*Photograph by Ken Grissom*

Fig. 16.9. Buckskinning is a participatory sport. As might be expected, tomahawk-throwing is a favorite pastime for the youngsters.—*Photograph by Ken Grissom*

and flintnapping. Scheduled activities included a Huguenot religious service and mass in French, trade canoe races, an eighteenth-century fashion show, cannon firing, tomahawk throwing, fencing matches, Punch and Judy show, numerous military drills and concerts by fife and drum corps, Indian and European folk dancing, bowling on the green, a concert of colonial choral music, massed pipes, and a thundering march of more than a thousand soldiers in nearly a hundred different French, British, American, and Indian units.

Despite the crush, a symbiotic relationship between buff and visitor developed. Several hundred sutlers, blanket and booth traders, met the exacting standards of the feast's Quality Control Committee:

You may sell only eighteenth-century and early nineteenth-century trade goods, Indian-made crafts, items handcrafted from natural materials, cultivated produce, herbs, or natural foods. No archaeological artifacts, bumber stickers and souvenir-type items, records or tapes, Civil War items, foreign-made items unless historically appropriate: i.e., Hudson's Bay blankets, English clay pipes, Canadian Indian crafts, etc., mass-produced items, T-shirts, photographs, posters, pictures, stationery, cards, and books—limited to a small selection related to your specialty: i.e., a gun dealer may sell a few books relating to guns, etc.

For them, the Feast of the Hunter's Moon was a profitable market. For the layman, Ouiatenon was a historical smorgasbord of foods, crafts, and costumes. And for the serious buff or museum interpreter (some of whom came from as far away as Louisbourg, Old Fort William, Greenfield Village, and Living History Farms), the event was like a reunion of old friends. The feast's vitality—and it is only one of many thriving events—testifies to the good health of the living-history movement generally.

NOTES

1. Hughie ("Poor Devil") Newman invited my Western Kentucky University class in museum studies to attend his winter rendezvous. Ten of us went to Beulah and had a thought-provoking and enjoyable experience.
2. "Poor Devil" gave a veritable workshop on the AMM's rules governing advancement.
3. All the Mountain Men at Hughie's rendezvous were more than willing to talk with us potential Pilgrims. Their generosity overwhelmed us. Each student had a similar experience to the one cited here.
4. Steve Laughbaum, interview with author, sometime on the afternoon of Saturday, February 19, 1983.
5. "Son of Davy Crockett," *Newsweek*, July 20, 1981, p. 61.
6. AMM membership material, 1983.
7. Ken Grissom, *Buckskins and Black Powder: A Mountain Man's Guide to Muzzleloading* (Piscataway, New Jersey: Winchester Press, 1983). I cannot praise this book enough. It will be a model for other buffs' organizations that need a basic handbook.
8. David Katzive, *Buffalo Bill and the Wild West* (New York: The Brooklyn Museum, 1981).
9. Carol Chidsey, "A History: The Green Rvier Rendezvous," *The Green River Rendezvous* 6:1 (July 10, 1935), a supplement to *The Pinedale Roundup* 78:40 (July 10, 1983), Pinedale, Wyoming.
10. I attended the Feast of the Hunter's Moon in 1981 and 1982 and talked with both officers of the Tippecanoe County Historical Association and participants and visitors at the festival. I also obtained a variety of material relating to the feast, including guides, reports, informal histories, and application forms for participants.

17
Prince Valiants

WHILE thousands of buckskinners, mountain men, Confederate guerrillas, and latter-day G.I. Joes were methodically trying to re-enact the past as realistically as possible, another group, the Society for Creative Anachronism (SCA), dedicated themselves to "re-creat[ing] the Middle Ages not as it was but as it should have been, doing away with the strife and pestilence and emulating the beauty, grace, chivalry, and brotherhood."[1]

Courtesy and chivalry are the S.C.A.'s hallmark. . . . Active participation involving courtesy and chivalry is what set us apart from other organizations. Each person in the Society is considered a lady or gentleman unless their actions prove them otherwise. Courtesy involves simple politeness, common sense, and the Golden Rule . . . treat others as you would wish to be treated. As you progress in the Society you will easily learn the customs and mores of each Kingdom and how history relates to our Current Middle Ages.[2]

The ladies and gentlemen of the SCA use anachronisms creatively to improve the quality of contemporary life. Their approach to the Middle Ages, the period of history from roughly the Fall of Rome to the seventeenth century, is straight out of Hal Foster's "Prince Valiant." And their premise is that a sojourn into this magical time will help the modern time traveler endure the altogether too obvious examples of strife and pestilence that characterize our modern world, the epoch of 1984.

For even experienced buffs, lords and ladies of the Society for Creative Anachronism frolic in a strange, distant world. Its members, therefore, go out of their way to welcome newcomers courteously. While most other buff groups now make it relatively difficult to join their organizations—the American Mountain Men require the pilgrim to do a year's probation, for example—the SCA offers all manner of assistance, beginning with *Queen Carol's Guide.* Early on, she empathizes:

The first time you attend a tournament or revel sponsored by the Society for Creative Anachronism, you may feel that you have wandered into a strange new world where customs and activities are overwhelming and confused. People in bright costumes rush hither and yon on unknown errands; tents and pavilions go up and fall down in disorderly heaps. Important-looking personages stride about giving unintelligible orders, and the newcomer stands astonished in the midst of this, not knowing where to go, what to do, or whom to ask [for] information.[3]

Carol goes on to explain the basic rules of chivalry that will help one "understand and enjoy your first Society event." There is information on clothing ("Everyone is required to wear Medieval dress or an attempt thereat"); safety ("Unless you are fighting, stay off the field at all times"); decorum ("It is rude to talk during court, to shout advice or comments, or while a herald is speaking"); hospitality ("Always ask permission before entering a pavilion or handling someone's equipment: a pavilion is a Lord's or Lady's Home Away from Castle; please don't enter or touch unless invited to do so"); and courtesy ("Treat your inferiors in rank, knowledge, and experience . . . as if they were your equals; treat your equals as if they were your superiors; treat the officers as representatives of the King; and treat the King and Queen with reverence due your sovereigns").[4]

SCA members take their re-created courts, revels, and tournaments seriously, but they also have fun. The atmosphere at a society event is warm and inviting. Cheslyn Martin, a graduate student of mine, slipped away from a tournament—a "Virgin Wars," sponsored by the Thorongil Shire (Montgomery, Alabama)—to telephone me.

"I don't want to come back. Being a knight's lady is a lot more fun than studying for an M.A."

She did return to her studies, but subsequently disappeared on weekends for a variety of "galops," "tournies," "investitures," and one "interbaronial peace."

The Society for Creative Anachronism was founded in 1966 at Berkeley, California.[5] Dave Thewlis and Ken de Maiffe, two students who had experimented with medieval weapons during a stint with the Air Force in Germany, brought their hobby home with them, where it generated some interest among their friends. On May Day, 1966, they threw a farewell party for Diana Paxton, who was going into the Peace Corps, and for fun they made it a medieval tournament. Everyone came in costume and had a great time, so they decided to meet again, in a park, six weeks later. Just before that event, a science

fiction writer, Marion Zimmer Bradley, came up with a name for the group: the Society for Creative Anachronism.

For this second tournament, more than two dozen warriors showed up, with a variety of neo-medieval weapons and armaments: rattan broadswords, a gladiator's net and trident, coat-hanger chain mail, and flatiron shields. They were joined by a mixture of other area residents; some were science fiction fans, and others were veterans of a Renaissance Faire that had begun in Los Angeles four years earlier. A good time was had by all. On Twelfth Night, 1967, the society held its first court. A king knighted a number of the more successful fighters; there was dancing, feasting, and a revel.

By combining medieval martial arts and courtly pleasures, the society had come up with a winning combination. The SCA movement rapidly spread from Berkeley across the nation, in the late 1960s, and became especially popular at colleges and universities with strong humanities departments. In 1969, the SCA was incorporated as a nonprofit educational organization "dedicated to researching and re-creating the customs, combat, and courtesy of the Middle Ages."[6]

During the next decade, the society grew to five thousand paid members and—roughly—ten thousand court followers and other social sycophants. The "Known World" (North America) was reorganized along feudal lines into shires, baronies, and kingdoms, and a complex national intrastructure was established. Compared to other buffs' organizations, the SCA spent, during the 1970s, what some members felt was an inordinate amount of energy on politics and organization. One serious member, Woodford of Lorien (Mike Woodford of Scottsdale, Arizona), even wrote an M.A. thesis in business administration on the SCA's management tangles.[7]

The society also began an ambitious pub-

Fig. 17.1. Knights of the Society for Creative Anachronism "bop and bash" for their own pleasure. The swords are made of rattan and do inflict real bruises.—*Stephen Lowry, Bowling Green, Kentucky*

lications campaign at the local, regional, and national levels. A quarterly, *Tournaments Illuminated* (published from 1967 on), covered a wide range of medieval topics. The 1982 winter issue, for example, included articles on medieval Japanese culture, perfumes and fragrances, dancing Christmas carols (lyrics and steps), medieval ships on modern seas (dhows, samuks, junks, etc.) tapestry weaving, sigillographica or armor decoration, a recently composed *rondel l'amore*, children's books on the Middle Ages, arrow fabrication, the merits of various cut-off dates for the society (1600, 1650, etc.), and a selection of car-

toons from the newsletters of various kingdoms—all very amusing. A pamphlet series, *The Creative Anachronist*, deals at greater length with subjects such as medieval eyeglasses and gaming. Rodema de Rohan and her husband Sir Raymond, Baron al-Barran of Albuquerque, New Mexico, in 1979 published a two-hundred-page guide to the SCA called *The Pleasure Book*.[8] The guide covered the organization's structure and events and devoted chapters to armor, calligraphy, cookery, costuming, dancing, decorative banners, games and amusement, heraldry, pavilions, and ballads. It also defined *anachronism* and interpreted the SCA's purpose from a member's point of view:

An anchronism is a tradition which has outlived its original purpose, but which survived just because it's a lot of fun. That's probably the best description of our group, since you can make anything you want from it. For some it's a means of serious research into Medieval culture, by trying to re-learn the skills, knowledge, and life-style of our ancestors. For others it's a hobby, a way of relaxing after a normal ("mundane") day, and an excuse to pursue interests and crafts they never found time for before. For many of us, it's the most interesting continuous costume party we've ever been to. A few members joined with an interest in history, drama, and folklore [having] found them dull as traditionally studied.[9]

Many living-history buffs from organizations other than the SCA would undoubtedly identify with one or more of these motives.

For more experienced members, the society published *The Fighter's Handbook* and *The Known World Handboke,* both of which quickly went out of print and had to be revised and re-issued. Since tournaments between knights in armor fighting with medieval weapons is one of the two major SCA activities, the book on the craft of fighting—by Kevin Perigrynne, *nom de plume* of Phillip McDown—was needed. It covers such topics as armor (shields, padding, helmets), weapons, field behavior, melees and wars, the basics of tourney fighting, first aid, and the etiquette of dying. *The Known World Handboke,* on the other hand, delves into more pacific pursuits. There are chapters on "Period Vocal Music for the Multitudes," "On the Making of a Parachute into a Pavilion," "Waggon-loading for the Compleat Idiot," and "How to Have Current Middle Ages Children Without Being a Prematurely Middle Age Parent."[10]

The Society for Creative Anachronism is meant to be fun. Its members time-trip primarily for pleasure. Even when they are seriously searching for the Grail, organizing a medieval feast, or "bop-and-bashing" each other with rattan swords, the tone at their

Fig. 17.2. A "medieval" tournament in the streets of Bowling Green, Kentucky. What these foot-soldiers lack in authenticity, they make up for in enthusiasm.—*Stephen Lowry, Bowling Green, Kentucky*

courts and tournaments is playful. They are modern counterparts of those golden knights and glowing maidens who captured so many hearts a century earlier at Philadelphia's Centennial Exposition. And despite the unabashed exotic flavor of their medieval events, these latter-day Prince Valiants and their ladies illustrate, through their enthusiasm, the essential attractiveness of living history as a form of recreation.

One of my graduate students, Debbie Bays, summed up the appeal of the buffs' movement after her first American Mountain Men rendezvous: "You know, I think living history is going to be *the* participatory sport of the future."[11]

NOTES

1. Carol of Bellatrix, *Queen Carol's Guide* (Berkeley, California: Society for Creative Anachronism, Inc., 1981), p. 2.

2. *Queen Carol's Guide,* p. 3.

3. *Queen Carol's Guide,* pp. 4–5.

5. My history of the SCA is based on Jack Fincher's "They Joust as if Knighthood Were Still in Flower Today,"

Fig. 17.3. To the victor belong the spoils. The Society for Creative Anachronism is characterized by courtesy, chivalry, and enthusiastic observance of the rites of courtly love.—*Stephen Lowry, Bowling Green, Kentucky*

Smithsonian 12:3 (June 1981): 95–103, and interviews with three early members, Debra Bennett, Mike Woodford, and Dave Schroeder.

6. *The Corpora and By-Laws of the Society for Creative Anachronism, Inc.* (Berkeley, California: The Society for Creative Anachronism, 1979).

7. Mike Woodford, *Trends of Change* (Scottsdale, Arizona: Mike Woodford, 1982).

8. *The Pleasure Book* (Albuquerque, New Mexico: Raymond's Quiet Press, 1979).

9. *Pleasure Book,* p. 11.

10. Kevin Perigrynne [Phillip McDown], *The Fighter's Handbook* (Berkeley, California: The Society for Creative Anachronism, 1978); and *The Known World Handboke,* a publication edited collectively by the Society for Creative Anachronism (Berkeley, California: The Society for Creative Anachronism, 1979).

11. Debbie said this to me as we were leaving the Beulah Rendezvous, Saturday, February 19, 1983.

18
Bivouac at Gadsby's Tavern

IN the spring of 1982, Suzanne Herlitz, the assistant curator of Gadsby's Tavern, a historic eighteenth-century inn at Alexandria, Virginia, had a fairly typical interpretive problem. She was responsible for the spring program there, and she was asked to recreate, on May Day weekend, some of the historic atmosphere that Gadsby's was famous for during the Revolutionary War era. George Washington himself had selected Gadsby's Tavern as the site of his birthday celebrations. Now, two centuries later, the staff wanted to evoke the warmth and gaiety that once characterized the tavern's bar, parlour, and assembly rooms.

The solution, Suzanne decided, could be provided in part by the Maryland Militia, an experienced re-enactment unit made up of volunteers from the Washington, D.C., area. Many of the militia's members were veterans of the American Revolutionary War Bicentennial. They had, in the course of eight years of part-time campaigning, perfected their living-history impressions. They had also had innumerable opportunities to interpret the realities of soldiering and camp life for a variety of contemporary audiences. In short, the militia was representative of the living-history buff's movement at its best. Why not have them bivouac in the tavern?

Bill Becker, the military unit's commander,

liked the idea. The militia had had extensive experience in outdoor camping, but little in a historic urban space. The tavern would be an ideal "laboratory." Perhaps his militia men and a few camp followers could, in such a setting, recreate the temporary billets so commonly used by both armies during the war.

So, for two spring nights, a dozen members of the Maryland Militia lived in the Gadsby Tavern's Assembly Room. They ate, drank, played cards, and socialized with each other and with visitors. The change in the tavern's atmosphere was immediately noticeable. Suzanne said that, when she first walked into the room, the space *felt* different: it seemed more "historical." Visitors had the same response. And the soldiers reveled in the opportunity to re-enact some "colonial R and R" in an authentic inn.

Gadsby's Tavern followed this successful program with a far more complex event: a traditional market, featuring a variety of civilian re-enactors that included a watchmaker, shoemaker, itinerant musician, and even a juggler. The tavern's restaurant erected a stand to sell roasted oysters and ale.

Such an event was possible, Suzanne explained, because local buffs had broadened their interests to include a selection of civilian impressions and period crafts. She was able

Fig. 18.1. **Experienced living-history military units constitute a valuable resource for historic sites like Gadsby's Tavern in Alexandria, Virginia, or Old Fort Niagara, where this photo was taken.**—*The 18th-Century Society, New Alexandria, Pennsylvania. Niagara Gazette photograph*

to stage a realistic historical event such as a country fair or an urban market with this informed and interested volunteer help. Since Gadsby's, like most open-air museums and historic sites, doesn't have the trained specialized interpretive staff necessary for complex events, enthusiastic, knowledgeable buffs are a godsend.[1]

Co-operation between the different segments of the living-history world is fast becoming the norm. Gadsby's Tavern is just one example of many that come to mind. For example, Old Beth Page, a fine open-air museum on Long Island, New York, turns itself into a Union Army training camp and depot for a long weekend each year. This provides an opportunity for re-enactors to experience the rigors of a Civil War "boot camp" in an authentic mid-nineteenth-century setting. For the staff of this Suffolk County museum, the training camp serves as a way of interpreting the larger historical context of the village. For at least a few days, Old Beth Page is an armed military camp, instead of a small Victorian town. It took courage to initiate this program. Old Beth Page is a county museum, and many of its staff members remember the debacles of the Civil War

Fig. 18.2 and 18.3. Members of the American Living History Association, on a campaign in Texas. Whether on campaign or simply rendezvousing, members of the association are dedicated to achieving an extremely high level of historical accuracy.—*American Living History Association, Inc., Austin, Texas*

Centennial and the subsequent National Park Service policy against any battle re-enactments on park land. They realized, however, that the public now includes a new generation of buffs who are earnest historians and a growing number of visitors who, having experienced the 1960s, now would appreciate more realistic and historically accurate museum programs—would like to know what the effect was *on the women and children of a small New York village*, seeing all their young men go off to a bloody Civil War, knowing full well that one in five or ten would not return. Today's history museums can't avoid these kinds of questions from the generation that experienced the Viet Nam War.[2]

Co-operation between historic sites and re-enactors really came of age on the Memorial Day weekend of 1983. The superintendent of Vicksburg National Military Park *invited* the American Living-History Association of Austin, Texas, to interpret the opening days of the siege of Vicksburg in 1863. The encampment was, for many experienced, serious re-enactors, the most historically accurate simulation to date. Michael Moore, secretary of the ALHA and editor of its journal *Phoenix* ("volunteer living-history programs, like the mythological bird, will rise out of the ashes of poor interpretation to that of high quality, useful historical, and especially living-history interpretation"),[3] worked closely with Edward Leachman, supervising park technician, to insure an extremely high level of historical accuracy. Several companies of the 23rd Alabama Infantry opposed the 47th Indiana Infantry in a fifty-hour "tactical situation." For two and a half days, the troops faced each other across a siege line in freshly prepared fortifications. The soldiers stood picket, sharpshot at each other when a target presented itself, built *cheveaux-de-frise*, positioned cotton bales and sandbags, and—when they could—slept, ate, played cards, and chewed the fat. During the re-enactment of an actual truce that occurred on May 22, 1863, the opposing forces also socialized between the lines, trading U.S. coffee for Confederate tobacco, and mutually complaining about the lack of whiskey. One night, the Alabama troops put on an old-fashioned minstrel show, while, across the line, the Indiana soldiers were listening to enlistment speeches aimed at recruiting freed blacks. Each soldier came prepared physically with authentic uniform and equipment and mentally with the information necessary to interpret a specific soldier who was present at the 1863 siege. Visitors passing down the trenches at night during a lantern tour met living facsimiles of the young men who had once lived and died in the Mississippi mud above Vicksburg. For re-enactor and visitor alike, it was an eerie experience: 1983 had suddenly became 1863.[4]

Vicksburg and similar re-enactments will be models for future events in and around historic sites, especially the numerous forts and battlefields scattered throughout North America that seek to update and improve their interpretive programs. As evidence of this positive trend, one need only look at the event and campaign calendars of the living-history magazines, journals, and newslet-

Fig. 18.4. Graduate-student interns engaged in research at The Homeplace 1850, in western Kentucky and Tennessee, are illustrative of the growing interest in living history among a new generation of academic historians. The Homeplace 1850 is a Tennessee Valley Authority living-history farm in the Land Between the Lakes area, bounded by Kentucky Lake and Lake Barkley, impoundments formed by TVA dams on the Tennessee and the Cumberland rivers.—*The Homeplace 1850, Golden Pond, Kentucky*

ters—they are filled with examples of co-operation between museums and buffs.

Serious re-enactors are also increasingly aware of the research potential of experimental living-history projects. A good recent example was carried out by Boat Number 17, a Rogers' Rangers unit formed four years ago to simulate French and Indian War soldiering. The unit's captain, Gregory Geiger, reported in the *F & I War* journal, that, although the unit's members were well aware of the way the original Rogers' Rangers dressed, ate, and marched, they didn't know specifically how they fought, especially in winter. In January 1757 and March 1758, Rogers's men fought two skirmishes against the French. Why not recreate, under similar conditions, the tactics used in these battles? That would include a long winter march on snowshoes, an ambush, a fire-fight with flint-locks, and a subsequent retreat and encamp-ment. Fifteen experienced re-enactors agreed to participate, so long as the research project was a "Class One" event, strictly "authentic and primitive."

On a bitterly cold January 22, 1983, in the Black Mountains along Lake George, New York, they began the experiment. The day was full of surprises. Among the most inter-esting: Rogers's cherished green uniforms were "incredibly loud in the winter woods," the "rifle was generally useless in this type of engagement," setting up an ambush was brutally difficult due to the cold, and the ele-ment of surprise was next to impossible to achieve—the crunch of snowshoes could be heard hundreds of yards away. In short, the experiment was a *great* learning experience that both answered and raised questions.[5]

The "Snowshoe Battle" is just one of many experimental research projects now under way involving re-enactors. As these living-history buffs delve deeper into the folklife of specific groups and periods, they invariably realize that the historical record is often thin and that experimentation may be a useful method of generating new data. Such proj-ects help to bridge the different worlds of living history and complement the more tra-ditional research of academic historians.

NOTES

1. Suzanne Herlitz, interviews with author, September 9 and 10, 1983, at Gadsby's Tavern.

2. Harrison Hunt, interview with author, July 18, 1983.

3. *Phoenix* 2:4 (Fall 1981).

4. Michael Moore, interview with author, May 10 and June 10, 1983.

5. George J. Geiger, "Battle on Snowshoes," in *F&I War* 2:1 (June 1983): 40–48.

Conclusion:
Computer Days and Digital Nights

ONE Sunday evening, after a supper of leftovers, I turned on the televison set. My daughter Anna had told me about a new program called "Voyagers." "You should watch it, Dad; it's about the same thing as your book—you know, time machines and history." She was absolutely right. "Voyagers," featured a young boy and his mentor who, by means of a talisman, travel back and forth in time and interact with famous people at crucial junctures in the past. They insure that historical events turn out the way the history books say they did. In the segment I watched, the heroes traveled to Hyde Park, New York, and to the year 1924. There they assisted Eleanor Roosevelt in persuading her crippled husband, Franklin, to walk again.

Anna liked the program. "You learn something about history, but it's fun." I liked the show, too, especially the humanization of the legendary FDR and Eleanor and the realism of their clothes, rooms, furniture, food, and general domestic scene. "Voyagers" helped me to visualize in my mind's eye a historical event that I had previously been able to imagine only in the sketchiest sort of way.

The premise of the show—that man can travel back in time and take an active hand in history—is, of course, not novel. It was used by Gregory Benford in *Time Scape* and Jack Finney in *Time and Again*, both of which were compelling, critically successful novels. For mortals, tinkering with history is a fascinating idea.

"Voyagers" also reminded me of a boyhood experience with time travel. I was listening, one weekend afternoon, to the radio, sometime in the late 1940s, when suddenly the announcer began to describe a battle under

Fig. C.1. T. J. Triplett takes a break from promoting the science of phrenology on a warm summer afternoon in Connor Prairie, an 1836 living-history village outside Indianapolis, Indiana.—*Connor Prairie Pioneer Settlement, Noblesville, Indiana*

way between Dutch and Spanish forces on the outskirts of Antwerp. I was horrified. Hadn't World War II ended years ago? If it had started again, wouldn't my dad have to go back into the Marines? What if he were killed this time? I nervously listened for a few more minutes, as Walter Cronkite made word-pictures of the fighting and then actually interviewed some soldiers with strange accents.

But it was more than I could stand, and I cried out the window to my father, who was working in the backyard: "The war's started again. They're fighting in Holland. It's on the radio."

Dad stopped working pretty fast and came up to my room. He listened calmly, then smiled. "Don't worry. It's just a radio program about history, called 'You Are There'.

Listen. You'll see it's about a war that was over, hundreds of years ago. You like to play soldiers. You should enjoy it." Well, I did enjoy it—and I was left with both a memory to last a lifetime and an enthusiasm for good historical simulations regardless of the medium: fiction, radio, television, film, theater, or living history.

As this book, *Time Machines: The World of Living History,* illustrates, mine is an enthusiasm shared by a varied company of interpreters, researchers, and buffs that must number at least a hundred thousand. Add to this group all the friends of living-history museums, armchair adventurers waiting impatiently for Thor Heyerdahl or Tim Severin's next voyage, and folk festival junkies—and you have a veritable army of living-history aficionados.

Fig. C.2. A ride through the snow by sledge at Old Fort William, on the north shore of Lake Superior.— *Old Fort William, Ontario Ministry of Industry and Tourism, Toronto, Ontario, Canada*

Fig. C.3. Adults—and a team of alert oxen—help with maple-sugaring at Washburn Norlands, a historic farm in Livermore Falls, Maine.—*Washburn Norlands Living History Center, Livermore Falls, Maine*

Fig. C.4. Loyalist farmers frolic, after the harvest, at Kings Landing, near Saint Johns, New Brunswick.—*Kings Landing Historic Settlement, New Brunswick, Canada*

Fig. C.5. One of the perks for the staff at living-history museums is the opportunity to time-travel after the tourists have gone away. Maritime fiddling fills the evening air at Kings Landing on such an occasion.—*Kings Landing Historic Settlement, New Brunswick, Canada*

What motivates otherwise normal people to don neolithic furs, medieval armor, buckram shirts, or brain-tanned skins and dash into the time warp of living history? What do they gain from years of farming behind cantankerous oxen, seasons of sailing smelly little ships on dangerous seas, and weekend bivouacs in the chill damp of a frontier forest or fort? Is all this activity just an ephemeral fad, or can we expect it to take root and grow into a mature tradition? Either way, is there any historical significance to living history.

Obviously, the first two questions deal with motivation and meaning and are best answered by the interpreters, experimenters, and buffs themselves. The last question, however, calls for a thesis, and I will suggest one that I believe makes sense.

Getting "living historians" to talk was no problem. People who enjoy vicarious time travel also take pleasure in sharing with outsiders their motivations for getting away from the present and recounting the meaningful rewards of their simulated but realistic ventures into the past. During many conversations along these lines, three reasons (and results) kept cropping up: a need to escape from the tyranny of abstract time; a nostalgic preference for the past—usually a particular epoch; and a curiosity about the nitty-gritty nature of everyday life in a specific historical period.

Living historians need to escape—if only for a day or two—from the late twentieth-century world of digital watches and omnipresent computers. The real "big brother" of 1984 is the clock, and it continually reminds one that time is money, and success is measured by the speed with which a job is done. The clock is often seen as a tyrant, proclaiming a speed-up on the assembly line of everyday life and proscribing even the most innocent of customs if they are found guilty of slowing down human activity or of keeping someone from making more money. Supermarkets are open twenty-four hours a

Fig. C.6. Some modern folk have a nostalgic preference for the past.—Connor Prairie Pioneer Settlement, Noblesville, Indiana

day; malls do business every Sunday; Christmas is hyped for three months; and football is played in the summer. Modern life is considered a rat race where everything has to be delivered overnight by air express, and time is measured in nanoseconds (1 / 9192631770 of an "old" second). Many of the living historians that I talked with often noted that a revolutionary "third wave" was indeed sweeping over them, uprooting their stabilizing traditions and leaving them future-shocked. They wanted desperately to slow down the pace of life and regain a sense of

Fig. C.7. These young visitors to Washburn Norlands bubble over with curiosity about the way people lived in Maine, a century ago. — *Washburn Norlands Living History Center, Livermore Falls, Maine*

Fig. C.8. For these Canadian students, Kings Landing glows with the timelessness of childhood. —*Kings Landing Historic Settlement, New Brunswick, Canada*

what Simone Weil called *enracinement,* or rootedness. The only way that seemed possible was simply to escape from the present into the timeless world of the past. To them, a medieval revel or a Civil War encampment has the potential for becoming an oasis of eternity in the desert of modern abstract time.

These modern time-travelers are not escapists. Hughie ("Poor Devil") Newman knows he must go back to the coal mines on Mon-

day, and Cheslyn Martin appreciates that her weekend SCA tournament will be only a memory as she returns to the classroom to sit through yet another graduate folklore class.

The liberating rewards of even temporary and vicarious time travel were blessed by the twentieth century's leading futurist, Buckminster Fuller, one evening at the Colonial Pennsylvania Plantation. One of Fuller's assistants, Meddy Gabel, worked for us as a

Fig. C.9. The realities of life and death in Walnut Grove, a small 1870s Iowa town, is what drew Jack Settle into becoming Living History Farms' resident cabinetmaker and undertaker.—*Iowa Living History Farms, Des Moines, Iowa. Photograph by Mimi Dunlap*

night watchman. He once told me that it was good to leave Bucky's twenty-second century, where he worked during the day, in Philadelphia, and commute back to the eighteenth century. One day in the summer of 1975, Gabel asked me if he could bring Fuller and Mrs. Fuller out to the plantation, along with some friends, to celebrate Bucky's eightieth birthday. Naturally I said yes, and the party was a great success. Fuller walked around our Quaker farm and asked a variety of questions about our research and interpretive goals. The idea of a "museum in the making," with its theme of open-ended scientific inquiry, really appealed to him. He told us how important time machines were going to be, in the future. They could, he said, help people adjust to the mind-numbing changes the technological revolution was introducing into modern life. It was healthy to stretch your imagination through the use of time machines, so long as you "escaped" into the future, as well as the past.[1]

Nostalgia was once a good, tough word for the deadly disease of homesickness. Two centuries ago, people died from nostalgia.[2] I often wish we could strip the word of its sentimental accretions; it would be a useful tool in the years to come.

Many living historians prefer the past to the present. They often say that they were born in the wrong century. Since people cannot control where or when they were born, time travel gives them the opportunity to practice a kind of reverse re-incarnation. Living history is a means of being born again in a more congenial time and place.

A number of buff organizations strongly recommend that their members adopt a historical persona. For example, in its *Corpora and By Laws*, the Society for Creative Anachronism "encourages members to develop a unique, historically valid persona, including a name and, if appropriate, an armorial device. To register and authenticate such names and devices, a College of Arms exists within the Society, performing these and other tasks."[3] So important is the persona concept to SCA members that they take pains to stay always in character—even to the extent of allowing their personas to take credit for the books they write. *Queen Carol's Guide* is a good example.

Often one comes across a classified advertisement in one of the buffs' magazines, announcing that a serious re-enactor is revising his "impression," another term for persona, and therefore has elements of his costume for sale. One sutler has even gone into the business of recycling authentic handmade period clothing from worn-out personas.

R. H. Griffiths, a serious buff who helped establish the North-South Skirmish Association, the Brigade of the American Revolution, and a French and Indian War unit of *Gens de Bois* shared his thoughts on the persona concept with me in a recent letter:

The persona trip involves learning the language, developing a credible history—where from, why here, parents—what did they do? What do you do? Why? The major mistake that many [buffs] make is to assume a persona that is based on the upper socioeconomic class. Being a poor person "ain't much fun" but most were—so try it—or shoot for "mechanik" status—be a damn good craftsman and build your own persona from that. The best living-history artist in this area [Virginia] is a cordwainer. He has studied in Europe (on a shoestring—pun intended) and has sought out *all* extant sources re shoemaking here in the states. He knows who he is, 18th-century wise, and makes a passable living at it when not demonstrating or teaching his skills.

Who *me?* Risiart ap Gruffydd (the original Welsh name).
Where from? Presteign, Radnorshire
Why here? Came as child—landed Philadelphia, 1743 (date fits age)
Why came? Parents had no work, religious difficulties, etc.
Trade? Trader / Gunsmith (can demonstrate this)
Politics, etc.—Able to discuss problems Quaker

majority in Pennsylvania causing for folks like me and the western settlers, etc.

And so it goes. Hope this has been some help.
R.H.G.[4]

In Jack Finney's fine novel *Time and Again*, his hero Si Morley is sent by a secret government project back to the New York City of the winter of 1882. Morley's purpose is to become a silent observer of the past, and he succeeds. The city he later describes to his superiors during a lengthy debriefing is riddled with political corruption, police brutality, poverty, and discomfort. Yet, he eventually decides that he prefers it to life in the 1970s. He returns and

. . . looked around the world I was in. At the gaslighted brownstones beside me. At the night-time winter sky. This, too, was an imperfect world, but—I drew a deep breath, sharply chilling my lungs—the air was still clean. The rivers flowed fresh, as they had since time began. And the first of the terrible corrupting wars lay decades ahead.[5]

And Si decides to stay forever. Fiction allowed Si an opportunity that many nostalgic buffs envy.

All serious living historians have a deep curiosity about the *texture* of life in the past. They want to know what it actually *felt* like to live, for example, on a Celtic farm and watch, as a Roman commander marched his company of foot soldiers north to man Hadrian's Wall. Were you afraid? Or were you more concerned with a sick lamb, a leaking roof, or the rain at haying time? How did your clothes feel? What did a porridge of melde taste like? What proverbs helped get you through hard times? What memories came to mind at midsummer? It's an impossible goal, of course, yet time travelers still attempt to reach it.

Every living historian I've talked to—and they number well over a thousand—harbors this fine-tuned curiosity. Some will even contend that Einstein's theory of time[6] has merit, and that we are like people in a boat drifting

Fig. C.10. Russ Leckband, potter at Living History Farms' Walnut Grove, enjoys a moment alone in his time-machine.—*Iowa Living History Farms, Des Moines, Iowa. Photograph by Mimi Dunlap*

along a winding river. Every day, we see evidence of the present, but past and future times are hidden from us around the river's bend. Still, they are there, waiting for us simply to step out of the boat and walk around the bend into the past. The problem is to figure out how to beach the boat and make our way through the undergrowth of our own "systems, both physical and cultural" (as Callahan puts it), which tie us like a spider's web to our own time. The goal is a "complete breakthrough" into the past, akin to a leap of

imagination that somehow will free us from the bonds of the present.

This dream has the characteristics of a secular mystical experience, and few living historians talk about it willingly. Yet, as you have no doubt noticed, all of the serious time travelers in this book—Hazelius, Goodwin, Tilden, Clawson, Deetz, Fortier, Lee, Babcock, Welsch, Hansen, Reynolds, Heyerdahl, Tonge, Villiers, Callahan, the de Haases, father and son, Large, Deloury, Sullivan, "Poor Devil," and Queen Carol—mention a

Fig. C.11. A housewife heats up her outdoor bake-oven at the Acadien Village, a regional folklife museum in northern New Brunswick. —*Acadien Historical Village, New Brunswick, Canada*

"moment in time" when the past seemed real.

Don Quixote would understand. Latter-day Sancho Panzas may scoff that it's an impossible dream, and most living historians would agree. But it is, nevertheless, a liberating illusion that helps them to overcome their temporal ethnocentrism and to empathize with ordinary people in the past. In a world mired in prejudice, time travel is an ethical act. An understanding, appreciation, and tolerance for our forebears may help us improve relationships with our foreign brothers and sisters in the here and now.

When I first started writing this book, my wife asked me if I had picked out a title. I replied, "How about *Into the Time Warp with History's Lunatic Fringe?*" We both laughed—nervously, for this is often the way living history is seen by outsiders. But they couldn't be more wrong. Living history is a medium of historical research, interpretation, and celebration that is absolutely right for our times. The medium has three characteristics that

Fig. C.12. Acadian women join in an *ecarderie*—a wool-carding frolic. Ethnic solidarity is an important byproduct of such work-gatherings. The staff of Acadien Village is made up of local residents, steeped in the Acadian traditions of their ancestors.—*Acadien Historical Village, New Brunswick, Canada*

will, I believe, insure its historical significance as an effective way of "doing" history.

Living history strives for what T. S. Eliot called "felt-truth." It challenges us to think *and* feel. To living historians, empathy is as important as understanding. The two most frequently asked questions at any living-history museum are "Do you live here?" and "What's it really like?" People today are not content to know just the bones of history; they want to sense its flesh and blood. Living history is the only mode of historical interpretation, research, and celebration that involves all the senses. As such, it forces us to experience the past as fully as possible. Of course, we can never be certain that the sights, sounds, tastes, textures, and smells of our re-created accounts of the past are authentic. The best we can do is to carry out our research as rigorously as possible and resist the temptation to claim too much for our time machines.

The medium is also very presbyterian. Living history lies outside the boundary of established academic and public history. It thrives on independence. Each museum, each project, and each unit makes its own covenant with historical truth and determines the way it will carry on its dialogue with the past. This form of populist democracy breeds a tough-mindedness. Living historians are more critical of themselves than are outsiders. The most damning criticism of living history by academic and public histo-

Fig. C.13. The craft of boat-building is preserved at Acadien Village in New Brunswick. Skilled ships' carpenters are valued as "keepers" of the Acadian way of life. For the people of northern New Brunswick, the village is their own folk museum.—*Acadien Historical Village, New Brunswick, Canada*

rians cannot match the hostility a serious buff will bestow on a "farb." One buff expressed this unswerving dedication to accuracy this way:

We have lived cheek-by-jowl with many, many re-creation groups. . . . Few are totally authentic; they compromise on important things and totally ignore the small. Some of this is excusable, if you know and recognize and admit that you aren't up to snuff due to cost, lack of time, etc. But willfully ignoring authenticity is a crime. In the field, such groups are known as *farbs* and are quickly dis-associated from the mainstream. Do it right, or try to do it right. It's not easy, but what is, if it's to be worthwhile?[7]

For living historians, it's not important where you went to school or what old-boy networks you belong to; the question is: do you have the right stuff?

Finally, living history rejects a linear view of the past. It argues that, before you can study the forest, you must become totally familiar with the trees. Living historians point out that the history establishment has often failed to study, interpret, and experi-ence the everyday reality of ordinary people in the past. Museums like Plimoth, experi-mental farms like Butser Hill, and dedicated buffs like the men and women of the Brigade of the American Revolution are attempting to remedy that neglect. The result is an empha-sis on new primary sources, especially mate-rial culture, and a willingness to try out novel techniques of research and interpretation. Lejre's use of imitative experiments and the Colonial Pennsylvania Plantation's attempt to interpret historiography itself are excellent examples. Living historians dart rapidly about that Bruegelesque painting of man's past, comfortably moving from one historical period to another. Their goal is not to discern a grand pattern of relationships, but to steep themselves in the historical context of a par-ticular place and time and come to under-stand, appreciate, and feel the life of the people who once lived there and then. When asked why they are attempting to communi-cate with their counterparts in the past, the living historians' quiet answer is: It's about time.

NOTES

1. Buckminster Fuller, interview with author, July 12, 1975, at the Colonial Pennsylvania Plantation.

2. See Jean Starobinski's "The Idea of Nostalgia," *Diogenes* 54 (Summer 1966): 81–103.

3. *Corpora and By-Laws* (Berkeley: Society for Creative Anachronism, 1980), p. 6.

4. R. H. Griffiths, letter to author, March 14, 1983.

5. Finney, *Time and Again*, p. 398.

6. Shallis, *On Time*, pp. 38–63.

7. R. H. Griffiths, letter to author, March 14, 1983.

Fig. C.14. Cod—the staff of life in the Maritime Provinces of Canada. Dry-curing cod is a significant craft, respected as a tangible link between the humble Acadians of yesterday and today.—*Acadien Historical Village, New Brunswick, Canada*

Appendix

Sources and Resources:
Of Each Kind, A Baker's Dozen

At least once every two weeks, I receive a telephone call or a letter from someone who has gotten involved in living history and needs direction.

"Is there a good guide, at least a bibliography?" they ask.

My answer is "Unfortunately, not just yet." Perhaps a comprehensive guide will follow this book.

In the meantime, I have included in the following appendix a selection of representative museums, organizations, books, magazines, articles, and sutlers involved with living history. There is a "baker's dozen" of each. Needless to say, the list is far from complete, but it should serve as a preliminary introduction to some of the best resources.

Entries are arranged in essentially the same way as this book: those that deal with the movement as a whole are first, followed by sources that focus on museums, experimental research, and the re-enacting of various historical periods.

Museums

Plimoth Plantation

A recreation of the Pilgrims' 1627 village, Plimoth Plantation is one of the two or three most exciting living-history museums in North America.

The enclosed village is harshly realistic; it really *looks* and *feels* medieval. The same attention to historical detail carries over to the simulated folk-life. Interpreters stay constantly in role and are believable as Pilgrims. They project an aura of spontaneity, of the sort that T. S. Eliot called "felt life." Walking into the village is akin to stepping into a historical drama. It's exhilarating.

My favorite times to visit the plantation are early spring, late fall, or on bad-weather days when the crowds are thin. For a truly absorbing ramble, the fewer other visitors there are, the better. On a slow day, you have the chance to talk at length with individual interpreters or poke around in the village's odd nooks and crannies. Special events such as weddings and Harvest Home are crowded, but worthwhile. A visit takes at least a day, especially if you tour the *Mayflower* and spend time in the museum's excellent store.

For information, write to Plimoth Plantation, P.O. Box 1620, Plymouth, Massachusetts 02061.

Fortress of Louisbourg

Awesome in scale, the Fortress of Louisbourg lies isolated at the end of Nova Scotia's beautiful Cape Breton Island. It's well worth the trip, especially if you are planning a Canadian maritime vacation.

Focusing on the year 1744, interpretation at Louisbourg varies from third-person animation to excellent static exhibits that tell the story of the site's restoration. The number and variety of the interpretive staff is daunting—the fortress was, after all, a small city, made up of soldiers, sailors, fishermen, merchants, and craftsmen of all sorts. You could spend a day just looking at all the different types of clothing.

Although the museum provides adequate orientation by means of a "time tunnel," Louisbourg has four excellent books and numerous brochures that, if read beforehand, would enrich a visit. Inside the fortress, canteens provide historically accurate eighteenth-century French food.

The serious living-history junkie should plan to spend at lease a couple of days at Louisbourg. The Feast of St. Louis, celebrated on August 25, is the highlight of the year and a great time to visit. However, biweekly candlelight tours during July and August are also superb ways to experience "a moment in time."

For information, write to Fortress of Louisbourg National Historic Park, Box 160, Louisbourg, Nova Scotia, Canada B0A 1M0.

Colonial Williamsburg

A pioneer in the field of living history, Colonial Williamsburg has been simulating life in the late eighteenth century for more then fifty years. Millions of Americans are familiar with the "old" colonial capital of Virginia: as dignified, courteous, and properly attired as a Southern gentleman.

There has been a change. The "new" Williamsburg is populated with women, blacks, workers, and other ordinary folk. The interpretive program is determined to communicate the city's social history.

Many of the museum's 550 costumed staff employ first-person interpretation in innovative and effective ways. Actors roam the streets, servants show visitors through the Governor's Palace; and in 1984, the first insane asylum in the United States, the Publick Hospital of 1773, will re-open.

In addition, the museum offers some of the finest crafts demonstrations in the nation, as well as lantern tours, concerts, plays, military tattoos, and a variety of seminars. You could spend months in Williamsburg and not experience all its programs. Off season, especially winter, is a good time to visit. The pace is slower and the crowds thinner.

For information, write to Colonial Williamsburg, P.O. Box C, Williamsburg, Virginia 23187.

Old Sturbridge Village

Situated in the hills of central Massachusetts, Old Sturbridge Village recreates the regional folklife of inland New England on the eve of the industrial revolution and the nineteenth century—a time when the atmosphere is no longer colonial; the United States is fiercely independent and beginning to look inward as it shapes its culture.

In addition to a complete traditional village, the museum also operates one of the finest living historical farms. Both are intensely rural and are wrapped in an aura of realistic nostalgia.

Sturbridge is one of the few living museums where the interpreters really look as if they had stepped out of a painting by an itinerant folk artist. Interpretation is generally in third person, but special events such as the town meeting often use role-playing.

This is a great place to get away from the late twentieth century and back to a cultural landscape that melds forest and field, meadow and green. A winter weekend is perfect.

For information, write to Old Sturbridge Village, Route 20, Sturbridge, Massachusetts 01566.

Old Fort William

In 1816, Old Fort William was the Grand Central Station of the Great North Woods. As headquarters of the North West Company, the fort was the center of a vast trading empire stretching from Montreal to the Pacific.

The company was the historical prototype of today's international conglomerates. Its fort was a microcosm of Canada: a miniature city in the wilderness, populated by French *voyageurs*, Ojibwa Indians, and Anglo-Scottish merchants.

Comparable to Louisbourg in scope, the fort contains more than forty buildings within its towering palisades and teems with entrepreneurial activity. There are carpenters, blacksmiths, armorers, tailors, and coopers at work; and in a huge canoe shed, thirty-six-foot Montreal freight canoes are being built of birch bark. The kitchens smell of bread, the tavern of wine. Shops are stocked with trade goods from Europe, and sheds are piled high with bundles of fur.

Animation is provided by almost a hundred and fifty interpreters, who use a variety of living-history modes, including very effective role-playing.

One day at the fort is not long enough: the site and the subject it interprets are too grand. Situated on the scenic north shore of Lake Superior, the fort is best visited as part of a cool summer vacation in western Ontario.

For information, write to Old Fort William, Vickers Heights P.O., Thunder Bay, Ontario, Canada P0T 2Z0.

Conner Prairie Pioneer Settlement

Situated on the northern outskirts of Indianapolis, Indiana, Conner Prairie Pioneer Settlement recreates life in an 1836 "first generation" frontier village. Its buildings and inhabitants are a heady mixture of immigrants from New England, the Hudson River Valley, Kentucky, and the eastern Midwest.

The community is a small town in the rough. Interpreters use first-person, a technique that was pioneered by Conner Prairie in the early 1970s. The orientation of visitors in the settlement's primitive schoolhouse has attained the status of a classic.

The museum contains more than thirty very different examples of original vernacular architecture on two hundred and forty acres. The atmosphere is realistic and contrasts nicely with the earlier, more eastern Old Sturbridge Village.

My favorite annual events are the re-enacted camp meeting and the 1836 election rallies. Both communicate the vigor of early American frontier religion and politics. Conner Prairie has its own blackpowder militia. They provide the fireworks on the museum's Fourth of July.

For information, write to Conner Prairie Pioneer Settlement, 13400 Allisonville Road, Noblesville, Indiana 46060.

The Homeplace 1850

Operated by the Tennessee Valley Authority, in its extensive recreation area Land Between the Lakes, the Homeplace is a representative family farm typical of western Kentucky and Tennessee just before the Civil War. As such, it is one of the few living-history museums portraying the folklife of the Upper South.

The Farm has sixteen structures, mostly log, and includes a superb "dogtrot" house and tobacco barn. Its setting is isolated from all modern intrusions, and the atmosphere is realistic. The Homeplace has the texture of an early daguerreotype.

Activities vary with the season. My favorites are the summer's-eve play party and the husking bee in late autumn. Besides farming and going about their daily 1850s lives, the staff also takes time out to celebrate a wedding and the visit of neighbors for a gospel sing.

Interpretation is basically third-person, and the staff is made up of a delightful mixture of older local residents and student interns. The orientation slide-show in a nearby earth-covered visitors' center is excellent.

Land Between the Lakes abounds in camp sites. A family weekend vacation with a day at The Homeplace is an ideal way to renew an acquaintance with history and nature. The Homeplace is a good example of the new generation of small living-history sites.

For information, write to Land Between the Lakes, TVA, Golden Pond, Kentucky 42231.

Washburn Norlands

Similar to TVA's The Homeplace, Norlands is also a small, successful living historical farm. It interprets Maine folklife during the 1870s, a period of peace and prosperity in inland New England.

The subject of an extensive article in the June 1983 *History News*, Norlands features a unique adult live-in program. Begun in 1977, the program is held on ten week-ends each year. Fifteen adults adopt the persona of two families and a collection of villagers—schoolteachers, preacher, blacksmith, pauper, widow, and so on. Billie Gammon, the program's director, notes that people today want to "experience another period in time." They see Norlands as a "'Fantasy Island,' a respite from the pressures of the 1980s." She cautions that the adult live-in is no vacation, or nostalgic trip to Grandma's. Rather, it is a voyage to a good but hard land in a fascinating period of history. The museum has, in addition to the adult live-ins, programs for children and student internships. It also welcomes summer visitors.

For information, write to Norlands, RFD #2, Box 3395 % Billie Gammon, Livermore Falls, Maine 04254.

Georgia Agrirama

The Georgia Agrirama depicts rural society in the southern "Pinebelt" region during the late nineteenth century. The open-air museum contains an 1870s subsistence herding farm, an 1890s progressive farm, and a small railroad town.

Activities include cane-grinding, sheep-shearing, log-rolling, and "frolics." The frolics feature traditional dancing, games, feasting, and storytelling.

Interpreters use third-person and encourage visitor participation, especially during the agrirama's county fair and Christmas celebrations. As is the case in other living-history museums, the agrirama's staff has carried out an extensive research program with the goal of establishing a solid historical base for its simulation of the material culture and traditional folklife of the region.

The museum's location is fortuitous—just off a north-south interstate highway. It is a good place to stop on the way to Florida, especially during the winter. A summer visit is worthwhile, if only to experience the good Deep-South heat. It helps you appreciate Faulkner.

For information, write to Georgia Agrirama, P.O. Box Q, Tifton, Georgia 31793.

Living History Farms

Situated on a six-hundred-acre site just west of Des Moines, Iowa, Living History Farms interpret the story of farmers and farming in the Midwest in five particular periods: 1700, the 1840s, the 1870s, 1900, and the near future. Each period except the first, which recreates an Ioway Indian lodge and farm, has several operating living-history components. The 1840s site, for example, has both a pioneer farm and a small general store. The 1870s area contains a town and a large progressive farm. The 1900 farm is one of the three best living historical farms in the nation; and the futuristic complex demonstrates conservation farming and energy-efficient technology.

Interpreters use third-person and help visitors adjust to the rapid time-traveling that a visit requires.

Special events occur every other weekend and range from plowing and corn-picking matches to generic seasonal festivals, such as "Old-Fashioned Fourth of July," Fall Harvest Days, homemade pie social, etc.

A visit to the farms is a trip into the heart of a region that just happens to be at the center of America's heartland. It is a piognant experience. Especially moving is the rural church that marks the site of Pope John Paul's pilgrimage to rural America in October 1979.

For information, write to Living History Farms, 2600 111th Street, Des Moines, Iowa 50322.

Village Historique Acadien

Situated on the northeast coast of New Brunswick, the Village Historique Acadien is a superb open-air museum on the Skansen model. From the Acadian tricolour at the entrance, to the French-speaking interpreters, the village proclaims its mission as *the* museum of Acadian culture.

For an American, it is a stimulating foreign place, filled with the unexpected. For example, farmers are skilled in marshland irrigation agriculture, fishermen still hand-process cod, housewives bake crusty Canadian loaves in outdoor ovens, and the French-speaking children scamper about in wooden clogs. The orientation exhibit features a moving sound-and-light show in the French style, and the museum's restaurant offers excellent local dishes.

The village quickly reveals its major theme: the function of traditional regional culture in a modern post-industrial nation. It is a contemporary, highly political message that the village's primarily French-Canadian audience deemed relevant. Only a few American museums seem willing to address this issue. Living History Farms is a good example. Village Historique Acadien is another.

For information, write to Acadian Historical Village, CP 820, Caraquet, New Brunswick, Canada E0B 1K0.

Kings Landing Historical Settlement

After the American Revolution, ten thousand British Loyalists fled the United States and settled along the St. John River valley in central New Brunswick, Canada. Over the next century, these political refugees developed a unique regional culture that remains, in substance and style, interestingly British-colonial. Kings Landing celebrates that culture in a beautifully situated folk park along the St. John River, just above Fredericton, the provincial capital.

The landscape is simply breathtaking; picture-postcard views open up wherever you walk. Many of the buildings, such as the water-powered sawmill and Quebec-style barns, are massive. Animators using generally third-person interpretation are drawn from the local area and project a deep attachment to their land and heritage.

Kings Landing contrasts interestingly with Old Sturbridge Village, its closest counterpart in scope and period of interpretation. Both are immensely relaxing places to visit. My favorite activities at the landing were a harvest service at St. Mark's Anglican Chapel-of-Ease, a pint of bitter at the Kings Head Inn, and an enjoyable summer's evening spent listening to dramatic readings of local writers. All *very* English.

For more information, write to Kings Landing Historical Settlement, P.O. Box 522, Fredericton, New Brunswick, Canada E3B 5A6.

Old-World Wisconsin

Located in a state forest just west of Milwaukee, Old-World Wisconsin is similar in purpose and scope to the New Brunswick museums. It interprets the immigrant experience in Wisconsin from 1845 to 1915, by means of a series of living-history farms and an 1870 village.

As might be expected, many of the ethnic enclaves there are from northern Europe, with an emphasis on the Scandinavian countries. It's possible to trace the history of Norwegian Americans as reflected through their farmsteads, for example, since the museum has moved in examples of Norwegian buildings and artifacts from key historical periods. The same is true of a number of other ethnic groups: German, Swedish, Danish, Finnish, and—most recently—New England Yankee.

The museum's interpreters use third-person and are generally engaged in traditional farming or crafts activities.

But it is the architecture that really sets the museum apart. A tremendous effort was made to move in stellar examples of European vernacular traditions, and it shows. You could spend a good week just comparing different architectual and decorative arts traditions.

A good time to visit the museum is June, for the Scandinavian Midsummer Celebration, or on winter weekends when the cross-country skiing trails open. In the best European tradition, the museum also has an excellent restaurant based in a magnificent 1897 octagonal barn. Old-World Wisconsin is the closest thing to Skansen in the United States.

For information, write to Old-World Wisconsin, Rt. 2, Box 18, Eagle, Wisconsin 53119.

Books

Shallis, Michael. *On Time.* New York: Shocken Books, 1983.

Shallis was a film director until 1970, when he began to study physics. In 1978, he received his doctorate in astrophysics from Oxford, where he now teaches. Shallis's book is an investigation into the scientific knowledge and human experience of time. The book's success derives from Shallis's ability to interpret current theories of time to the educated layman, often by helping the reader to visualize the subject through the use of metaphors. This learning experience is not easy, for our "commonsense" concept of time as objective, linear, and simple is an ethnocentric one, rooted in our culture and sense of history. Nevertheless, transcending our dated ideas and experience of time can be exhilarating, akin to looking back to earth from outer space.

Finney, Jack. *Time and Again.* New York: Simon and Schuster, 1970.

Considered one of the five best mysteries ever written, *Time and Again* brings H. G. Wells's *Time Machines* up to date. Finney's hero, Si Morley, travels back to the New York City of 1882 on a secret government project. Not only does Finney explain the feasibility of this time travel, he also brings alive the historical culture of New York by the brilliant device of having Si depict it in words *and* pictures. In fact, Finney calls his book an "illustrated novel." The result is a near-total suspension of the reader's normal disbelief in time travel. Finney captures the good feelings that come with a successful simulation of life in another time.

Fortier, John. *Fortress of Louisbourg.* With color photographs by Owen Fitzgerald. Toronto: Oxford University Press, 1979.

Co-winner of the American Association for State and Local History's Award of Merit, *Fortress of Louisbourg* looks like a coffeetable book, but it far transcends that genre. Fitzgerald's fifty-eight photographs capture the color and texture of life in the fortress during the mid-1740s. But it is John Fortier's text that sets the book apart. The former director discusses in an engrossing style the site's history, restoration, and interpretation. Fortier's text, essentially an essay, is one of the most persuasive arguments for living history to date.

Coles, John. *Experimental Archaeology.* New York: Academic Press, a subsidiary of Harcourt, Brace, Jovanovich, 1979.
John Coles is the foremost historian of the field of experimental archaeology. A reader in European Pre-history at the University of Cambridge, his *Archaeology by Experiment* (London: Hutchinson, 1973) codified the methodology for valid experimentation. *Experimental Archaeology* is essentially a critical history, in which Coles describes hundreds of successful experiments in chapters that focus on voyages, subsistence, settlement, arts and crafts, and, finally, daily life and death. Well illustrated and documented, Coles's book is definitive. Although it could easily stand as a reference, Cole's prose is free of technical jargon and is crafted like a novel. *Experimental Archaeology* is, as they say in England, *a good read.*

Heyerdahl, Thor. *Kon-Tiki.* Chicago: Rand-McNally and Company, 1950.

Heyerdahl's account of his 4,300-mile crossing of the eastern Pacific on a raft is a classic. Although few archaeologists accept his thesis today, Heyerdahl nevertheless is recognized as an innovative scholar, a pioneer in the field of experimental archaeology, and a courageous and ethical man. *Kon-Tiki* was a bestseller throughout the world and a re-reading of it reminds you why: Heyerdahl is a gifted storyteller whose style at once captures the reader's imagination. The seventh person on the raft with Heyerdahl and his five companions is the reader.

Severin, Tim. *The Brendan Voyage.* London: Hutchinson and Company, Ltd., 1978. (Arrow paperback edition, 1979).

A geographer and medieval scholar educated at Oxford and Harvard, Tim Severin built a large leather curragh and sailed it from Ireland to Newfoundland in 1976–1977. He sought to retrace the fifth-century voyage of Saint Brendan. Severin's account of the recreation of the curragh and the harrowing voyage across the North Atlantic in it is reminiscent of *Kon-Tiki*—exciting, yet modest, well written and carefully considered. In addition to the narrative, Severin, an experienced sailor, provides a scholarly appendix on the design, manufacture, and performance of his craft.

Finney, Ben. *Hokule'a.* New York: Dodd, Mead and Company, 1979.

Finney, a Harvard-educated professor of anthropology at the University of Hawaii, in 1976 sailed a reconstruction of an ancient double-hulled Polynesian canoe from Hawaii to Tahiti and back—six thousand miles in all. The voyage proved without doubt that Polynesians could have deliberately sailed throughout the Pacific, transplanting their culture to its many archipelagoes. *Hokule'a* is a record of Finney's voyage and the effect the trip had on modern Hawaii and native Hawaiians. The book is a case study in experimental and applied anthropolgy. Although Finney's theory of Pacific migrations contradicts Heyerdahl's, *Hokule'a*, like *Kon-Tiki*, is a thought-provoking, exciting book.

Reynolds, Peter. *Iron-Age Farm.* London: British Museum Publications, Ltd., 1979.

The only published study of an experimental farm, Reynolds's volume is a remarkable report that draws the serious reader into the everyday life of Iron-Age England by a careful re-examination of the ordinary farmer's home, outbuildings, livestock, crops, crafts, food, and seasonal work patterns. Reynolds's portrait is based on data generated by Butser Ancient Farm Research Project, one of the most complex experimental archaeological programs to date. Reynolds writes for both scholar and layman, in the clear-headed prose that characterizes the best British interpretations of modern science.

Klinger, Robert, and Richard Wilder. *Sketchbook '76.* 1967. Reprint. Union City, Tennessee: Pioneer Press, 1974.

This modest fifty-three-page book was a first. Originally published privately in 1967, *Sketchbook '76* provided Revolutionary War period re-enactors and interpreters with sketches, notes, and patterns of historically accurate uniforms and equipment originally used by the American foot soldier, between 1775 and 1781. Klinger and Wilder based the examples used in their book on original artifacts, thereby establishing a model for authenticity that was followed by thousands of living-history buffs during the Bicentennial years. *Sketchbook '76* was quickly followed by several dozen other similar guides to the material culture of particular periods. Klinger and Wilder helped "professionalize" the field of living history.

The Book of Buckskinning. Edited by William Scurlock. Texarkana, Texas: Rebel Publishing Company, 1981.

Muzzleloader Magazine's editor, Oran Scurlock, Jr., asked ten experienced buckskinners to write essays on the basic components of their "sport." The result was a unique compendium containing articles on philosophy, getting started, rendezvous and shoots, guns, clothing, accoutrements and equipment, skills, crafts, the lodge, and women's activities. Scurlock's book is essentially a collection of sketchbooks. His choice of contributors was informed; each was knowledgeable and articulate. The result is a highly useful manual for "pilgrims" on the road to becoming accomplished buckskinners, as well as an invaluable primary source for historians of the living-history movement.

Grissom, Ken. *Buckskins and Black Powder.* Piscataway, New Jersey: Winchester Press, 1983.

Outdoor writer for the *Houston Post,* Ken Grissom is a highly regarded buckskinner. He calls his book a "mountain man's guide to muzzleloading." Without question, *Buckskins and Black Powder* is the model for future living-history guides. Comprehensive, well written, and beautifully illustrated with several hundred photos and line drawings, Grissom's volume sets the standard for the field. Grissom takes his subject seriously and examines buckskinning in the context of contemporary American popular culture. He also speaks with the authority of an insider, in an informal, yet informed, style. In his preface, Grissom acknowledges that there is probably "no way to duplicate, in the twentieth century, the experience of having to shift for yourself a thousand miles deep in a vast wilderness . . . yet, if a man has the sense to yearn for a simpler and more natural life— never mind that it's unattainable—I say his heart is good." *Buckskins and Black Powder* gently helps the pilgrim on his way.

Loeb, Robert, Jr. *Meet the Real Pilgrims.* Garden City, New York: Doubleday and Company, 1979.

Working closely with the staff of Plimoth Plantation, Robert Loeb has written for youth an excellent introduction to the everyday life of Plimoth Plantation in 1627. The book takes the form of a tour, led by Loeb, in which the reader meets a selection of Pilgrims, all very earthy, and all speaking a colloquial Elizabethan English. The device is effective. Events that heretofore were legends become human, involving *real* people with work that needs to be done, stories they want to tell, and a village they want you to see before you return to your modern world. A series of inviting photographs helps the reader visualize this brave new world. Loeb followed up this volume with a similar one, *New England Village,* which was chosen as a Notable Children's Trade Book by the National Council for the Social Studies.

Bond, Nancy. *The Best of Enemies.* New York: Atheneum, 1978.

Also for youth *The Best of Enemies* is set in Concord, Massachusetts, during the Bicentennial. The plot is intriguing; a teen-ager, Charlotte Paige, finds herself involved in an explosive confrontation between American re-enactors, for whom living history is recreation, and an odd assortment of British troops, who seem bent on refighting the Revolutionary War. The result is a highly original mystery that interestingly deals with one of living history's primary themes—the line between fantasy and reality. Bond won the Newberry Honor Award for her earlier *A String in the Harp,* a book that also explores the theme of time travel.

Articles

Becker, Carl. "Every Man His Own Historian." In *Every Man His Own Historian.* New York: F. S. Crofts, 1935.

Carl Becker, in his Presidential Address to the American Historical Society in December 1931, coined the term *living history.* Becker argues that the "essence of history is the memory of things said and done," and that it is therefore obvious that "every normal person, Mr. Everyman, knows some history." Each individual and each generation imaginatively creates its own "living history, the ideal series of events that we affirm and hold in memory, since it is so intimately associated with what we are doing and with what we hope to do." Today, the living-history movement uses the term *living history* as a noun that refers to a particular mode of imaginatively creating history, whereas Becker uses *living* more as an adjective to describe the vitality of the historical instinct. Both uses of the term, Becker would have been the first to admit, are valid.

Lowenthal, David. "The American Way of History." In *Columbia University Forum,* vol. 9. New York: Columbia University Press, 1966.

A professor of geography at University College, London, Lowenthal was one of the first scholars to examine critically the American way of "imaginatively creating" history. In this article, he challenges Americans with the observation that "what is old is looked at as special, 'historic,' different. Not wanting to be

different, Americans anathematize the past. In the process, they become conscious of antiquity as a separate realm. And as the past was cut away from the present, history emerged as an isolated object of reverence and pleasure. For all its deliberate relevance, History Land remains detached, remote, and essentially lifeless."

Deetz, James. "The Reality of the Pilgrim Fathers." *Natural History* 57:6 (November 1969).

Director of research at Plimoth Plantation, archaeologist James Deetz contends that "A step into the time capsule of re-created Plimoth evokes a living community of Pilgrims—its smoky odors, animal noises, and household clutter—and dispels our misconceptions about colony life." His article then goes on to describe the research base and mode of interpretation that make Plimoth Plantation a valid and powerful experiment in presenting history to the general public.

"History Lives." *Museum News* 53:3 (November 1974).

With this issue of the journal of the American Association of Museums, living history becomes respectable as a mode of interpretation. In a series of articles by William T. Alderson ("Answering the Challenge"), Peter Cook ("The Craft of Demonstration"), Robert Ronsheim ("Is the Past Dead?"), and Holly Sidford ("Stepping into History"), *Museum News* presented the strengths and weaknesses of living history. Ronsheim's cautionary essay was especially prophetic in a Bicentennial Era that saw living history becoming a bowdlerized fad.

Kelsey, Darwin. "Harvests of History." *Historic Preservation* 28 (1976).

Kelsey, a cultural geographer and director of museum administration at Old Sturbridge Village, argues that the living historical farm is a new hybrid variety of historic site that seeks to preserve material and nonmaterial culture in context and in process. The simulated environments of LHFs are not only unique institutions for preserving cultural intangibles, they are also effective experimental laboratories for teaching subjects previous scholars had written off as "best left to the imagination." Living historical farms provide, Kelsey argues, "in addition to strict intellection and cognition, experimental modes of knowing—knowing through sight, sound, smell, touch, taste."

Hawes, Edward. "The Living Historical Farm in North America: New Directions in Research and Interpretation." *ANNUAL* of the Association for Living Historical Farms and Agricultural Museums II (1976).

A professor of history at Sangamon State University in Springfield, Illinois, Hawes wrote the first lengthy academic analysis of the living historical farm. His audience was the international open-air museum community, and this paper was later delivered at a congress of agricultural museum officials held in Prague. In it, Hawes examines the history and theory underlying LHFs and discusses their research, educational, interpretive, and preservation functions. He examines the problems LHFs are facing and predicts the directions they may take in the future.

Anderson, Jay. "Immaterial Material Culture: The Implication of Experimental Research for Folklife Museums." *Keystone Folklore* 21 (1976–77). Reprinted in *Material Culture Studies in America*, edited by Thomas J. Schlereth. Nashville: The American Association for State and Local History, 1982.

The author, who was then chief of research and interpretation at Living History Farms in Des Moines, Iowa, suggests that experimental archaeology as practiced at Butser Hill and Lejre might be utilized by living-history museums. He argues that, in addition to "correcting our perception of the past, experimental archaeology can also teach us much about contemporary postindustrial cultural behavior and the mental and physical distance we have put between our forefathers and ourselves." Museums such as Plimoth Plantation and the Colonial Pennsylvania

Plantation are not only "repositories for the material culture of the past, but also catalysts for questioning one's own culture . . . they have the potential to become powerful mediums for encouraging in visitors the habit of disciplined self-analysis."

Fortier, John. "Thoughts on the Re-creation and Interpretation of Historical Environments." *Schedule and Papers,* the Third International Congress of Maritime Museums. Mystic Seaport, Connecticut, 1978.

Drawing on his experience as superintendent of the Fortress of Louisbourg, John Fortier presents a clearly reasoned, delightfully expressed essay on the potential of living history as a "personal approach to understanding the past." He introduces the concept of role-playing: "If the goal of a museum village is to recreate a real place, it follows that the lives of the original people, as well as the landscapes and furnishings they knew, are relevant and deserve to be recalled." But Fortier also counts the costs and cites Louisbourg as a case study in what and what not to do when undertaking a serious living history program. "Historical reality," he notes, is "elusive and momentary. It may exist in its ideal form only for as long as the swing of a door, or the moment it takes for a costumed figure to disappear around a street corner. Yet that moment can bring a sense of timelessness, a realization of the humanity we share with our ancestors, that will not be like anything else you can experience."

Elder, Betty Doak. "Behind the Scenes at Living History Farms." *History News* 34:12 (December 1979).

This entire issue of *History News* was devoted to Elder's story of what happened when Pope John Paul II visited 340,000 people at Living History Farms, October 4, 1979. According to Jerry George, director of AASLH, Betty got two stories: "One was the story I sent her for, about what happens to a museum staff and facility when suddenly hundreds of thousands of people are descending on it for such an unprecedented event as a Pope's presence.

But also, there's the story she saw when she got there, about how the visit brought out what such a museum and the historical experience it presents can mean for the human spirit." For many, that Thursday in October was one of living history's finest and most publicized hours. Elder's piece captures the excitement and the inner meaning of that day.

Carson, Cary. "Living Museums of Everyman's History." *Harvard Magazine* (Summer 1981).

Carson, director of research for Colonial Williamsburg, sees living museums as a way of taking "history directly to the people." And the "history" Carson means is the "new social history" that champions as significant the everyday lives of ordinary people. He argues that, as living museums, "collections of ordinary, everyday activities re-created the basic life experiences that serve as focal points for the new social history—birth, education, work, marriage, diet, disease, and the provision of clothing, housing, and material possessions." Carson concludes that "Like it or not, museums are forums, not attics. Their visitors' enthusiasm for thoughtful history has gone far to assuage the misgivings of attic-loving professionals."

Deetz, James. "The Link from Object to Person to Concept." *Museums, Adults, and the Humanities.* Washington, D.C.: The American Association for Museums, 1981.

In this short article, Deetz relates living history to contemporary anthropological theory in much the same way that Carson connects it with the new social history. Deetz notes that living-history museums have the potential to interpret not only material culture, but culture itself, the concepts underlying the objects. Visitors to such museums might be viewed as "anthropological fieldworkers going in to experience a community and elicit from it what they could." Museum interpreters then become "informants" who could share an insider's view of past cultures. Plimoth Plantation's experience at the frontier of interpreting history was one that other sites could usefully emulate.

Leone, Mark. "The Relationship between Artifacts and the Public in Outdoor History Museums." *Annals,* New York Academy of Science. 1981.

Mark Leone, an archaeologist at the University of Maryland who often applies Marxist interpretation to contemporary museums, visited Shakertown at Pleasant Hill, Kentucky, and used the experience to suggest that our history museums could be evaluated as complex artifacts that promote a particular ideology. "For instead of being warehouses of artifacts needing further analysis or as neutral masses of potential information, such museum presentations can be seen as fully operating parts of modern American culture . . . (museums) can be a clue to the ideological part of our own society, in this case our conception and use of the past and its relationship to the present."

Anderson, Jay. "Living History: Simulating Everyday Life in Living Museums." *American Quarterly* 34 (Fall 1982).

This is the first published article that treats all aspects of living history, "an attempt to simulate life in another time," as a unity. The author suggests three primary motivations for simulating history: interpretation, research, and serious play. Numerous examples are given for each branch of the living-history movement, which he feels has a potential role to play in American culture and its history.

Magazines and Journals

Living History Magazine

This new magazine is the only one that addresses the entire world of living history and seeks as its audience all serious living-history reenactors and interpreters. The magazine is a heavily illustrated glossy quarterly, runs more than fifty pages, and costs ten dollars a year.

Write to *Living History,* Circulation, P.O. Box 2309, Reston, Virginia 22090.

Its premiere issue, Summer 1983, contained six

articles of about two thousand words each and dealt with the 1981 bicentennial of the siege of Yorktown, programs aboard the U.S. *Constellation* in Baltimore, a National Park Service weekend in Fort McHenry in 1861, and reports on the re-enactment of Saylor's Creek, the last major battle of the Civil War, and the fifth annual "Great War Recreation" in Pennsylvania. In addition, the magazine includes book reviews, a calendar of events such as Plimoth Plantation's 1621 Harvest Home and the fortieth anniversary of the D-Day landings, notes on equipage and clothing, profiles of model units, and interviews with leaders in the living-history field.

Living Historical Farms Bulletin

The *Living Historical Farms Bulletin* runs about sixteen pages, appears every other month, and is published by the Association for Living Historical Farms and Agricultural Museums. A subscription costs eight dollars a year.

Write to ALHFAM, Smithsonian Institution, Washington, D.C. 20560.

Now in its fourteenth year, the bulletin contains "ALHFAMIANA," information about regional living-history workshops, seminars, and conferences, descriptions of new living museums, programs, and organizations, book reviews and thumbnail sketches of new publications. The bulletin's focus is primarily on outdoor museums and its audience of professional interpreters.

Tournaments Illuminated

Published quarterly by the Society for Creative Anachronism, *TI* runs to more than forty pages and costs twenty dollars per year.

Write to S.C.A., Office of the Registry, P.O. Box 743, Milpitas, California 95035.

Seventy numbers of *TI* have appeared since 1965. Generally, issues include about twenty short articles of about 1,500 words. Their range is fascinating. Recently, articles have examined the brewing of sake, manufacture of safe combat arrows, a discussion of the actual duration of the Middle Ages, sigillographica or the craft of seals, dancing Christmas carols, and books for children. *TI* contains much artwork, especially schematic drawings and cartoons, many of which are really humorous to seasoned knights and ladies.

Muzzle Blasts

One of the oldest of the magazines dealing with living history, *Muzzle Blasts* has been published by the National Muzzle Loading Rifle Association since 1939. It is a monthly, runs about seventy pages, and costs sixteen dollars a year.

Write to NMLRA, P.O. Box 67, Friendship, Indiana 47021.

MB is heavy on advertisement, often with several hundred per issue and annoucements from clubs throughout the nation. The magazine is a no-nonsense publication of obvious value to the serious individual interested in black powder rifles, and many subscribers are also living-history buffs.

Black Powder Report

Formerly the *Buckskin Report*, BPR is a sixty-page monthly, published "by buckskinners for buckskinners." Its editor, John D. Baird, is also a founder of the National Association of Primitive Riflemen, at whom *BPR* is aimed.

Write to 220 McLeod Street, P.O. Box 789, Big Timber, Montana 59011. Subscriptions are eighteen dollars a year.

Normally, *BPR*'s twenty features are devoted to living-history subjects such as pemmican, buckskin clothing, winter camping, the problems of authenticity, and—of course—muzzle-loaders. NAPR's rendezvous are announced and reviewed regularly, as are books on the fur trade period. *BPR* is in its twelfth year of publication and is recognized for the high standards set by its editors.

Muzzleloader

Similar to *Black Powder Report*, but with a more eastern focus, is *Muzzleloader*. Published since 1971 by Oran Scurlock, *Muzzleloader* is a seventy-page bimonthly that features a high proportion of articles with a historical bent, such as "Plains Indian Art of the Fur Trade Era," "Germanic Flintlock Rifles," and "Fort Niagara Falls Again." Subscriptions are nine dollars and fifty cents a year.

Write to Rebel Publishing Company, Route 5, Box 747-M, Texarkana, Texas 75503.

A regular feature for women by Shari Wannemacher indicates *Muzzleloader*'s interest in attracting the family trade.

Blackpowder Annual

The *Blackpowder Annual* is published by Dixie Gun Works of Union City, Tennessee, one of the oldest of the living-history sutlers. *BA* runs more than a hundred glossy pages and contains a mixture of twenty articles reflecting the varied interests of black-powder advocates. The second— 1984—issue included features on "Survival of a Revival: The NMLRA's First 50 Years," "Time-Tripping into the Eighteenth Century," "Blackpowder Turkey Tactics," and "In Search of Beaver Tail Stew."

BA costs two dollars and fifty cents and is available from Pioneer Press, P.O. Box 684, Union City, Tennessee 38261, or at newsstands, in autumn.

Its editor, Sharon Cunningham, notes her readers' preference for features on black powder hunting and historical and nostalgia pieces. *BA* clearly reflects those interests.

F & I War

Published by the 18th-Century Society, *F&I* emphasizes the 1750–1763 period, but contains articles on the pre-Revolutionary and Revolutionary War periods (1764–1783), as well. Edited by Ray Washlaski, an experienced re-enactor, *F&I* is a heavily illustrated quarterly, costing ten dollars per year.

Write to 18th-Century Society, Box 264, RD 1, New Alexandria, Pennsylvania 15670.

The magazine runs about seventy pages and generally features eight articles, all focusing on living-history concerns. Recent articles examined the problems of establishing authentic camps, an experimental winter campaign on snowshoes, a report on the Fort de Chartres Rendezvous, and blanket-style leggings. *F&I* can be described as a "pure" living-history magazine, of interest primarily to the very serious buff. It's in its third year.

The Courier

This modest newsletter is the official publication of the North West Territory Alliance. I've included it among the longer, more prodigious glossies because *The Courier* ably represents a score of similar less expensive, more focused publications. It appears ten times a year and costs just four dollars.

Write to *The Courier*, 380 Hawthorn, Glen Ellen, Illinois 60137.

Now in its eighth year, *The Courier* contains not only announcements of upcoming events, but specific features on subjects such as correct bagpipe tunes for the NWTA's period, dueling etiquette, and advice to the novice on how to handle criticism of one's uniform. *The Courier's* tone is informal and ripe with humor.

The American Star

The American Star, published by the Society of Mexican War Historians, is similar to *The Courier*. Tightly focused on the 1830–1849 period, *AS* is a bimonthly, runs about sixteen pages, and contains articles on subjects such as military insignia of the 1840s, infantry uniforms and equipment of the Mexican War, and reviews of books and even articles in other journals. Edited by Kevin Young, an example of the new breed of living-history interpreter ("I haven't fired a shot in mock anger for four years"), *AS* costs twelve dollars a year.

Write to *The American Star*, P.O. Box 1837, San Antonio, Texas 78296.

Scores of similar publications dot the living-history landscape. *AS* is a good example of one that is clearly devoted to high standards of authenticity.

Camp Chase Gazette

One of the oldest magazines published solely for Civil War buffs, *CCG* is edited by William Keitz, who began the *Gazette* in 1972 in an effort to improve interpretation of the Civil War period. The *Gazette* runs about thirty-six pages, is published monthly, and costs fifteen dollars a year.

Write Camp Chase Publishing, 3984 Cinn-Zanesville Road N.E., Lancaster, Ohio 43130.

CCG generally presents five features. A recent representative issue contained a Civil War diary, a Christmas letter from the front, instructions for making an authentic confederate oilcloth, and some thoughts on "the past campaign year" and the difficulty of truly "reliving history." *CCG* also contains detailed announcements of upcoming campaigns, critiques of specific events, and an excellent letter section called "Camp Gossip."

The Post Dispatch

Neal and Laura Blair, its editors, call *The Post Dispatch* the "Magazine of American Living History, 1860–1900."

A bimonthly costing ten dollars per year, it is available from *The Post Dispatch*, 310 West College Drive, Cheyenne, Wyoming 82007.

First published in 1979, *PD* is primarily concerned with the "living history, soldier, civilian and lady of the frontier west." Nobly, the *PD* has included a substantive number of articles on the folklife of the Native American, the civilian, and on women. It is well illustrated, runs about thirty-six pages, and provides a mixture of historical features, such as specifications for an 1878 Army bunk and advertisements for tours of Indian War sites. Recently, *PD* featured a series of articles on living history in Australia.

The Point

First published in 1974, *The Point* is a bimonthly magazine of the World War II Historical Re-enactment Society. About thirty pages long, *The Point* costs twelve dollars per year.

Write *The Point*, 3448 Tedmar Avenue, St. Louis, Missouri 63139.

Each issue is made up entirely of reports from individual units and advertisements submitted by members and World War II surplus suppliers. In addition, there are informal features by members on such topics as converting cheap WW II U.S. garrison caps into mock Russian "pilotka" or the realistic possibility of joining with European units in a D-Day campaign. Reading *The Point* is akin to listening in on a conversation between serious living-history re-enactors. As such, *The Point* is a valuable primary source.

Living-History Organizations

Association for Living Historical Farms and Agricultural Museums

Mercifully referred to as ALHFAM (Al' făm), this organization was founded in 1970 and is based in the Smithsonian Institution. It was the first group actually to use the term *living history* in its title. ALHFAM has about 250 active institutional and individual members. Most are associated with outdoor museums. It publishes a bi-monthly *Bulletin* and a record of its yearly meeting, the *Annual*. In addition to its annual conference, usually held in June at a major North American museum, ALHFAM regularly sponsors regional workshops that emphasize practical instruction in living-history interpretation. Recently, ALHFAM has sought to encourage membership from museums and organizations that are not necessarily agriculturally oriented. Annual dues are eight dollars for individuals. For information, write to ALHFAM, Smithsonian Institution, Washington, D.C., 20650.

Society for Creative Anachronism

The Society for Creative Anachronism was founded in 1966 at Berkeley, California, and since has grown to approximately 15,000 active members. It is highly organized along feudal lines into shires, baronies, and kingdoms. Frequent tournaments and courts are held at the local and regional level. Once a year, more than 6,000 members gather for a week to fight the Pennsic Wars in a meadow outside Slippery Rock, Pennsylvania. SCA publishes a quarterly, *Tournaments Illuminated*, and a variety of other guides and manuals, some of which are characterized by well-honed advice and grace. SCA differs from most other living-history organizations in that it has, from the start, encouraged membership from both sexes. A sustaining membership is twenty dollars. For information, write to the Society for Creative Anachronism, 1277 Fallenleaf Drive, Milpitas, California 95035.

Sealed Knot Society

Founded in 1968 by historian Peter Young, the Sealed Knot Society attracted widespread attention as the pre-eminent re-enactment group in Europe. It has an active membership of more than 2,000 who are organized in roughly 40 English Civil War units of "horse, foote, dragoones, and trayne of attillerye." The level of authenticity is high and serves as an inspiration to similar American organizations. The primary activity of the SKS is re-enacting specific battles of the period from 1640 to 1645. Generally, units are paid "by the siege," an economic arrangement that seems to please both contractor and SKS members and may serve as a model in North America, as agencies such as the National Park Service here temporarily employ re-enactment groups as living-history interpreters. For information, write to British Jousting Centre, Chilham Castle, Nr. Canterbury, Kent, England CT4 8D8.

National Muzzle Loading Rifle Association

Established in 1933, the National Muzzle Loading Rifle Association now numbers more than 25,000 members. While an all-pervading interest in muzzle-loading rifles, both antique and reproduced, is the chief characteristic of the association and its monthly journal *Muzzle Blasts,* there has been from the start a concurrent enthusiasm for the pioneers and soldiers who once used these firearms. Members speak of their participation in NMLRA events as an "experience in heritage." Twice a year, in spring and fall, more than 10,000 members convene at Friendship, Indiana, for a week of sharpshooting and fellowship. Recently, a "primitive camp" has been established at these matches for the several thousand members who wish to rendezvous more authentically. Annual membership is sixteen dollars. For information, write to the National Muzzle Loading Rifle Association, P.O. Box 67, Friendship, Indiana 47021.

National Association of Primitive Riflemen

Founded a decade ago by John Baird, editor of *The Blackpowder Report,* the National Association of Primitive Riflemen has grown to 6,500 members. They rendezvous yearly at a wilderness site somewhere in the West. In 1983, more than 3,000 members trekked fifty miles into a national forest near Glacier National Park, along the Canadian border. The NAPR covers a wide period of history—from pre-Revolutionary War days to the period when cartridge guns were popular for buffalo hunting. The NAPR uses "old time" rules for its matches— offhand shooting, open sites, loading from the pouch, etc., and charcoal-drawn targets. Although the NAPR encourages living history, it doesn't limit itself to purists. Rather, its events stress an informal enjoyment of history and old-fashioned shooting. Membership costs eighteen dollars per person per year. For information, write to the National Association of Primitive Riflemen, 220 McLeod Street, P.O. Box 789, Big Timber, Montana, 59011.

American Mountain Men

The American Mountain Men began in 1968 and now numbers more than a thousand active members. The AAM focuses on the period from 1800 to 1840 and stesses authenticity. Requirements for membership are difficult; the AAM is the Marine Corps of black-powder groups. They solicit "men who are willing to step back in time and live life as man was meant to live it, a Free Individual, a true Son of the Wilderness." Members are loosely organized and participate in seasonal rendezvous, often under strenuous conditions. It takes at least a year for a "pilgrim" to qualify for full membership. For information, write to the American Mountain Men, Box 259, Lakeside, California, 92042.

The 18th-Century Society

A comparatively young organization, the 18th-Century Society was formed in 1981. Its focus is on the 1750s and 1760s, but it counts as members individuals and units interested in interpreting early and later periods in the eighteenth century. The society has more than a thousand members, scattered over North America, with a concentration in the Northeast and Midwest. Annual events include a seminar at the Bushy Run Battlefield outside Pittsburgh and rendezvous at Fort de Chartres, Illinois, and Friendship, Indiana. Associated with the society is an umbrella military re-enactment organization, The Forces of Montcalm and Wolfe. The society publishes *F & I War.* Memberships are ten dollars yearly. For information, write to the 18th-Century Society, Box 264, RD 1, New Alexandria, Pennsylvania 15670.

North West Territory Alliance

A midwestern organization, the North West Territory Alliance was founded in 1974 in Racine, Wisconsin. The alliance concentrates on the Revolutionary War period (1776-1783) and limits membership to serious units interpreting the history of that era. It is unusually active and sponsors demonstrations, concerts, fashion shows, and encampments at numerous midwestern rendezvous and festivals. The largest is the Feast of the Hunter's Moon held at Fort Quiatenon, outside Lafayette, Indiana. NWTA publishes *The Courier,* an excellent newsletter. It encourages serious interpretation of camp life and has a high percentage of women members. For information on the NWTA and a unit near you, write to *The Courier,* 380 Hawthorn, Glen Ellen, Illinois 60137.

Brigade of the American Revolution

Founded in 1963, the Brigade of the American Revolution has more than a thousand members enrolled in approximately 125 units. Membership is limited to units—British, Loyalist, Hessian, French, Spanish, and Continental—however, many women, children, and craftsmen join the Brigade's Civilian Corps. The brigade's standards of authenticity are extremely high. BAR units sponsor about two events a month, as well as an annual cantonment in New Windsor, Connecticut, and a spring "School of the Soldier," an advanced workshop in living-history interpretation. The brigade also published a fine magazine, *The Dispatch,* but it ceased publication with the Yorktown campaign and the formal end of the Bicentennial. For more information, get in touch with Adjutant John Muller, 7 Crescent Place, Ho-Ho-Kus, New Jersey 07423.

1840s Living History Association

Typical of many new organizations that focus on a specific period and stress authenticity, the 1840s Living History Association has several hundred members, primarily in the Southwest. They specialize in the social and military history of the period from 1830 to 1850. The association puts out a modest journal, *The American Star,* and sponsors encampments at a variety of sites associated with the Mexican War. Membership is twelve dollars yearly. For information, write to Kevin Young, 1840s Living History Association, P.O. Box 1837, San Antonio, Texas 78296.

American Living History Association

A slightly older counterpart of the 1840s Association is the American Living History Association. It focuses on the period 1830 to 1870, especially the Civil War years. Michael Moore, one of its founders, calls the ALHA a "museum without a site." The several hundred members are unapologetic purists who consider themselves living-history interpreters, not re-enactors. The ALHA began publishing a quarterly, *Phoenix,* in 1980. It runs about thirty pages and provides members with various aspects of living history. The ALHA has recently worked closely with the National Park Service in providing interpretive encampments at both Gettysburg and Vicksburg. Membership dues are ten dollars a year. For more information, write to the American Living History Association, P.O. Box 7355, Austin, Texas 78712.

North-South Skirmish Association

One of the oldest of the living-history organizations, the North-South Skirmish Association, was founded in 1950, to provide a vehicle for competition with Civil War firearms. It now has more than 175 units and three thousand individual members. Twice yearly, the N-SSA holds a national skirmish at its 250-acre home range, Fort Shenandoah, in Virginia. Most members are, to some degree, military buffs, collectors, and marksmen. The N-SSA has published a bimonthly journal, *The Skirmish Line,* since 1955. While the focus of the N-SSA is on target shooting, the majority of its units are authentically uniformed and equipped, and the camp life aspect of its events have become progressively more historically accurate. Memberships are twelve dollars annually. For information, write to the North-South Skirmish Association, 4815 Oglethorpe Street, Riverdale, Maryland 20737.

World War II Historical Re-enactment Society

The World War II Historical Re-enactment Society was incorporated in 1976 and since then has sponsored more than one hundred battle re-enactments. It holds an annual National Battle in mid-October. Membership is more than fifty units and nearly a thousand individuals. The society has published a bimonthly magazine, *The Point,* since 1974. It contains unit reports, announcements of upcoming campaigns, and advertisements. Although the society has increasingly provided demonstrations or impressions for the public, often at military bases, the majority of its events are closed, carefully supervised battle re-enactments. Memberships are twelve dollars a year. For more information, get in touch with John Ong, 3432 Sunset Drive, Madison, Wisconsin 53705.

Sutlers

Dixie Gun Works

For almost thirty years, Turner Kirkland's Dixie Gun Works has been selling antique guns and replicas and muzzle-loading supplies from its headquarters in Union City, Tennessee. Its annual catalogue is as thick as a big-city telephone directory and runs close to six hundred pages. Almost every item is illustrated and described in detail. While the works at first catered primarily to muzzle-loader enthusiasts and buckskinners, its inventory now has expanded to include artifacts such as hot-air balloon kits, armor helmets, and nearly five hundred books. The works is a highly professional but nevertheless down-home operation. Most of its employees are delightfully pictured in the catalogue, often wearing a *voyageur* cap or holding a long rifle. For information, write to Dixie Gun Works, Gunpowder Lane, Union City, Tennessee 38261.

Navy Arms Co.

Val Forgett, founder of Navy Arms, began serious marketing of modern mass-produced replica black-powder firearms in 1957. An experienced member of the North-South Skirmish Association, Forgett wanted to purvey a line of replicas both authentic and safe. His thirty-page catalogue is a glossy wish-list for the serious re-enactor. For information, write to Navy Arms Co., 689 Bergen Boulevard, Ridgefield, New Jersey 07657.

The Hawken Shop

Art Ressel, a serious collector, acquired the famous Hawken-Gemmer gun factory, which had closed in 1915, and reopened the company in 1971, as The Hawken Shop. Ressel began making production guns that were absolutely authentic. They are weapons with both "show and blow." Ressel also supplies a variety of accessories, forged items, clothing, and trade silver—all of interest to the muzzle-loader. For information, write to the Hawken Shop, 3028 North Lindbergh, St. Louis, Missouri 63074.

Track of the Wolf

A good example of one of the many new companies devoted to the buckskin trade is the Track of the Wolf. It publishes a one-hundred-and-fifty-page catalogue that is heavy on books, historical-clothing kits, and rendezvous equipment. The Wolf also features a good selection of firearms. For information, write to Track of the Wolf, Box Y, Osseo, Minnesota 55369.

La Pelleterie

Pat and Karalee Tearney are very serious living-history professionals, and their superb ninety-page catalogue shows it. The Tearneys provide "custom-tailored historic reproductions and recreations of historic costume" from the eighteenth and nineteenth centuries. They provide both historical headnotes and photographs for all their items. The result is a handy guide to historic clothing for both the layman and the experienced re-enactor. The Tearney catalogue is the Neiman Marcus of the living-history trade. For information, write to La Pelleterie, P.O. Box 127, Highway 41, Arrow Rock, Missouri 65320.

Avalon Forge

John White joined a Revolutionary War regiment and was disillusioned by the lack of suitable accoutrements. In 1975, he and his wife, Kay, started Avalon Forge, first as a hobby, now as a part-time job. Their goal is to provide well-researched and well-documented goods of the period from 1760 to 1780. The forge's clientele is about 60 percent buffs and the remainder museums and historic sites with living-history programs. The twenty-five-page catalogue of eighteenth-century military and camp equipment documents virtually all Avalon Forge items with a reference source. For information, write to Avalon Forge, 409 Gun Road, Baltimore, Maryland 21227.

Buffalo Enterprises

Carole Roberson and Raymond Moore began their cottage industry in 1972. As living-history impressionists, they always dreamed of starting a living-history farm, but instead "ended up developing the business." Buffalo Enterprises is a full-time enterprise, best known for period clothing from the French and Indian, Revolutionary, and Civil War eras. The owners like to emphasize that they make and sell *clothing*, not costumes. Their seventy-page catalogue is both charming and informative. The enterprise is an excellent example of what the new, serious sutlers are attempting: a much higher standard of historical accuracy. For information, write to Buffalo Enterprises, 308 West King Street, East Berlin, Pennsylvania 17316.

The Sutler of Mount Misery

Legend has it that G. Gedney Godwin, Inc., was given permission to put up his tent at any and all Brigade of the American Revolution encampments. His reputation for historical accuracy is well established and his seventy-six-page catalogue, covering the French and Indian and Revolutionary War periods, is a textbook on what is correct. For information, write to G. Gedney Godwin, Inc., Box 100, Dept. L, Valley Forge, Pennsylvania 19481.

C & D Jarnagin Co.

The Jarnagins have done for the Civil War re-enactor what Godwin has accomplished for the Revolutionary War era: theirs is the standard against which other suppliers of Civil War uniforms and equipment are judged. Their thirty-page catalogue, really just a price list, exudes authenticity. One needs to be very knowledgeable about military uniforms, just to peruse it intelligently. For information, write to C & D Jarnagin, Route 3, Box 217, Corinth, Mississippi 38834.

James & Son

An old family business that began by providing costumes for Philadelphia's mummers and, later, for stage actors, James & Son branched out during the Bicentennial and began to outfit serious historical re-enactors. They now manufacture "authentic military clothing from WW II and back." This includes some of the lesser-studied periods, such as World War I, the Spanish-American War, the Indian campaigns, and the War of 1812. Much of their business is with overseas re-enactors, especially in Germany. For information, write to James & Son, Military Clothier, 1230 Arch Street, Philadelphia, Pennsylvania 19107.

Amazon Drygoods

Janet Burgess's complete name for her company is the Amazon Drygoods, Vinegar & Pickling Works. She is "purveyor of items for the nineteenth-century impression, and also serves the owners of old homes, the history buff, the staffs of historic homes, the multi-centennials of small towns, and lovers of Victoriana . . . with the heaviest emphasis on the hoop skirt era and the bustle eras." There isn't a firearm in the Amazon catalogue. Rather, it brims with domestic items: there are parasols, hand-crocheted mitts, Edwardian underthings, and pages of yard goods. By providing authentic goods to those whose hobby is history, Burgess makes a profit, and everyone benefits. For information, write to Amazon Drygoods, 2218 E. 11th Street, Davenport, Iowa 52803.

The Calico Corner

When Kathleen York and her husband, Dave, became active in Civil War re-enacting in 1975, Kathleen was surprised at the paucity of historically accurate clothing for women. She has tried to fill that need by opening a shop that could supply both dressmaking materials and finished articles and by writing two excellent Civil War Ladies Sketchbooks. Recently, she has also begun buying and selling used clothing. "If you are new to re-enacting or leaving the hobby, outgrowing your clothes or switching armies, please telephone me at home or visit me at Midwest re-enactments in the sutler camp." York heralds a new and welcomed day in the world of living history: the marketing of army and civilian *surplus* reproductions! For information, write to the Calico Corner, 513 East Bowman Street, South Bend, Indiana 46613.

George A. Peterson

From his Virginia store, George Peterson sells a full line of World War II and American re-enactment uniforms, headgear, field equipment, insignias, medals, and related material. Ironically, this is not old army surplus, the stuff that, as kids and —later—as students, we used to buy cheap. Peterson sells brand-new, mint-condition, accurate reproductions to re-enactors, many of whom have studied originals in museums and are therefore sticklers for authenticity. An experienced buff, Peterson does handle genuine surplus for all of America's twentieth-century wars, since his clientele includes collectors as well as re-enactors. However, few would commit the curatorial sin of campaigning in antiques! For more information, write to George A. Peterson, National Capital Historical Sales, Inc., 7904 "F" Yarnwood Ct. (Fullerton Industrial Park), Springfield, Virginia 22153.

Acknowledgments

During the writing of this book, many individuals and organizations gave generously of their advice and information, and many others made available pictorial materials for use here. Author and publisher make grateful acknowledgment to each one—to those named or quoted in the text and to those cited here:

The Agricultural History Center, the University of California, Davis, Cal.; *Americana* Magazine, New York, N.Y.; the American Association of Museums, Washington, D.C.; the American Living History Association, Austin, Tex.

Todd Buchanan, Santa Ana, Cal.

Colonial Williamsburg Foundation, Williamsburg, Va.; *Colonial Williamsburg Today,* Williamsburg, Va.; *Columbia University Forum* and Columbia University, New York, N.Y.; Connor Prairie Pioneer Settlement, Noblesville, Ind.

The 18th-Century Society, New Alexandria, Pa.; the Essex Institute, Salem, Mass.

Ken Grissom, Seabrook, Tex.

Horreus de Haas, the Polder Project, Bilthoven, the Netherlands; Hans-Ole Hansen, Lejre Historical Archaeological Center, Lejre, Denmark; Henry Ford Museum, the Edison Institute, Dearborn, Mich.; *Historic Preservation* and the National Trust for Historic Preservation, Washington, D.C.; The Homeplace, 1850, Golden Pond, Ky.

Ireland of the Welcomes, Dublin, Ireland.

Joe Kalal, St. Louis, Mo., and K. Nicholas Thoman; Kings Landing Historical Settlement, New Brunswick, Canada.

Living History Farms, Des Moines, Ia.; Stephen C. Lowry, Bowling Green, Ky.

Mackinac Island State Park Commission, Lansing, Mich.

The National Geographic, Washington, D.C.; the National Muzzle Loading Rifle Association and *Muzzle Blasts,* Friendship, Ind.; New York State Department of Commerce; Nordiska Museet, Stockholm, Sweden.

The Old Fort, St. Helen's Island, Montreal, Canada; Old Fort Niagara, Youngstown, N.Y.; Old Sturbridge Village, Sturbridge, Mass.; Ontario Ministry of Industry and Tourism, Ontario, Canada, and Old Fort William.

Parks Canada and the Fortress of Louisbourg National Historic Park, Louisbourg, Nova Scotia, Canada; Plimoth Plantation, Plymouth, Mass.

The Smithsonian Institution, Washington, D.C.

K. Nicholas Thoman and Joe Kalal, St. Louis, Mo.

Village Historique Acadien, New Brunswick, Canada.

Washburn-Norlands Living History Center, Livermore Falls, Me.; World War II Historical Re-enactment Society and Allen Fishbeck, Florissant, Mo.

Author and publisher also gratefully acknowledge permission from the following for use here of the materials credited to them:

The American Association of Museums, for excerpt from "The Link from Object to Person Concept," by James Deetz, in *Museums, Adults, and the Humanities,* by Zipporah W. Collins (Washington, D.C.: American Association of Museums, 1981). Copyright © 1981 by the American Association of Museums.

The Christian Science Publishing Society, for excerpt from "What It Was Like on an Early American Farm," by Peter Tonge, in the *Christian Science Monitor,* August 22, 1975. Reprinted, by permission, from the *Christian Science Monitor.* Copyright © 1975 by the Christian Science Publishing Society. All rights reserved.

Curtis Publishing Company, for excerpt from "We Sailed the Columbus Ship," by Robert Marx, in the *Saturday Evening Post,* January 26, 1963. Reprinted, with permission, from the *Saturday Evening Post.* Copyright © 1963 by the Curtis Publishing Company.

Rand McNally & Company, for Figure 7.1, from *Kon-Tiki,* by Thor Heyerdahl. Copyright © 1950 by Thor Heyerdahl. Copyright renewed 1978 by Thor Heyerdahl. Published in the U.S. by Rand McNally & Company.

TIME, Inc., for excerpt from "A Last Bicentennial Bash," copyright © 1981 by TIME, Inc. All rights reserved. Reprinted by permission from TIME.

Index

Broach, Buz, 155
Brooks, Bill, 61–62
Brown, Bill, 146–147
Bruegel, Peter, 11
Buckskin Report, 160
Buckskins and Black Powder (1983), 160, 201
Buckskinners, 137, 157–165
Buffalo Enterprises, 210–211
Burcaw, G. Ellis, 23
Burger, Valie, 9–10
Butser Hill Ancient Farm Research Project: history, 96–99; demonstration farm, 105, 192

C & D Jaragin Company, 211
Calico Corner, The, 211
Callahan, Errett, 123–125; *Old Rag Report* (1973), 123; Coconino Project, 123–124; Pamunky Project, 124–125; *Wagner Basalt Quarries Report* (1974), 124; at Colonial Pennsylvania Plantation, 125, 131, 188
Callender, Donald, Jr., 103–105
Camp Chase Gazette, 153, 160, 206
Campbell, H. Dean, 116–118; *A Second Impression* (1974), 117, 118
Canada, museums, 61–70, 198–199
Carson, Barbara, 81
Carson, Cary, 30, 81–204
Centennial Exhibition (1876): Hazelius' tableaux, 25; New England state exhibit, 25; tournament, 135–136
Chase, Darryl, *Selected Living Historical Farms, Villages, and Agricultural Museums in the United States and Canada* (1976), 39
Chidsey, Carol, 165
Chorley, Kenneth, 31
Christian Science Monitor, 104
Civil War Centennial: buffs, 137–139; history, 141–143
Clark, George Rogers, 144
Clawson, Marion, 37–38
Cline, Walter, *The Muzzle-Loading Rifle: Then and Now* (1941), 136–137
Coconino Project, 123–124
Cody, William F., 136, 160–161
Colby, Jean, 118
Coles, John: *Archaeology by Experiment* (1973), 87; *Experimental Archaeology* (1979), 87, 91, 200; goals of experimental archaeology, 87–88; methods, 107–108; evaluation of projects, 129–131
Collins, Zipporah, 57
Colonial Pennsylvania Plantation: history, 101–105, 185, 192; mentioned, 77
Colonial Williamsburg: history, 29–33; mentioned, 35, 60, 62, 68, 196
Columbia University Forum, 202
Columbus, Christopher, 114, 115–116
Connecticut Yankee in King Arthur's Court, A (1889), 10
Courier, The, 206
Creative Anachronist, 169

Cunliffe, Barry, 130
Custis-Lee Mansion, 36
Cutler, Edward, 28, 29

D-Day re-enactment, 153
Deakin, Tom, 146–147
Deetz, James: at Plimoth, 47–52, 57, 60–61, 73, 202, 204
Deloury, Barbara, 147
Denmark, museums, 21, 93–96
Dispatch, The, 146
Dixie Gun Works, 210
Donnelly, Joseph P., 116–117
Dorson, Richard, 81
Dow, George Francis, 26–28
Dramatizations: at Old Fort William, 69–70; Old Sturbridge Village, 79; Fort Mackinac, 79

1840s Living History Association, 209
18th-Century Society, The, 208
Einstein, Albert, 11, 187
Elder, Betty Doak, 203–204
Eliot, T. S., 191
Elizondo, Carlos Etayo, 115–116
England, museums, 22, 93–99, 104–105, 129–131
Essex Institute: history, 27–28; mentioned, 33
Evans, George Ewart, 91
Everyman His Own Historian (1935), 202
Experimental Archaeology (1979), 87, 91, 200
Experimental archaeology, 12, 87–88, 200. *See also* specific archaeologists, projects, in Part 2

F & I War, 150–153, 160, 177, 206
Fakelore, 22
Farb, 141, 192
Farming. *See* Agricultural history
Farming in the Iron Age (1976), 99
Farmers' Museum at Cooperstown, 33, 35
Feast of the Hunter's Moon, 161–165
Felt-truth, 191
Finland, museums, 17
Finney, Ben, *Hokule a* (1979), 200
Finney, Jack, *Time and Again* (1970), 11, 179, 187–188, 192, 199
First-person interpretation: at Plimoth, 51–52, 67; at Old Fort William, 69–70; by buffs, 186–187
Folklife: interpretation at Old Sturbridge Village, 78–79
Folklorismos, 22
Ford, Henry, 28–29
Fort Mackinac, 68, 79
Fort Ouiatenon, 161–165
Fort Snelling, 68
Fort Sumpter, 142
Fortier, John, 61–62, 71; *Fortress of Louisbourg* (1979), 199–200, 203
Fortress of Louisbourg (1979), 61–63, 199–200
Forty-Seventh Indiana Infantry, 176